Impact of Climate Change

Editors

Dr. Mamta Sharma   Dr. Hukam Singh

Dr. Upendra Singh

Pustak Bharati
Toronto Canada

Editors : Dr. Mamta Sharma
Dr. Hukam Singh
Dr. Upendra Singh

Book Title : Impact of Climate Change

Cover Picture : By Dr. Anil Kumar Chhangani, D.Sc

Published by :
Pustak Bharati (Books India)
180 Torresdale Ave, Toronto Canada M2R 3E4
email : pustak.bharati.canada@gmail.com
Web : www.pustak-bharati-canada.com

Published for
Raj Rishi Government Autonomous College,
Alwar, Rajasthan, India

Financial Assistance
Rashtriya Uchchatar Shiksha Abhiyan
(RUSA-2.0)

Copyright ©2023

ISBN : 978-1-989416-41-9

ISBN 978-1-989416-41-9

90000

9 781989 416419

PREFACE

"Our planet is slowly dying, and if we don't do anything about it soon enough, it would eventually begin to deteriorate and everything would be used. The world would become a barren place without any resources. We need to cater to the needs of our planet, and we need to change our life styles so that it becomes beneficial to the planet. We need to become much more eco-friendly, so that no harm is dealt to the planet by our existence. Many people don't realize that they waste large amounts of energy and other resources in various unnecessary things that could otherwise be saved."

This series of books is an extension of the 3 days international conference on **Multidisciplinary Approach Towards Sustainable Development And Climate Change For A Viable Future (ICMSDC-2022)** held from 12th -14th August 2022 at Raj Rishi Government Autonomous College, Alwar, Rajasthan.

We are very happy and delighted to publish our series of books which are accumulation of research papers of knowledgeable experts in the field of sustainable development and climate change.

Climate change is the most significant challenge to achieving sustainable development, and it threatens to drag millions of people into grinding poverty. At the same time, we have never had better know-how and solutions available to avert the crisis and create opportunities for a better life for people all over the world. Climate change is not just a long-term issue. It is happening today, and it entails uncertainties for policy makers trying to shape the future.

There is a dual relationship between sustainable development and climate change. On the one hand, climate change influences key natural and human living conditions and thereby also the basis for social and economic development, while on the other hand, society's priorities on sustainable development influence both the greenhouse gas emissions that are causing climate change and the vulnerability.

Climate policies can be more effective when consistently embedded within broader strategies designed to make national and regional development paths more sustainable. This occurs because the impact of climate variability and change, climate policy responses, and associated socio-economic development will affect the ability of countries to achieve sustainable development goals. Conversely, the pursuit of those goals will in turn affect the opportunities for, and success of, climate policies.

With these books, we aim to reach to as many people as we can, and spread awareness about sustainable development and climate change and its in-depth analysis through our didactic research papers. We hope that the thought with which ICMSDC-2022 was executed is taken forward through this series of books and the inception of an idea of saving the environment is rooted in the minds of our readers.

The articles in these books have been contributed by eminent research scholars, scientists, academicians and industry experts whose contributions have enriched this book series. We thank our publisher, Pustak Bharati, Toronto, Canada for joining us in this initiative and helped in publishing this series of books.

Finally, we will always remain indebted to all our well-wishers for their blessings, without which ICMSDC-2022 and series of these book would have not come into existence.

Financial Assistance provided by Rashtriya Uchchatar Shiksha Abhiyan (RUSA-2.0) is gratefully acknowledged.

Dr. Mamta Sharma
Dr. Hukam Singh
Dr. Upendra Singh

Contents

Greener Living : Healthy Life

Dr. Mamta Sharma*,
Dr. Hukam Singh**
Dr. Upendra Singh ***

Introduction

Go Green and Save Green

The new decade is upon us, and many of us have the same goal in mind: to be more eco-friendly. Living a more sustainable lifestyle can be very rewarding – but also a bit daunting. Thankfully there are three easy-to-follow stepping stones that we can apply to everyday life: reduce, reuse and recycle. Green living is a lifestyle that strives to create balance in preserving and protecting Earth's natural resources, habitats, human civilization and bio-diversity. The pros of choosing green living are clear, more sustainable living, reduced climate change and establishing better habits and creating a healthier home for future generations on planet earth. In simple terms living green and sustainably means developing a lifestyle that works with nature rather than against it and does no long-term or irreparable element of the ecological system. By reducing, reusing and recycling we can decrease air and water pollution which become a very big problem internationally, conserve materials for continuous reuse in making new products and can reduce demand for mining and extraction of virgin materials. Reduce means to cut back on the amount of trash we generate, Reuse means to find new ways to use things that otherwise would have been thrown out, Recycle means to turn something old and useless in to something new and useful. Recycling is vital for cleaning up the environment and keeping our communities clean. By reusing recycled items to produce new products we reduce the impact we have on over mother land. The principal of reducing waste, reusing and recycling resources and products and known as "3 Rs".

Impact of Climate Change

The advancing climate crisis is one of the greatest problems the humanity is facing today. In order to stop it, not only great projects and new technologies are needed, but also care and concern for the environment in our micro activities. It is a task that we can cope with by changing our daily habits. It is about the growing amount of rubbish and waste we generate, The 3R principal comes to our aid- reduce, reuse, recycle. The 3R's works together to reduce the waste generated and for the improvement of the waste management process. Reduce reuse, and recycle helps in reducing the amount of CO_2 in the atmosphere and Save the environment. Recycling, as well as waste reduction, can cut CO_2 by millions of tons every year. Recycling and composting reduce trash that is destined for the landfill that would have emitted greenhouse gases while the decomposing. Reduces greenhouse gas emissions that contribute to global climate change, helps sustain the environment for future generations. The 3Rs Hierarchy ranks our environmental actions based on greatest positive impact on the environment beginning with reduce, followed by reuse, recycle and then final disposal. Earth is the only home we have, and it is our duty to keep it in good shape. Taking more than we give the earth has impacted negatively on our planet and this has come at a cost. The earth's ecosystem are an intricate, well-balanced system where everything works together to ensure continuous support of life on earth. Thus the 3Rs that Reduce, Reuse & Recycle are points of action that show steps to be taken to lower the amount of waste generated, improve waste management and to make our planet a healthier place. It is important to produce as little waste as possible, but when we do produce waste, determine how much of it can actually be recycled, clean it off and throw it in the recycling bin.

Detour

Reduce consumption, what You do need of things that makes pollution on the earth. People should reduce. waste low waste zero waste. Find solution for clean surrounding and becomes eco-friendly. Improve health of the environment. Use biodegradable material where we are environmentally safe and ecological. Green environment can be saved, conserved by creating awareness. Blue planet on which healthy environment changing behavior and lifestyle to reduce the amount of pollution and waste generated. Resources and energy conservation, waste reduction and ecological balance protecting the earth from pollution.

Refuse, Reduce, Reuse, Repurpose, Recycle that offers improvement to the environment. Reuse today then no problem to reduce tomorrow. Recycling leads to a significant reduction in greenhouse emissions and global warming Recycling leads to a significant reduction in greenhouse emissions and global warming helps to keep the surrounding neat. Renewable energy "clean energy or green power or sustainable energy because it doesn't pollute the air or the water. Wind power, solar energy, tidal energy (Ocean energy), bio energy ((biomass), geothermal energy, hydropower etc. are naturally renewed. Solar operated charging system for motor vehicles. Biogas system for lighting purpose and cooking. Hydropower system for electricity and irrigation purpose. Thermal power station for electricity & produce Ash bricks. Hybrid car (E.V. & diesel), solar of operator trains in Tamandu, Nuclear power plant reuse of hot water etc Promotes sanitation, sanitary landfill, use cloth napkins and plates instead of paper. Use organic pesticides & organic fertilizers. Field waste, animal waste and agro industrial waste by reduce & reuse by treatment process and transportation process Green life style for healthier planet. For that thinking green, living green and save green. Benefits of green Promotes sanitation, sanitary landfill, use cloth napkins and plates instead of paper, use organic pesticides. &organic fertilizers field waste, animal wrote and Argo Industrial waste by reduce & reuse by treatment process and Transportation process.

Green life style for Heathier planet. For a that thinking Green, living green and save green.

❖ **Benefits of green lives :**
- Reduces pollution and global emissions.
- Helps to conserve electricity.
- Conserve natural resources.
- Green living is economical.
- Lead a healthier life.

❖ **Green living Practices :**
- By organic food.
- Go plastic free.
- Thinks twice before shopping.
- Make sure your big purchases.
- Use water wisely, water resources conserved, save water.
- Drive less drive green.
- Save energy.
- Enjoy gardening and truly go green.
- Buy local, use local produce.
- Reduce the use of paper. Go digital.
- Avoid dry cleaning.
- Teach kids to care for the world.
- Educate others.
- Together we can save the planet.
- Maximizing recycling: newspapers, books and magazines.
- Reduce own carbon footprint - reduce global temperature.
- Plant trees, Save trees.
- Watch less Television, walk more, ride a bicycle.

At the same times, two more R; can be added to the three basic 3R ones.

- Rethink can be added to the start of the list. It means we should thank about the way our actions impact the environment.

- Recover is sometimes added to the end of the list. it refers to the act of putting waste products to use for example, decompose garbage products methane gas, which can be recovered and burnt do produce energy

what do we mean by all the above?

- Reduce means minimize the amount of waste we create.
- Reuse refers to using items more than once
- Recycle means putting a product to a new use instead of throwing it away.
- Rethink is about Considering how our actions affect the environment.
- Recover refers the practice of putting waste products to use
- Landfill of a site where waste materials are disposed of

SAVE THE EARTH AND SAVE THE FUTURE

References
Source of knowledge is the internet and it is highly acknowledged.

*Associate Professor (Zoology)
**Professor
*** Associate Professor (Chemistry)
Raj Rishi Government (Autonomous) College,
Alwar, Rajasthan 301001,India.
email : mamta810@gmail.com;
drhukamsingh63@gmail.com ;
dr.usingh09@gmail.com

2. Exploring Nutritional and Biochemical Traits of *Pseudomonas Syringae* pv. *Tagetis* for its Identification in Seeds of French Marigold (*Tagetis Patula*)

Pinky Gurjar* and Laxmi Kant Sharma

Abstract

The present study has investigated presence of *Pseudomonas syringae* pv. *tagetis* (*Pst*) in seeds of French marigold (*Tagetis patula*) by use of its biochemical traits. Total twenty five bacterial colonies were obtained from the diseased seeds of marigold and identified as *Pseudomonas spp.* through numerous biochemical tests. Further these were confirmed as *Pst* on the basis of LOPAT test, carbohydrate utilization, HR (hypersensitive reaction) and pathogenicity tests. The discoloured and symptom showing seeds were plated on nutrient agar medium and total 39 bacterial colonies were selected on the basis of colony morphology and response on King's B medium. From these isolates, totally 25 colonies were sorted for further identification test. They were gram negative, rod shaped, belonged to group 1b of LOPAT and utilized glucose, mannitol, inositol but unable to consume sucrose and starch in medium. Their host and pathogenicity test confirmed the pathovar as *Pseudomonas syringae* pv. *tagetis* (*Pst*).

Keywords : Bacterial leaf spot, French marigold, *Pseudomonas syringae* pv. *tagetis*, biochemical test, *Tagetes patula*

1. Introduction

Tagetes patula or French marigold is a famous member of family Asteraceae; native to North and South America and known for its extensive use in assembly of garlands, prettification and other well-known purposes like for extraction of pigment and oil. It is also popular as a source of medicines and some therapeutic purposes (Riaz et al. 2020). Besides being used as insecticide, fungicide, bactericide and larvicide for other crops, it is attacked by many pathogenic bacteria which annually results in heavy yield losses

(Aktar and Shamsi, 2014; Politi et al., 2012; Zhang et al., 2013; Salehi et al., 2018; Mir et al. 2019).

The pathovars of *Pseudomonas syringae* have a wide host range as they are known for infecting mostly economically important crop species, thus it is considered as the most common pathogen of plants (Lamichhane et al. 2015). Additionally, regular occurrences of diseases caused by *P. syringae* pathovars remain as a global threat to production of different crops (Xin et al. 2018; O'Malley and Anderson 2021.) such as diseases of zinnia, common ragweed, sunflower and Jerusalem artichoke (Shane and Baumer, 1984) have been a matter of concern. One of the latest examples of such distressing effects of this pathogen is bacterial leaf spot (BLS) disease caused by pathovar *tagetis* in French marigold grown worldwide including India.

BLS is a devastating disease of marigold and is triggered by bacterium *Pseudomonas syringae* pv. *tagetis*. It is a seed-borne disease as it transmits from seeds to seedling and plant. It was first detected in the United States in the year 1978 and till then it has been reported from many countries of the world and causes heavy destruction of yield by infecting juvenile plants of marigold (Styer et al., 1980).

The notable characteristic symptoms of this disease start with black spots development on cotyledon of saplings and necrosis of leaves enclosed by irregular circles of chlorotic soft tissue. In some severe cases distortion of apical growth resulting in death of the infected plant is also observed. It shows variability in symptom development pattern also as sometimes little; moist, dark-green spots are emerged on lower side of leaves which later covers upper layer also with brownish drawn-out de-coloration (Hellmers, 1955).

As mentioned above, the marigold has immense importance as a source of medicinal compounds, details on its microbial pathogens and their early identification process is a necessity to decide approaches of crop protection so that monetary losses can be prevented, particularly for small-scale producers.

Materials and Methods
• Field Survey and Sampling
For collecting samples of French marigold, two field surveys were performed in the year 2019-2020 and total 117 samples of seeds were collected from fields of different districts of Rajasthan state. In initial investigation, the seeds were sorted on the basis of paleness of cotyledons, wrinkles or any other spot.

• Screening of the Pathogen
Out of the 117 samples, 76 samples showed discoloration and spots on seeds which later yielded in isolation of 39 bacterial colonies. On application of specific identification methods, 25 colonies were identified as *Pseudomonas syringae* pv. *tagetis* (Pst) which were further confirmed by host and pathogenicity assays. Before doing biochemical tests, the seeds' surface was sterilized by treating with 90% (v/v) ethanol for 1 min and then with 1% (v/v) NaOCl for next 5 min. Further, seeds were cleansed with autoclaved distilled water. Such decontaminated seeds were directly plated on nutrient agar (NA) medium and left for incubation at 28±2°C for next for 2-3 days. The different bacterial lumps grown under the seeds were picked and transferred on semi selective King's B (KB) medium for further identification process.

The isolates which showed *Pst* type colony appearances were exposed to many biochemical tests.

• Nutritional and Biochemical Analysis
As stated above 25 bacterial isolates were selected for their reaction towards Gram's- stain, KOH solubility, and catalase activity, LOPAT test (Levan production, Oxidase activity, Potato soft rot, Arginine dihydrolase activity, and Tobacco hypersensitive response) for early identification of pseudomonas spp. (Klement et al., 1990; Peix et al., 2018; Patyka et al., 2019). In addition to these initial tests, the isolates were confirmed for Esculin hydrolysis, Gelatin liquefaction, Indole production and utilization of metabolites like Ethanol, Erythritol, D-Galctose, Gluconate, myo-Inositol etc. (Lydon et al., 2011).

The isolates were tested for development of fluorescence also by streaking on KB (King's medium B) and observed under UV light (Mohan and Schaad, 1987). Likewise, leaves, stems and seeds showing symptoms of *Pst* were disinfected and their small parts were transferred on NA and tested for nutritional and biochemical features as stated above.

- **Pathogenicity Test (Host Test)**

The isolates showing characteristic test of *Pst* were assessed for pathogenicity test on French marigold and other hosts such as Jerusalem artichoke (*Helianthus tuberosus* L.), sunflower (*Helianthus annuus* L.), a willow- leaf sunflower (*H. salicifolius* A. Dietr) and common ragweed (*Ambrosia artemisiifolia*) (Robinson et al. 2004). The leaves of host plants were punctured and the bacterial suspension maintained at 1×107 CFU/mL was injected in the middle vein while the control was inoculated with sterile tap water only (Rhodehamel and Durbin 1985; Peix et al., 2018). The inoculated leaves were then placed in at $25 \pm 2°C$ and looked every day for development of any necrotic or pathogenic symptoms (Schaad and Kendrick, 1975; Saettler et al., 1989).

Results and Discussion

The *P. syringae* pv. *tagetis* hosts members of family Asteraceae and incites apical chlorosis and bacterial leaf spots (Gulya et al., 1982; Hellmers, 1955; Rhodehamel and Durbin, 1985; Rhodehamel and Durbin, 1989; Shane and Baumer, 1984). Formerly also, it has been isolated from various plants and from weeds showing apical chlorosis. On the contrary, it is assessed for antagonistic activity for controlling Canada thistle in soybean and woolly leaf bursage in cotton (Budde and Ullrich et al. 2000; Sheikh et al.., 2001; Gronwald et al., 2002). In this study, overall 76 seed samples displayed atypical colour and spots on seed coat which further brought out 39 types of bacterial colonies. From these isolates, 25 colonies were developed on NA medium and characterized as *Pst* on the basis of their response for nutritional and biochemical analytic tests as shown in table no. 1. The colonies developed on NA were whitish, mucoid, raised, smooth and glistering (Fig. 2 A and C).

All the isolates were Gram's negative and positive for KOH and catalase test and rod shaped (Fig. 1 B and Fig. 2 B&D). The isolates produced a yellow – green to blue fluorescence on King's B (KB) medium, confirming that the isolates are fluorescent pseudomonads

(Mohan and Schaad, 1987). This pigment has been used as characteristic of many *P.* syringae strains (Lamichhane and Varvaro, 2013; Tymon and Inglis, 2017; Fuenzalida-Valdivia et al. 2022).

These fluorescent pseudomonads were looked for their group on the basis of LOPAT test and they were -+--+ (Fig. 1) and confirmed their position in LOPAT group Ib (Young and Fletcher 1997). Suzuki et al. (2003) also used LOPAT and other test to differentiate *P. syringae* pv. *pisi* from *Pst* in infected pea plants. The most studied *P. syringae* bacterial models had same pattern in some other study viz. *P. syringae* pathovar from tomato (Whalen et al. 1991) and cauliflower (Weibe et al. 1993) showed same response for KB medium and LOPAT test.

The results of morphology of colony and LOPAT directed that all the purified colonies are strains of *Pseudomonas syringae*. The results of different phenotypic (biochemical) tests lead to the confirmation of pathovar. Further positive results for D-Galctose, Gluconate, Glucose, inositol, mannitol, sorbitol utilization and negative results for starch hydrolysis and Glycerol and sucrose specified that all isolates are *Pst* which was further confirmed by host and tobacco HR test. In previous studies too, similar responses of biochemical and hypersensitivity reactions of *Pst* have been observed in marigold and other plants (Lydon et al. 2011; Song et al. 2015). Also, pathogenicity test showed development of chlorosis and necrosis with spot in different hosts tested (Table no. 2). In earlier studies also similar pattern has been observed in various members of family Asteraceae (Rhodehamel and Durbin 1985; Lydon et al. 2011; Suzuki et al. 2003; Zhang et al., 2002). Even there are surprising reports of symptom development by this pathogen in plants of Brassicaceae, Solanaceae and Cucurbitaceae family (Gulya et al. 1982). There are reports that host range of pathovars of *Pseudomonas syringae* is expanding frequently like in *Ageratum, Cirsium, Cordyline, Anemone, Argyranthemum Fuchsia, Lavandula, Arabidopsis thaliana, Geranium, Helianthus,* and *Tagetes* (Zavala et al. 2022). This is the reason the *P. syringae* has attracted scientists due to its diverse host range and toxin production (Xin et al. 2018).

In some key studies, the selective characteristics of pathogen of marigold were established on the basis of specific biochemical features (Jeevan et al. 2021). For *B. altitudinis*, *P. aeruginosa*, *B. aryabhattai*, *B. wiedmannii* and many more, biochemical characterization method was applied successfully (Margarita et al. 2017; Shah et al. 2022). In experiments exploring antimicrobial properties of *Pst*, it was identified and distinguished on the basis of nutritional requirements Grădilă et al. 2022). For other pathovars of *P. syringae* biochemical and pathogencity tests have made its early identification easier as commended in various studies (Chaturvedi et al. 2018; Jangir et al. 2018; Chaturvedi et al. 2015). Though there are developments of enormous advanced techniques for identification of bacterial pathogens from plants, the LOPAT, biochemical and pathogenicity tests are still important as colony type and difference in carbon source utilization plays a significant role in deciding pathovar of a species (Marques et al. 2016; Tymon and Inglis, 2017; Gomila et al. 2017; Chaturvedi et al. 2018; Saint-Vincent et al. 2020). Thus, the present study has established identification of *Pseudomonas syringae* pv. *tagetis* on by exhausting its biochemical traits.

Conclusion :

We have performed an inclusive phenotypic and biochemical analysis of 25 strains of *Pseudomonas syringae* pv. *tagetis* isolated from the seeds of French marigold. The strains showed ability to utilize D-Galctose, Gluconate, Glucose, inositol, mannitol and sorbitol as sole carbon source in medium. We established an early detection of this seed borne pathogen of marigold as yet there is no effective control measure known for this pathogen other than use of infection free seed lots in the field.

The significance of LOPAT and other biochemical tests has been established in many molecular detection experiments also and in our study we successfully demonstrated that these methods are vital to decide pathovar of *Pseudomonas syringae*. We have provided an extensive detail of these test methods and results which may be proven as a great source of reference in further studies.

Table no. 1: Nutritional and Biochemical analysis of strains of *Pseudomonas syringae* pv. *tagetis* isolated from seeds of French marigold

S.no.	Carbohydrate source	Response	S.no.	Carbohydrate source	Response
1.	D-Arabinose	N	16.	Mannitol	Y
2.	Cellobiose	N	17.	Quinate	Y
3.	Citrate	N	18.	Ribose	Y
4.	Ethanol	Y	19.	Sorbitol	Y
5.	Erythritol	N	20.	Starch	N
6.	D-Galctose	Y	21.	Succinate	Y
7.	Gluconate	Y	22.	Sucrose	N
8.	Glucose	Y	23.	Trehalose	N
9.	Glutarate	N	24.	Triacetin	N
10.	Glycerol	N	25.	L-Valine	N
11.	Fructose	N	26.	D-Xylose	Y
12.	*myo*-Inositol	Y		Other charateristics	
13.	2-ketogluconate	N	27.	Esculin hydrolysis	N
14.	Lactate	N	28.	Gelatin liquefaction	N
15.	*myo*-Inositol	Y	29.	Tobacco Hypersensitivity test	Y

Table no. 2: Pathogenicity test on French marigold and other members of Asteraceae family and hypersensitivity reaction (HR) on tobacco leaves

Isolates	Pathogenicity reaction					Hypersensitivity reaction on tobacco
	French Marigold	Sunflower	Jerusalem artichoke	Willow leaf sunflower	Common ragweed	
Pseudomon	H	M	H	H	H	+
as syringae	M	M	M	H	H	+
pv. *tagetis*						

Rating scales were as follows: H- High (disease index 4.1to 5.0); M-Moderate (2.6 to 4.0); L- Low (1.1 to 2.5); and 0-None (1.0); + Infiltrated area becomes necrosis.

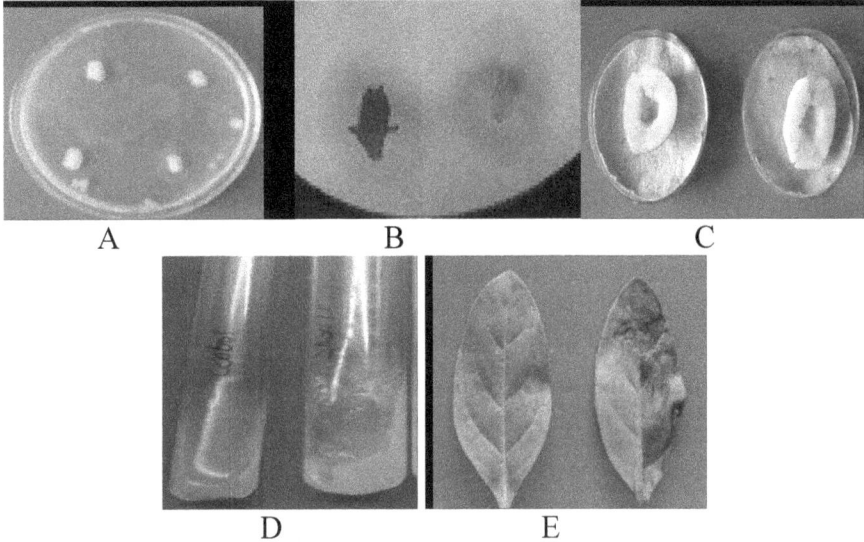

A

B

C

D

E

A : Levan negative
B : Oxidase positive
C : Potato soft rot negative
D : Arginine hydrolysis
E : Tobacco HR test

Fig. 1: Results of LOPAT explain that the response of pathogen *Pseudomonas syringae* pv. *tagetis* was -+--+ that includes it in **LOPAT 1B group**

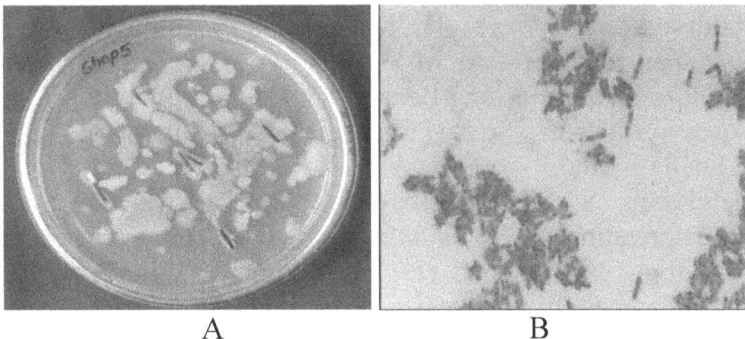

A

B

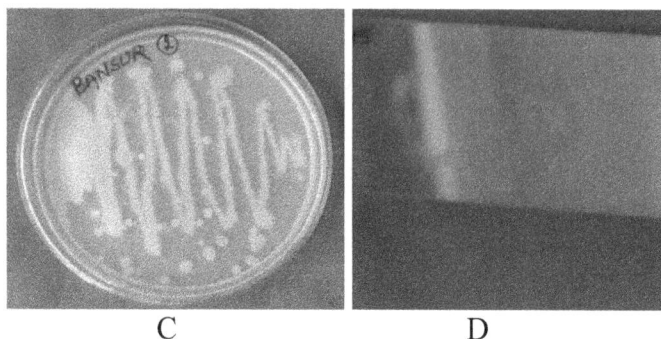

C   D

Fig. 2: Results of colony morphology, Gram's staining and KOH solubility test

A: White, glistening and mucoid colonies of *Pseudomonas syringae* pv. *tagetis* on NA

B: Rod shaped colonies in Gram's staining

C: Whitish glistening colony on NA

D: Bubbles indicating KOH solubility test

References

1. Aktar M, Shamsi S. 2014. Report on alternaria blight of *Tagetes erecta* and Ta*getes patula* caused by *Alternaria alternata* (Fr.) Keissler. J. Asiat. Soc. Bangladesh, Sci. 40(1): 133–140. https://doi.org/10.3329/jasbs.v40i1.31740

2. Budde IP, Ullrich M. S. 2000. Interactions of *Pseudomonas syringae pv. glycinea* with host and nonhost plants in relation to temperature and phytotoxin synthesis. Mol. Plant-Microbe Interact. 13:951-961.

3. Chaturvedi S, Agrawal K, Kulshrestha S, Narayan A. 2018. Molecular Identification of *Pseudomonas syringae (savastoni)* pv. *phaseolicola* in Mung Bean (*Vigna radiata* L. Wilczek) Seeds Grown in Rajasthan State, India. Int. J. Curr. Microbiol. App. Sci. 7(11):1859-1866.

4. Chaturvedi S, Kulshrestha S, & Agrawal KP. 2015. Characterization of *Pseudomonas savastoni* pv. *phaseolicola* in seed lots of mung bean (*Vigna radiata* L. Wilczek) collected from Rajasthan, India. Int. Res. J. Biological Sci. 4(10):57-61.

5. Fuenzalida-Valdivia I, Gangas MV ,Zavala D, Herrera-Vasquez A, Roux F, Meneses C, Blanco-Herrera F. 2022. Draft Genome Sequence of *Pseudomonas syringae* RAYR-BL, a Strain Isolated from Natural Accessions of Arabidopsis thaliana Plants. Microbiol. Resour. Announc. 11: e01001-21.
6. Jangir R, Sankhla IS, Agrawal K. 2018. Characterization, incidence, transmission and biological control of *Ralstonia solanacearum* associated with soybean [*Glycine max* (L.) merrill] in Rajasthan, India. Res. Crop. 19(3):472–479.
7. Jeevan U, Kurian PS, Sreelatha U, Mathew D, Narayanankutty C. 2021. Morphological, symptomatological and molecular charac-terization of Enterobacter cloacae causing bacterial wilt in African marigold (*Tagetes erecta* L.). Indian Phytopathol. 75: 279-285. doi:10.1007/s42360-02100414310.1007/s42360-021-00414-3
8. Lamichhane JR, Messean A, Morris CE. 2015. Insights into epidemiology and control of diseases of annual plants caused by the *Pseudomonas syringae* species complex. J. Gen. Plant Pathol. 81(5): 331–350. doi:10.1007/s10327-015-0605-z
9. Lamichhane JR, Varvaro LA. 2013. New medium for the detection of fluorescent pigment production by pseudomonads. Plant Pathol. 62: 624–632.
10. Margarita G, Antonio B, Magdalena M, Elena GV, Jorge L. 2017. Clarification of Taxonomic Status within the *Pseudomonas syringae* Species Group Based on a Phylogenomic Analysis. Front Microbiol. 8:2422 URL=https://www.frontiersin.org/article/10.3389/fmicb.2017.02422 DOI=10.3389/fmicb.2017.02422 ISSN=1664-302X
11. Marques E, Borges, RCF, Uesugi, CH. 2016. Identification and pathogenicity of *Pseudomonas cichorii* associated with a bacterial blight of gerbera in the Federal District. Horticultura Brasileira. 34:244-248. DOI http://dx.doi.org/10.1590/S0102-053620160000200015
12. Mir RA, Ahanger MA, Agarwal RM. 2019. Marigold: From Mandap to Medicine and from Ornamentation to Remediation. Am. J. Plant Sci. 10(2) 309-338. https://doi.org/ 10.4236/ ajps.2019.102024
13. Mohan SK, Schaad NW. 1987. An improved agar plating assayfor detecting *Pseudomonas syringae* pv. *syringae* and P. s.

pv.*phaseolicola* in contaminated bean seed. Phytopathol. 77:1390–1395

14. Gradila M, Dinu S, Jaloba D, Ciontu VM, Bartha S. 2021. Experimental treatment of biopreparattion based on *Pseudomonas syringae pv. tagetis* for weeds control. Nardi Fundulea, Romania Romanian Agricultural Research. pp 39. www.incda-fundulea.ro First Online: November, 2021. DII 2067-5720 RAR 2022-130

15. O'Malley MR, Anderson JC. 2021. Regulation of the *Pseudomonas syringae* Type III Secretion System by Host Environment Signals. Microorganism*s*. 9(6):1227. https://doi.org/10.3390/microorganisms9061227

16. Peix A, Ramírez-Bahena MH, Velazquez E. 2018. The current status on the taxonomy of Pseudomonas revisited: An update. Infect. Genet. Evol. 57: 106–116.

17. Politi FA, Figueria CM, Aruio AM, Sampieri BR, Mathias MI, Szabo MP, Bachara GH, Santos LCD, Vilegas W, Pietro RC. 2012. Acaricidal activity of ethanolic extract from aerial parts of *Tagetes patula* L. (Asteraceae against larvae and engorged adult females of *Rhipicephalus sanguineus* (Latreille, 1806). Parasit Vectors. 17 (5):295.

18. Riaz M, Ahmad R, Rahman NU, Khan Z, Dou D, Sechel G, Manea R. 2020. Traditional uses, Phyto-chemistry and pharmacological activities of *Tagetes Patula* L. J. Ethnopharmacol. 255: 112718. doi:10.1016/j.jep.2020.112718

19. Robinson JM, Lydon J, Murphy CA, Rowland R, Smith RD. 2004. Effect of *Pseudomonas syringae* pv. *tagetis* Infection on Sunflower Leaf Photosynthetic and Ascorbic Acid Relations. Int. J. Plant Sci. 165(2): 263–271. doi:10.1086/382799

20. Saint-Vincent PM, Ridout M, Engle NL, Lawrence TJ, Yeary ML, Tschaplinski TJ, Newcombe G, Pelletier DA. 2020. Isolation, Characterization, and Pathogenicity of Two *Pseudomonas syringae* Pathovars from *Populus trichocarpa* Seeds. Microorganisms. 8(8):1137. https://doi.org/10.3390/microorganisms8081137

21. Shah D, Khan MS, Aziz S, Ali H, Pecoraro L. 2022. Molecular and Biochemical Characterization, Antimicrobial Activity,

Stress Tolerance, and Plant Growth- Promoting Effect of Endophytic Bacteria Isolated from Wheat Varieties. Microorganisms. 10: 21. https://doi.org/10.3390/microorganisms10010021

22. Song ES, Kim SY, Chae SC, Kim JG, Cho H, Kim S, Lee BM. 2015. PCR-based Assay for the Specific Detection of *Pseudomonas syringae* pv. *tagetis* using an AFLP-derived Marker. Res. Plant Dis. 21(1): 1-5. http://dx.doi.org/10.5423/RPD.2015.21.1.001

23. Suzuki A, Togawa M, Ohta K, Takikawa Y. 2003. Occurrence of white top of pea caused by a new strain of *Pseudomonas syringae* pv. *pisi*. Plant Dis. 87:1404-1410.

24. Tymon LS, Inglis DA. 2017. Identification and pathogenicity of *pseudomonas syringae* genomospecies 1 phylogroup 2B causing leaf spots and fruit warts on cucurbite in Western Washington, U.S. J. Plant Pathol. 99(3):713-722.

25. Whalen MC, Innes RW, Bent A, Staskawicz BJ. 1991. Identification of *Pseudomonas syringae* pathogens of Arabidopsis and a bacterial locus determining avirulence on both Arabidopsis and soybean. Plant Cell. 3: 49–59.

26. Wiebe WL. 1993. Characterization of *Pseudomonas syringae* pv. *maculicola* and Comparison with P. s. tomato. Plant Dis. 77: 414.

27. Xin XF, Kvitko B, He SY. 2018. *Pseudomonas syringae*: What it takes to be a pathogen. Nat. Rev. Genet. 16: 316–328.

28. Young JM and Fletcher MJ. (Eds) 1997. International Collection of Microorganisms from Plants: Catalogue Accession 1-12989 (3rd Edn), Manaaki Whenua Landcare Research, Auckland, pp 271

29. Zavala D, Fuenzalida I, Gangas MV, Peppino Margutti M, Bartoli C, Roux F, Meneses C, Herrera-Vasquez A, Blanco Herrera F. 2022. Molecular and Genomic Characterization of the *Pseudomonas syringae* Phylogroup 4: An Emerging Pathogen of *Arabidopsis thaliana* and *Nicotiana benthamiana*. Microorganisms. 10: 707. https://doi.org/10.3390/microorganisms10040707

30. Zhang JX, Lin BR, Shen HF, Pu XM, Wang ZW, Zeng DQ, Huang N. 2013. First Report of Bacterial Soft Rot on *Tagetes*

patula Caused by *Dickeya dieffenbachiae* in China. Plant Dis. 97(2): 282-282.

31. Gronwald JW, Plaisance KL, Ide DA, Wyse DL. 2002. Assessment of *Pseudomonas* syringae pv. tagetis as a biocontrol agent for Canada thistle. Weed Sci. 50:397-404.

32. Gulya TJ, Urs R, Banttari EE. 1982. Apical chlorosis of sunflower caused by *Pseudomonas syringae* pv. *tagetis*. Plant Dis. 66:598-600.

33. Hellmers E. 1955. Bacterial leaf spot of African marigold (*Tagetes erecta*) caused by *Pseudomonas tagetis* sp. n. Acta Agric. Scand. 5:185-200.

34. Rhodehamel NH, Durban RD. 1985. Host range of strains of *Pseudomonas syringae* pv. *tagetis*. Plant Dis. 69: 589-591.

35. Rhodehamel NH, Durbin RD. 1989. Two new hosts of *Pseudomonas syringae* pv. *tagetis*. Plant Dis. 73:368.

36. Shane WW, Baumer JS. 1984. Apical chlorosis and leaf spot of Jerusalem artichoke incited by *Pseudomonas syringae* pv, *tagetis*. Plant Dis. 68:257-260.

37. Styer DJ, Durbin RD. 1982. Isolation of *Pseudomonas syringae* pv. *tagetis* from sunflower in Wisconsin. Plant Dis. 66:601

38. Patyka V, Pasichnyk L, Butsenko L, Petrychenko V, Zubachev S, Dankevych L, Gnatiuk Y, Huliaiva H, Tokovenko I, Kalinichenko A. 2019. Express Diagnostics of Phytopathogenic Bacteria and Phytoplasmas in Agrophytocenosis. (Eds) Suszanowich D, Patyka V and Wyd-wo I. Drukarnia Swietego Krzyza, Opole, Poland. ISBN 978-83-7342-684-9.

39. Klement, Z. 1963. Rapid detection and the pathogenicity of pathogenicity of phytopathogenic Pseudomonas. Nature. 199:299-300.

40. Lydon J, Kong H, Murphy C, Zhang W. 2011. The Biology and Biological Activity of *Pseudomonas syringae* pv. *tagetis* Pest Technol. 5(1):48-55.

41. Salehi B, Valussi M, Morais-Braga M, Carneiro J, Leal A, Coutinho H, Vitalini S, Kręgiel D, Antolak H, Sharifi-Rad M, Silva N, Yousaf Z, Martorell M, Iriti M, Carradori S, & Sharifi-Rad J. 2018. *T*agetes spp. Essential Oils and Other Extracts: Chemical Characterization and Biological Activity. Molecules

(Basel, Switzerland). *23*(11):2847. https://doi.org/10.3390/molecules23112847

42. Sheikh T, Wheeler TA, Dotray PA, Zak JC. 2001. Biological Control of Woollyleaf Bursage (*Ambrosia grayi*) with *Pseudomonas* syringae pv.*tagetis*. Weed Technol. 15(2):375–381. doi:10.1614/0890-037x(2001)015[0375:bcowba]2.0.co;

**Department. of Botany,
Raj Rishi Govt. College , Alwar, (Raj.)
email : *pink.g.1993@gmail.com**

3. Chemicals and their Impact on Environment

Dr. Sudha Sukhwal Shringi

Abstract

Chemicals play a vital role in our everyday lives, from the food we eat to the products we use. However, the release of certain chemicals into the environment can have negative impact on human health and the ecosystem. The use of certain chemicals can have severe consequences for the environment and the organisms that depend on it. Therefore, it is important to use chemicals responsibly and to take steps to reduce the release of harmful chemicals into the environment. Due to these chemicals in the long run there is effect on climate and over the years if left unattended this can be a big factor for change in earths climate and global warming. Steps must be taken to reduce harmful chemicals usage and focus on using environment friendly ones.

Keywords : Chemicals, Pollution, Environment

Introduction

Chemicals and the environment are closely interconnected, as chemicals play a significant role in many human activities, such as industry, agriculture, and transportation. Chemicals can have a significant impact on the environment. They can contaminate air, water, and soil, and can also harm plants and animals. Some chemicals, such as pesticides and fertilizers, are designed to be used in the environment and can have negative effects on ecosystems if not used properly. Other chemicals, such as industrial pollutants and toxic waste, are released into the environment through accidents or improper disposal. These can also have harmful effects on wildlife, as well as on human health. Additionally, some chemicals can have long-lasting effects on the environment and can persist for many years. It is important to use chemicals responsibly and to properly manage and dispose of them to minimize their impact on the environment.

Introduction to chemistry and environmental science can provide an understanding of the ways in which chemicals are used and released into the environment, as well as the potential impacts these chemicals can have. This knowledge can then be used to develop strategies for reducing or preventing these negative impacts, such as regulations and best practices for chemical use and disposal. Chemicals are used in a wide range of products and processes, from everyday items such as cleaning supplies and personal care products, to larger-scale industrial operations such as manufacturing and agriculture. These chemicals can be released into the environment through a variety of means, including leaks, spills, and improper disposal. Some chemicals can have a direct impact on human health, such as those that are carcinogenic or toxic. Others can have an indirect impact, such as by harming the environment and the organisms that live within it. This can ultimately affect human health and well-being, as well as the health of the planet.

Chemical pollutants can have different effects on different organisms and environments. For example, heavy metals can be toxic to fish and other aquatic life, while pesticides can harm bees and other pollinators. Different chemicals also have different persistence in the environment. Some chemicals can degrade quickly, while others can last for many years, and even centuries.

To mitigate the negative impacts of chemicals on the environment, there are a variety of actions that can be taken, such as regulations and guidelines for chemical use and disposal, education and outreach programs, and development of alternative products and technologies. For example, the European Union has implemented the REACH regulation (Registration, Evaluation, Authorization and Restriction of Chemicals) which aims to improve the protection of human health and the environment from the risks that can be posed by chemicals.

Impact on Environment

Chemicals can have a significant impact on environmental pollution in various ways. Some common examples include:

Air pollution: Certain chemicals, such as sulfur dioxide, nitrogen oxides, and volatile organic compounds (VOCs), can be released into the air during industrial processes and contribute to the formation of smog and acid rain.

Water Pollution : Chemicals can contaminate water sources through industrial and agricultural runoff, as well as through leaks and spills. For example, pesticides and fertilizers can run off into rivers and streams, harming aquatic life and making water unsafe for human consumption.

Soil Pollution : Chemicals used in agriculture and industry can contaminate the soil, making it difficult for plants to grow and reducing the ability of the soil to support a diverse ecosystem.

Plastic Pollution : plastics are made from chemical compounds and its accumulation in the oceans and on the land, can cause harm to marine life, animals and birds and also affect human health and livelihoods.

Persistent Organic Pollutants (POPs) are chemicals that are extremely toxic, persistent in the environment, and can travel long distances. These chemicals can have harmful effects on human health and the environment, and they can accumulate in the food chain, leading to dangerous levels of exposure for animals and humans.

Endocrine Disruptors : Certain chemicals can mimic or interfere with the body's hormones, leading to a range of health effects such as developmental disorders, cancer, and reproductive problems.

Climate Change : Some chemicals, such as chlorofluorocarbons (CFCs), can contribute to the depletion of the ozone layer, while others, such as carbon dioxide and methane, are greenhouse gases that contribute to global warming.

Microplastics : Microplastics are small particles of plastic that are smaller than 5mm and can be ingested by marine organisms and also can enter our food chain via sea food, these can have hazardous effects on human health.

Some examples of chemicals that can cause environmental pollution include pesticides, lead, and industrial pollutants such as polychlorinated biphenyls (PCBs).

Pesticides are used to protect crops and control pests, but they can also harm beneficial insects, birds, and other animals. In addition, pesticides can contaminate water and soil, making it difficult for plants and animals to survive.

Lead is a toxic metal that was commonly used in paint and gasoline in the past. Although its use has been greatly reduced, lead is still present in the environment and can harm human health and wildlife.

Ways to Reduce Impact of Chemicals

To reduce the impact of chemicals on environmental pollution, there are several strategies that can be employed:

Substitution : Finding safer alternatives to harmful chemicals is an effective way to reduce pollution. For example, using bio-based pesticides instead of synthetic pesticides can reduce the impact of agriculture on the environment.

Source Reduction : Reducing the amount of chemicals used and/or the rate at which they are released into the environment can significantly reduce pollution.

Recycling and Waste Reduction : Reducing the amount of waste produced can decrease the amount of pollution that is generated. For example, recycling paper, plastic and metals instead of throwing them away can help reduce pollution.

Proper Disposal : Properly disposing of chemicals can prevent them from entering the environment and causing pollution.

Regulations and laws : Government regulations can play a crucial role in reducing pollution and protecting the environment, by implementing laws and regulations that set standards for chemical use, and penalties for violating those standards.

Public Awareness : Raising public awareness of the dangers of chemical pollution and the importance of reducing pollution can help bring about positive changes in behavior and attitudes.

It's important to note that, protecting the environment from chemical pollution is a complex task that requires the collaboration of governments, industry, and the public. By working together and taking a holistic approach, we can reduce the impact of chemicals on the environment and protect human health.

Here are a few additional ways to reduce pollution by putting in extra efforts and by creating awareness.

Clean Energy : transitioning to clean energy sources, such as solar and wind power, can help reduce pollution from fossil fuels and curb greenhouse gas emissions.

Transportation : Encouraging the use of public transportation, biking, and walking, and promoting the use of electric and hybrid cars can help reduce air pollution from vehicle emissions.

Green Infrastructure : Incorporating green spaces and natural features, such as trees, rain gardens, and green roofs, into urban areas can help reduce pollution and improve air and water quality.

Industrial Design : Re-designing industrial processes to use fewer resources and generate less waste can significantly reduce pollution.

Water conservation: Reducing the amount of water that is used can help reduce pollution by decreasing the amount of pollutants that are present in water sources and reducing the amount of energy that is needed to treat the water.

Proper Waste Management : Properly managing waste, through sorting, recycling, composting, and reusing, can help reduce pollution and conserve resources.

Consumer Choices : Every day choices on consumer products, packaging and food we buy, can impact the pollution and waste, by choosing eco-friendly products and packaging, we can reduce pollution.

International Cooperation : Reducing pollution often requires cooperation between countries, as pollution knows no borders. International agreements and protocols, such as the United Nations Framework Convention on Climate Change and the Paris Agreement, are important mechanisms for addressing global pollution problems.

Overall, there are many ways to stop pollution, from individual actions to policy changes. It's important to take a multi-faceted approach to pollution control and to involve everyone in the effort to create a cleaner and more sustainable future.

Environmentally friendly chemicals are substances that are less harmful to the environment than traditional chemicals. They may be biodegradable, non-toxic, or made from renewable resources. Examples include plant-based cleaning products, non-toxic pesticides, and biodegradable plastics. These types of chemicals can help reduce pollution and protect ecosystems.

Some Additional Examples of Environmentally Friendly Chemicals Include :

Enzymes : These are proteins that can be used to replace harsh chemicals in cleaning products, helping to break down stains and grime while being less harmful to the environment.

Citric Acid : This naturally occurring acid can be used as a pH adjuster and preservative in cleaning products and food, and is a safer alternative to harsh chemical acids like sulfuric acid.

Baking Soda : A natural abrasive, baking soda can be used as a scouring powder in cleaning products and can also be used as a deodorizer.

Solvents : Some solvents such as ethanol, propanol, and butanol are less toxic and more biodegradable than traditional solvents such as benzene and toluene.

Conclusion

Overall, an understanding of the relationship between chemicals and the environment is important for developing sustainable and responsible practices that protect human health and the planet. It's important to note that chemicals can also contribute to climate change. Some chemicals, such as carbon dioxide and methane, are greenhouse gases which trap heat in the atmosphere and contribute to global warming. The use of fossil fuels, which are a major source of these gases, is a major contributor to climate change.

Lastly, it is also important to consider the global aspect of chemicals and environment. Many countries, particularly developing countries, may lack the infrastructure and resources to properly regulate and manage chemicals. This can lead to increased risks to human health and the environment, as well as contribute to global environmental issues such as the pollution of international waters and the destruction of biodiversity.

In conclusion, chemicals and the environment are closely interconnected, and the effects of chemicals on the environment can be complex and far-reaching. It is essential to understand the sources, uses, and impacts of chemicals, as well as the strategies and actions that can be taken to minimize these impacts, to ensure the protection of human health and the planet.

References

1. "Persistent Organic Pollutants: An Overview" by R. Harner and M.J. Schenker in Environmental Science & Technology, vol. 38, no. 17, pp. 3939-3945, 2004.
2. "Chemicals in the Environment: Assessing and Managing Risk" by D.E.G. Irvine, R.C. Buck, and D.J. Wilson in Nature, vol. 479, pp. 323-329, 2011.
3. "The impact of chemical pollutants on wildlife, habitats and ecosystems" by R.D. Everett in Environmental Pollution, vol. 202, pp. 8-16, 2015.
4. Environmental Protection Agency (EPA): https://www.epa.gov/ chemical-research
5. National Institutes of Health (NIH): https://www.niehs.nih.gov/ health/topics/index.cfm
6. World Health Organization (WHO): https://www.who.int/ environmental_health_emergencies/chemical_risks/en/

Associate Professor
Department of Chemistry
Rajrishi College Alwar, Rajasthan,
India

4. Responsibilities of Teachers in the Perspective of Environmental Protection

Dr. Chiinkhanniang Tombing

Abstract

Awareness of environmental protection is not a recent idea. Due to rapid industrialization, urbanization and pollution the living conditions of the people in the world have been deteriorated gradually and very rapidly. It is seriously degraded and there is creating an imbalance and disharmony. At the point when common assets of environments are exhausted, environment is considered to be corrupted and harmed. There are a number of different techniques that are being used to prevent this, including environmental resource protection and general protection efforts.

So a great need is being felt to create awareness for the protection of the environment by redesigning the objectives, methods and curriculum in the field of education.

Education is regarded as an important instrument and means for generating proper awareness and adequate knowledge and skills regarding environment protection. In that case a teacher plays vital role in growing or inculcating awareness among the students. The teacher should motivate and train the students to acquire and spread knowledge and skills that would help the society to solve inter-related environmental problems and prevent their occurrence.

Keywords : Environmental degradation, Development, Resource, Protection, Awareness.

Introduction :

Environmental degradation is the disintegration of the earth or deterioration of the environment through consumption of assets, for example, air, water and soil, the destruction of environments and the eradication of wildlife. Awareness means to help social groups and individuals acquire a knowledge of and sensitivity to the total environment and its related problems. Environment includes both living and non-living objects in the world, their interactions and the products of these interactions. Men is the most dynamic element in the ecosystem because he changes most of the other elements in the environment. Even after realizing well about the relation of man with nature and environment, the modern community of human being does not protect his environment and is responsible for its pollution. Due to rapid industrialization, urbanization and pollution the living conditions of the people in the world have been deteriorated gradually and very rapidly. Here we feel for a great need of Environmental Education (EE) which helps to learn the survival capacity or strategies for the present or future generation. "Environmental Education is a way of implementing the goals of environmental protection. Environmental Education is not a separate branch of science or subjects of study. It should be carried out according to the principle of life-long integral education." (Finnish National Commission for UNESCO, Report of the Seminar on Environmental Education, Janni, Finland, 1974).

The young learners in today's world are preparing for life and for work tomorrow. Their life styles differ very widely and the situations in which they acquire knowledge, skills and attitudes relevant to life and work also differ very remarkably. Now the question arises that how can environmental education objectives be infused into the curriculum so that not only sound educational principles of acquisition and transfer are followed but also that receivers are able to synthesize their experiences in various disciplines into a meaningful environmental awareness context. In order to provide right knowledge and to develop right attitude towards environmental education the teachers play a vital role. The teacher should motivate and train the students to acquire and spread knowledge and skills that would help the society to solve inter-related environmental problems and prevent their occurrence. It should co-relate the topics of environmental issues while teaching the subjects. It can be helpful to create environmental protection awareness among the public to safeguard its own environment from the adverse environmental damage.

Objectives :

The study has some objectives –

1) To focus on the process of practicing the environment-related awareness

2) To understand the role of a teacher towards students in respect of environmental education.
3) To mention the status of environmental education in different institutional level.
4) To elaborate the methods of environmental education teaching.

Responsibility of a Teacher to make Aware Students about the Environmental Protection.

It is the duty of the teacher to show always the right direction to the society. In fact, he can develop a healthy attitude among the students towards building a healthy environment. Hence, all teachers in the institutions are expected to play a significant role in the environmental conservation and sustainable development. Teachers has to foster love and sympathy for the natural environment among their students, and to train them to appreciate the nature.

A teacher should play the following roles in the conservation and sustainable development of the environment:

- Motivate and train the students to acquire and spread knowledge and skills that would help the society to solve inter-related environmental problems and prevent their occurrence.
- Organize seminars and workshops on environmental issues like soil erosion, population explosion and deforestation.
- Discuss environmental issues alongwith simple teaching activities through which learners understand the importance of environmental resources.
- Teach the inter-dependence of living things and the relationship between the needs of the society and the interaction with the environment.
- Select, develop, and implement curricular materials which make students aware of how man's cultural activities (religious, economic, political and social aspects) influence the environment from an ecological perspective and how individual behavior impacts the environment from an ecological perspective.
- Make students aware of the need for environmental issues, investigation and evaluation as a pre-requisite to sound decision making.
- Tell students about the relationship between a healthy life and pure natural environment.

- Organize field-trips to Zoos, National parks, polluted cities, polluted rivers, birds' sanctuaries and deforested sites.

The young learners belong to an age-group which is a very crucial stage in their life. Their spontaneity, curiosity, creativity and activity, in general should be used to promote teaching-learning in their immediate environments with a view to developing desirable knowledge, skulls and attitudes. Education should take into consideration the social, intellectual, emotional and physical maturity of the individual as well as the socio-economic needs of their community. Education should emphasize on a basic minimum to be achieved in respect of each and every individual and should also have enough scope for flexibility and local adjustments to permit each institution to go as far beyond the basic minimum as its circumstances permit. There should be scope for developing problem-solving ability among the students. The activities requiring the development of problem-solving ability are the basis of any instruction aimed at developing abilities particularly demanded for effective improvement. The very nature of environmental studies makes it imperative that the planning of teaching-learning activity should be such that the classroom becomes a laboratory for living and learning as students search for information and react to this experience. There should be provision for continuous evaluation of activities in the teaching-learning situation. Teacher's observation during problem-solving situation is very important. The teacher should evaluate how far the students are able to develop awareness about environmental pollution and the method of controlling the same.

Practical work and Activities undertaken by the Institution for Environmental conservation and Sustainable Development.

For a long-term development of our environment, we should give our efforts very much practically, not theoretically. In this regard educational institution can play a vital role represented as below :

- **To inculcate the Environmental Values in a Learner**

Human values are closely integrated with human life. They are inter-twined with our day-to-day chores. No human life is possible without values. How much of virtues and vices are filled in depends solely on the parents, teachers, circumstances, environment, and sometimes even geographic location. However everyone can be inculcated with human values by the parents, teachers, friends and even strangers. Self education of human values is also possible by meeting, learning and reading about, great individuals living a holistic life.

At institutional level we can produce or apply a very good method named as **"Brain Storming method"** by which it is easily possible to inculcate the environmental values among the present and future generation or group of students for sustainable development.

Brain-storming is a strategy or technique for allowing a group to explore ideas without judgment. In practice the students may be asked to sit in a group for solving a problem and attacking it without any inhibition from many angles: in fact, literally storming it with a number of possible ideas and solutions. The technique should be applied in the whole class at a time. The students get the opportunity for divergent thinking and they become very active and conscious about the problem. During the session the teacher should observe and encourage them with strolling. Thus internal discussion becomes very much lively and fruitful. As all the students can participate at that time, so the participants are inspired through creative thinking.

Some type of motivating questions should be put forward to the students to make them think divergently. And various creative solutions may come-out from this brainstorming session.

Besides this, there are many different methods to help the students to know the ways of improving environment. Some of them are mentioned below :

(a) Small-Group project method
(b) Field-trip method
(c) Outdoor study method
(d) Creative thinking
(e) Experiential learning
(f) Use of exhibits
(g) Inquiry learning
(h) Community programmes
(i) Environmental Educational Forum
(j) Problem-solving method

(k) Story-telling
(l) Collaborative approach
(m)Celebration of Environmental Calendar, etc.

Through the implementation of such various practical works, methods, celebration of environmental calendar, etc. Our young generation can develop and sustain the habitable environment for our future, if we the teachers community try to retain and continue the practice as a never ending process. So, we have to make our students to realize that they are part of the problem, and therefore they have to be part of the solutions.

Work and Activities

- Collection of plants and flowers.
- Survey of animals and their modes of living.
- Observation of growth of plants and maintenance of record book.
- Writing essays-poems on forest and natural environment.
- Preparing posters on global warming.
- Preparing charts and crap-books on environment related issues.
- Organizing debates, exhibition and discussion on environmental issues.

Conclusion

Teachers can help nurture the love for the environment through formal and informal educational tools. Institutional authorities have to ensure that environmental education is a significant part of the curriculum for all stages of education seminars, field-trips, competitions and faires on environmental themes help the students identify their interest in nature and choose a related career. What the students learn early in life for cleanliness, conservation and use of resources would stay with him all his life.

Voluntary groups may be formed in each institution which can be the medium for the message of clean air, clean water, and clean environment. Visit areas to help local community can make understand the concept of Blue and Green bins. Organize drawing competitions and seminars to encourage students in the Green Good Deeds. Students can join local RWAs, and identify NGOs and Nature Clubs in their area to participate in Green Good Deeds. Plant saplings and make the area green. Inspire others also in doing so. Involving teacher would mean reaching-out to several students.

Reaching-out to students would mean we have initiated a mass movement in our aim to save the environment. And it would also mean reaching-out to future generations. Students should have the energy, the initiative and to create inquisitiveness to learn more. Spread awareness about protection of ozone layer, and ozone depleting substances. Plant and nurture trees in institutions and neighborhood. Students should be taught to avoid cutting or damaging trees or flowers on plants. Institutions may audit air quality, and educate students on pedestrian etiquette and responsibility. Institutions may make involve the young students in the whole process of new concepts and trend setting requirements of the society. The idea is to go about doing this through teachers. Once the teachers are made aware of the challenges of the future, the knowledge is passed onto the students simply and easily.

References :
1. Brainstorming - Mind Tools content Team, Retrieved from – http://www.mindtools.com/brainstom.html
2. Das, B.N. (2014) : Trends and Issues in Indian Education, Dominent Publishers and Distributors Private Ltd., New-Delhi, India, ISBN: 978-93-82007-02-9 (HB), 978-93-82007-54-8 (PB), P-375,376,378.
3. How to inculcate Human values-Retrieved from-www.wikihow.com/inculcate-Human-values.
4. How to Run a Brainstorming Meeting ? Scott Berkun, Retrieved from–http://scottberkun.com/essays/34-how-to-run-a-brainstorming-meeting/
5. Mangal, S.K. (2006) : Advanced Educational Psychology, 2nd Edition, Prentice Hall of India, Private Ltd., New-Delhi-110001, ISBN – 81-203-2038-7,P-350-351.

Associate Professor,
Deptt. of Education, Imphal College,
(Under Manipur University)
Govt. College, Airport Road, Imphal West, Manipur.
email : ckniangtombing@gmail.com

5. Kinetics of the Uninhibited and Resorcinol Inhibited with Coo Catalysed Autoxidation of Sulfur (Iv) in Alkaline Heterogenous Medium

Manoj Kumar[1]
Manju Bala Yadav[1]
D.S.N.Prasad[2]

Abstract

The kinetics of resorcinol inhibited CoO catalysed S(IV) autoxidation in the pH range 7.50 to 8.50 medium have been investigated and a rate law &free radical mechanism have been proposed based on the observed results and inhibition parameters. In all situations, the reaction's order and rate constants were calculated, meanwhile, the reaction was determined to be first-order. The impact of various temperatures & pH levels were explored also. We reported resorcinol as a significant inhibitor for SO_2 autoxidation in the pH range of 7.50 to 8.80. The Arrhenius equation was used to get the value of apparent activation energy (E_a) ($K= A.e^{-E_a/RT}$).

$$\frac{-d[S(IV)]}{dt} = \frac{(k_1 + k_2 [CoO]) [S(IV)]}{1 + B [Resorcinol]}$$

Introduction

In atmospheric chemistry, one of the serious global problems is acid rain, in which the pH of the rainwater decreases. It is a common occurrence in several industrially developed countries in the northern hemisphere. Through the process of moist depositions, it has extremely detrimental effects on plants, aquatic creatures, soil, structures, and materials. Acid rain is formed by ammonium, carbon, nitrogen, and sulfur chemicals in the atmosphere reacting with water molecules to produce acids. The kinetics of dissolved sulfur dioxide oxidation has been the focus of several recent reviews due to its role in acid rain chemistry[1-3]. Studies in India and abroad have shown that anthropogenic sources in the atmosphere are the major contributors of SO_2 and NO_x which are transformed into acids such as HNO_2, HNO_3, H_2SO_3, and H_2SO_4. The atmospheric reactions of SO_2 and NO_x etc. are major acid rain precursors and responsible for the acidification of various forms of atmospheric water[4,5].

34

The oxidative transformation of sulfur dioxide into sulfuric acid is the primary cause of acid precipitation in the atmosphere. Oxidation is catalysed by dissolved trace metal ions and suspended particulate particles in the aqueous phase. Which are created in the atmosphere by photochemical reactions between O_3 and H_2O_2 in the gaseous phase. A large number of organic and inorganic chemical species are released into the atmosphere by anthropogenic and natural sources. The subsequent photochemical and thermal reactions of these species in gas and aqueous phases form the backbone of atmospheric chemistry[6]. The oxidation of aqueous sulfur dioxide into acid sulfate is catalysed by trace metal ions found in all atmospheric systems.

Metal oxides are a component of suspended particulate matter (SPM) that is discharged into the atmosphere as a result of combustion activities. In this regard, the catalytic role of numerous metal oxides in acidic media, such as CoO[7], Co_2O_3[8], Ni_2O_3[9], CuO[10], MnO_2[11], and Cu_2O[12] has been thoroughly investigated. The kinetics aligned with the rate law for the first five oxides (1).

$$-d[S(IV)]/dt = (k'_1 + k''_2 [H^+]^{-1})[Catalyst]\ [S(IV)] \quad (1)$$

Where k'_1 and k''_2 are the rate constants for HSO_3^- and SO_3^{2-} autoxidation, respectively.

Rate inhibition by organics such as ethanol owing to scavenging of oxy sulfur radicals engaged in radical autoxidation is an interesting property of many radical reactions, and specifics of the process may be found in papers[13-18] and reviews[19-22]. Bigelow et al., (1988)[23] postulated a radical mechanism for CoO and Co_2O_3 by preventing the CoO, Co_2O_3, and Ni_2O_3 catalysed autoxidation reaction in an alkaline medium. Aleya and Backstromet al.,(1929)[24] looked researched how aliphatic alcohols including ethanol, isopropanol, secondary butanol, and benzyl alcohol hinder sodium sulfite oxidation under alkaline environments. Alcohols, which are abundantly found in both urban and rural environments, are classified as volatile organic compounds (VOCs) postulated by Hussain, F. et al.,.(2018)[25] and J.ziajka, W. Pasiuk-bronikowskaet al., (2003)[26]. Through their interactions with hydroxyl, nitrate, and sulfate radicals, they play an important role in troposphere chemistry[26,27]. The interaction of alcohols with SO_2 oxidation intermediates could have an impact on the development of acidity in the atmosphere. Organics such as acetic acid[21], oxalic acid[21], alcohols[28,29], carboxylic acid[30,31], ammonia, formic acid[32-34], aniline[35], benzamide[36], sodium benzoate[37], ascorbic acid[37], organic compounds[38], VOCs[39-42,48], and diesel truck particles[43] decrease the pace of numerous radical processes. The pH of water on the Indian subcontinent ranges from 6.5 to 8.5. This needs to research into S(IV) autoxidation in alkaline medium pH ranges.

Most studies have mentioned the role of organics in the metal ion catalysed autoxidation of S(IV) in aqueous media. The inhibitory impact of resorcinol on metal oxide catalysed aqueous sulfur dioxide autoxidation has yet to be investigated. There is very little research founded on the effect of organics on the cobalt oxide catalysed autoxidation of S(IV) in an aqueous heterogeneous alkaline solution. To characterize the nature of the process, we investigated the kinetics of S(IV) autoxidation catalysed by CoO in the pH range 7.50 - 8.50 and the influence of resorcinol in an aqueous heterogeneous alkaline media.

Experimental

The procedure for the experiment was the same as previously reported[41,42] and is summarized in this paragraph. A conductivity (doubled distilled) water solution was used to prepare all of the chemical solutions. A "150 ml Erlenmeyer flask" was used for the reactions, which were carried out with the lid open so that oxygen from the atmosphere could flow through. When the target temperature of $30\pm0.10^{\circ}C$ was desired, the flask was positioned in a beaker with an inlet at the bottom and exit at the top. Standard Na_2SO_3 solution was mixed into the reaction mixture together with buffer and catalyst (metal oxide) in the necessary volume to start the reactions. To avoid the reaction from becoming oxygen mass transfer controlled, we used a magnetic stirrer set to 1600 ± 100 rpm to continually agitate the reaction mixture. There were no pH fluctuations during the experiment, which allowed for a better understanding of how reactions proceed. To achieve the necessary pH, 100 ml of buffer containing 10 cm^3 of Na_2HPO_4 (0.08 mol dm^{-3}) and KH_2PO_4 (0.02 mol dm^{-3}) alkaline medium was utilized. Aliquots of S(IV) were taken occasionally and titrated iodometrically in slightly alkaline media to monitor the kinetics. Replica measurements were frequently within +10% of each other in terms of accuracy. MS Excel-2010 was used for all calculations and graphs in the trials.

Product Analysis

Sulfate was found to be the only product of oxidation in the qualitative tests. "The reaction mixtures containing catalyst and S(IV) inappropriately buffered solutions were constantly stirred for a sufficiently long time to ensure complete oxidation of sulfur(IV)," according to the quantitative analysis. CoO was filtered out after the reaction was finished, and sulfate was calculated gravimetrically by precipitating sulfate ions as $BaSO_4$ using standard procedure[43].

According to the product analysis, sulfate recovery was 98+2% in all cases, which is consistent with Eq. (2)

$$S(IV)+0.5O_2 S(VI) \longrightarrow \dots\dots\dots\dots\dots\dots \quad (2)$$

Results

1. PreliminaryInvestigation

The kinetics of both uncatalysed and CoO catalysed reaction were studies in alkaline medium in the pH range 7.5 to 8.50. In both cases, the kinetics was first order in [S(IV)] and the treatment of kinetics data is based on the determination of first order rate constant k_1 from log [S(IV)] versus time (t),plots as shown in Fig.1.

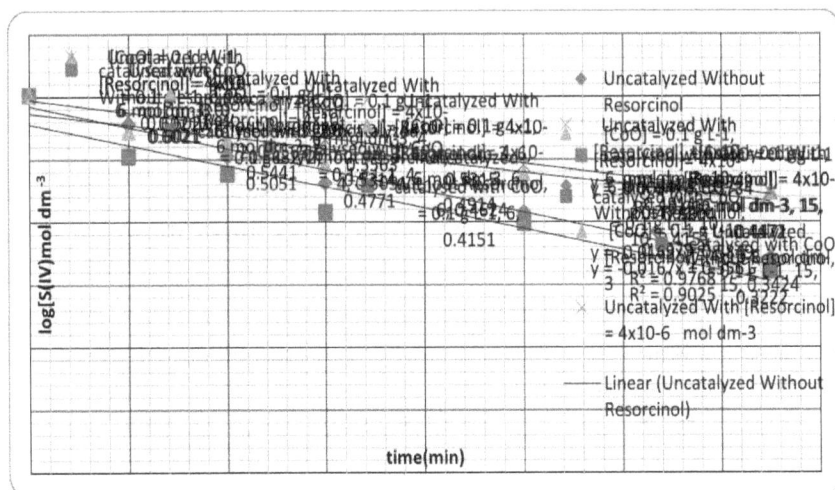

Fig.1: The disappearance of [S(IV)] with time in air-saturated suspensions at[S(IV)] = $2x10^{-3}$mol dm^{-3}at Temp.= 30^{0}C and pH=7.50in phosphate-buffered medium

2. Uncatalysedreaction : In ths study the reaction was studied without adding CoO.

3. Dependence of Sulphite :

The detailed dependence of the reaction rate on [S(IV)] was studied by varying it is in the range 1×10^{-3} to 8×10^{-3} mol dm^{-3}at pH = 7.50, time =30°C in phosphate buffer medium.

The kinetics was found to be first order in [S(IV)] as shown in Fig.1, log [S(IV)]v/s time plots were linear. The Value of first order rate constant, $k_1$are given in Table- 1,are seen to be independent of [S(IV)] and are in agreement with the rate law (3):

$$-d[S(IV)]/dt = k_1[S(IV)]\ldots\ldots\ldots\ldots(3)$$

Table-1:The values of $k_1$for uncatalysed reaction at different [S(IV)] at pH = 7.50,Temp.= 30°C in phosphate-buffered medium

[S(IV)]mol dm^{-3}	0.001	0.002	0.004	0.006	0.008
10^4 k_1s^{-1}	6.837	6.496	6.332	6.706	6.117

4. [Resorcinol] dependence:

The main goal of this research was to see how different organic inhibitors affected the reaction rate of sulfur(IV) autoxidation in a phosphate-buffered medium. Resorcinol was chosen as one of the organic inhibitor compounds for this study. On increasing the concentration of resorcinol from 2×10^{-7} to 1×10^{-3} mol dm^{-3}, the rate of reaction was decreased. However, in the presence of resorcinol, the nature of the [S(IV)] dependence remained first order and did not change. The first-order rate constant k_{inh} was defined by rate law (4) in presence of resorcinol.

$$-d[S(IV)]/dt = k_{inh}[S(IV)] \ldots\ldots\ldots\ldots\ldots\ldots (4)$$

The values of k_{inh} at different [Resorcinol] are given in table-2

Rate law (4) specified the values of first-order rate constant k_{inh} in the presence of decreasing, with rising [Resorcinol] following the rate law (5).

$$k_{inh} = k_1 /(1+B[Resorcinol]) \ldots\ldots\ldots\ldots (5)$$

where **(B) is inhibition parameter** for rate inhibition by resorcinol.

By rearranging the equation (5) we get

$$1/k_{inh} = 1/k_1 + B[Resorcinol] / k_1 \ldots\ldots\ldots\ldots(6)$$

Following Eq. (6), the plot of $1/k_{inh}$ versus [Resorcinol] was found to be linear with a non-zero intercept, fig.-2

Where intercept = $1/k_1$ and slope = B/k_1. The values of $1/k_1$ and B/k_1 were found to be 2.2×10^3 s & 4.2×10^6 $mol^{-1}dm^3$ s at pH =7.50, and Temp.= $30^{\circ}C$. The slope/intercept relationship provides us with the value of the inhibitory parameter (B), which was determined to be 1.9×10^3 mol^{-1} dm^3.

Table-2: The values of k_{inh} at different [Resorcinol], [S(IV)] = 2×10^{-3} mol dm^{-3}, pH = 7.50, Temp. = $30^{\circ}C$, Na_2HPO_4 = 8×10^{-2} mol dm^{-3}, KH_2PO_4 = 2×10^{-2} mol dm^{-3}

[Resorcinol] mol dm^{-3}	2×10^{-7}	5×10^{-7}	3×10^{-6}	4×10^{-6}	7×10^{-5}	2×10^{-4}	5×10^{-4}	1×10^{-3}
$10^4 k_{inh}$ s^{-1}	8.58	6.94	4.18	3.87	3.34	3.19	2.27	1.53
$1/k_{inh}$ s	1166	1440	2439	2591	2994	3135	4405	6536

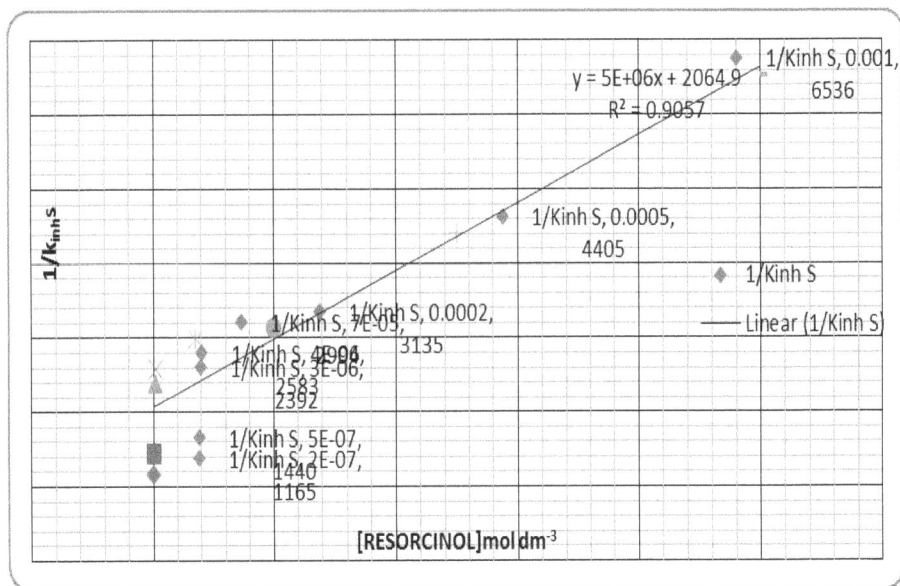

Fig.2.Effect of Resorcinol at [S(IV)] =2×10^{-3}mol dm^{-3} at Temp. = $30^{\circ}C$, pH= 7.50 in phosphate-buffered medium

5. CoO - Catalysed Reaction :

First of all the kinetics of CoO catalysed reaction on the autoxidation of sulfur(IV) was investigated in the absence of inhibitor-resorcinol at pH = 7.50 and Temp. = 30°C in alkaline phosphate-buffered medium.

6. [S(IV)] Variation :

[S(IV)] was varied from 1×10^{-3} to 10×10^{-3} **mol dm**$^{-3}$ at two different but static[CoO] of 0.1 and 0.2g L^{-1} was carried out at pH =7.50 and time = 30°C the results show that first order in [S(IV)] plots were linear.

7. [CoO] Variation :

The effect of [CoO] was studied by varying [CoO] from 0.1g dm^{-3} to 0.5g dm^{-3} at [S(IV)] of 2×10^{-3} mol dm^{-3} at pH = 7.50 and Temp.= 30°C in alkaline phosphate-buffered heterogeneous medium. The first-order rate constants' values k_{cat} for S(IV) autoxidation were observed at different [CoO] at pH = 7.50, Temp.= 30°C are given in table-3.

The character of dependence of k_{cat} on [CoO] shown in fig-3 indicates the two-term rate law.

$$\text{dt d[S(IV)]} = k_{cat} [S(IV)] = (k_1 + k_2 [CoO]) [S(IV)] \ldots \ldots (7)$$

or

$$k_{cat} = k_1 + k_2 [CoO]$$

From the graph plots in fig-3. "The values of intercept are equal to k_1 and the slope is equal to k_2 were found to be **1.5×10^{-3} s and 9.3×10^{-3} mol^{-1} dm^3 s,** respectively at pH = 7.50 and Temp.= 30°C in an alkaline phosphate-buffered medium."

Table-3: The value of k_{cat} at different [CoO] at S(IV)] = 2×10^{-3} mol L^{-1}, pH = 7.50, time = 30°C

[CoO]g dm^{-3}	0.1	0.2	0.3	0.4	0.5
$10^4 k_1 s^{-1}$	7.07	9.87	12.30	16.11	20.33

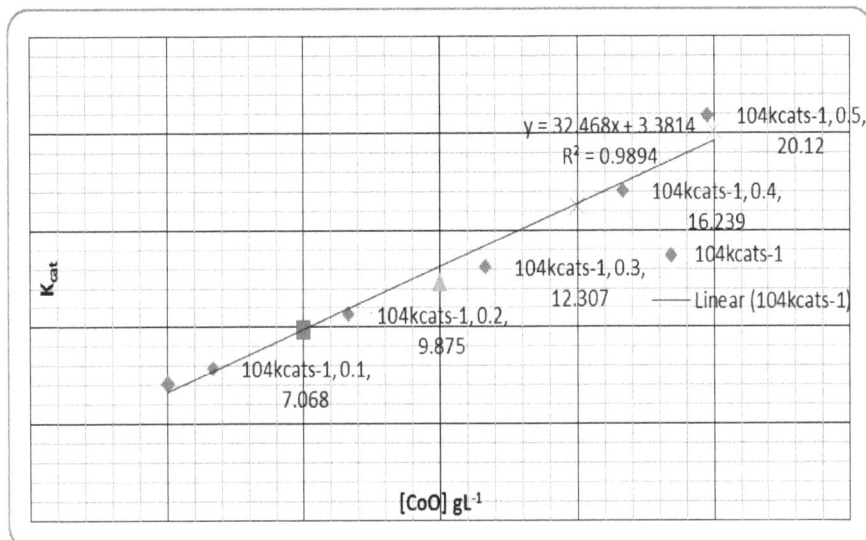

Fig. 3. Effect of CoO at [S(IV)] = 2×10^{-3} mol L^{-1}, pH=7.50 and t= 30°C, in phosphate in phosphate-buffered medium.

8. Rate of reaction studies in the presence of resorcinol :

The effect of [Resorcinol] on CoO catalysed S(IV) autoxidation [Resorcinol]variation was carried out from 2×10^{-7} to 1×10^{-3} mol dm^{-3} at two diverse [CoO] that is 0.1 and 0.2 g dm^{-3} but fixed [S(IV)] = 2×10^{-3} mol dm^{-3} at pH = 7.50 and Temp.= 30°C in alkaline phosphate-buffered medium. The results indicate that increasing the [Resorcinol] concentration decreases the rate of reaction i.e., on the other hand, inhibition happens.

In the presence of resorcinol, a comprehensive examination of the rate dependence on [S(IV)], [CoO], and pH found that the kinetics persist first order in equally [S(IV)] & [CoO] and are independent of pH. The results are given in Table-4.

A graph was plotted between [CoO] versus k_{cat} and was found linear with a non-zero intercept. **The intercept and slope values are found to be 2.9x10^{-3} s^{-1} and 4.7x10^{-3} g^{-1}dm^3 s^{-1}.**

The dependence of observed results for the reaction follows the following rate law in presence of resorcinol. Eq.(8).

$$\frac{-d[S(IV)]}{dt} = \frac{(k_1 + k_2[CoO])\,[S(IV)]}{1 + B\,[Resorcinol]} \quad (8)$$

$$\text{where} \quad k_{inh} = \frac{k_1 + k_2[CoO]}{1 + B[Resorcinol]} = \frac{k_{cat}}{1 + B[Resorcinol]} \quad (9)$$

$$\frac{1}{k_{inh}} = \frac{1 + B\,[Resorcinol]}{k_{cat}} \quad (10)$$

$$\frac{1}{k_{inh}} = \frac{1}{k_{cat}} + \frac{B\,[Resorcinol]}{k_{cat}} \quad (11)$$

By producing a second graph between $1/k_{inh}$ versus [Resorcinol], a linear line with a non-zero intercept was obtained **Fig.4.** The intercept $= 1/k_{cat}$ and slope $= B/k_{cat}$ values obtained from the graph are 2.4×10^3 s and 4.4×10^6 mol^{-1} dm^{3}s, respectively. The value of the inhibition parameter (B) can be computed using these values: **inhibition parameter (B) = slope/intercept, which equals B = 1.83×10^3 mol^{-1} dm^3.**

Table-4.: Variation of CoO at [S(IV)] = 2×10^{-3} mol dm^{-3}, [Resorcinol] = 4×10^{-6} mol dm^{-3}, pH = 7.50, Temp.= 30°C in phosphate-buffered medium.

[CoO](g L^{-1})	0.1	0.2	0.3	0.4	0.5
$10^4\,k_{cat}$s^{-1}	3. 60	5.81	8.39	9.08	13.16

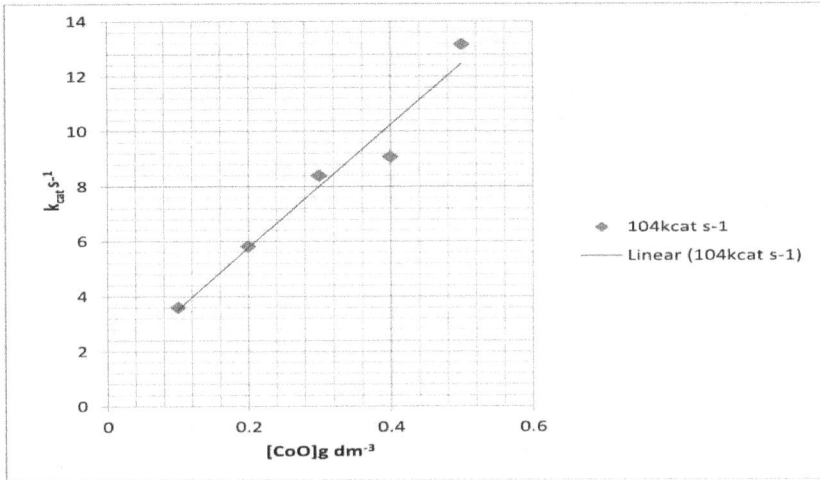

Fig. 4: Effect of [CoO] at S(IV) = $2x10^{-3}$ mol dm^{-3}, [Resorcinol] = $4x10^{-6}$ mol dm^{-3} at pH =7.50 and t = 30°Cin phosphate-buffered medium.

Table-5. The variation of [Resorcinol] at [S(IV)] = 2×10^{-3}mol dm^{-3}, [CoO] = 0.1 g dm^{-3}, Temp. = 30°C, pH = 7.50 in phosphate-buffered medium.

[Resorcinol] mol dm^{-3}	$2x10^{-7}$	$5x10^{-7}$	$2x10^{-6}$	$4x10^{-6}$	$7x10^{-5}$	$2x10^{-4}$	$5x10^{-4}$	$1x10^{-3}$
10^{-4}kinhs^{-1}	8.47	6.79	3.73	3.60	3.20	3.01	2.16	1.47
$1/K_{inh}S$	1181	1473	2681	2778	3125	3333	4761	6803

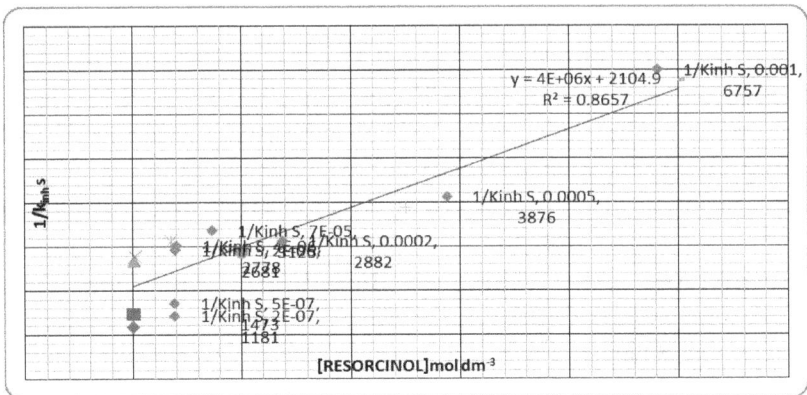

Fig. 5. Effect of [[Resorcinol] at S(IV) =2x10^{-3}mol L^{-1}, CoO= 0.1 g L^{-1}, pH =7.50, and at 30°C, in phosphate buffered medium .

By producing a second graph between $1/k_{inh}$ versus [Resorcinol], a linear line with a non-zero intercept was obtained (fig-5)The intercept $=1/k_{cat}$ and slope $= B/k_{cat}$ values obtained from the graph are 2.4×10^3s and 4.4×10^6 mol^{-1} dm^{3}s, respectively. The value of the inhibition parameter (B) can be computed using these values: **inhibition parameter (B) = slope/intercept, which equals B = 1.83×10^3 mol^{-1} dm^3.**

9. Variation of pH:

Variation of pH in the range 7.50 to 8.50 in phosphate buffer medium was studied at $S(IV)=2x10^{-3}$, [CoO]=0.1gL^{-1}, [RESORCINOL]=$4x10^{-6}$ at t=30°C and the result show that be reaction is independent of pH. (Table.6). The effect of [buffer] was examined by varying the concentration of both Na$_2$HPO$_4$ and KH$_2$PO$_4$ in such a way that the ratio [Na$_2$HPO$_4$]/[KH$_2$PO$_4$] remained same, So that pH remained fixed . The values showed that the rate of the reaction to be insensitive to the buffer concentration.

Table-6:Variation of pH at [S(IV)] = 2×10^{-3} mol dm^{-3}, CoO=0.1 g dm^{-3}, [Resorcinol] = 4×10^{-6} mol dm^{-3}, Temp. = 30°Cin alkaline buffer medium.

pH	7.50	7.85	8.20	8.40
10^4 k$_{cat}$s^{-1}	3.60	3.67	3.88	3.95

10. Effect of temperature :

k_{obs} values were determined at three distinct temperatures ranging frc 30°C to 40°C. Table-7,shows the results. Variation of temperature $[S(IV)] = 2\times10^{-3}$ mol dm^{-3}, CoO=0.1 g dm^{-3}, [Resorcinol] = 4×10^{-6} n dm^{-3}, pH=7.50, Na$_2$HPO$_4$ = 8×10^{-2} mol dm^{-3}, KH$_2$PO$_4$ = 2×10^{-2} mol dm^{-3} The apparent empirical energy of activation was determined to be 68. KJ mol^{-1} using these measurements.

Table-7 :Effect of temperature on k$_{obs}$ air saturated suspensions at S(IV)] = 2×10^{-3}mol dm^{-3}, [CoO] = 0.1 gdm^{-3}, [Resorcinol] = 4×10^{-6} mol dm^{-3},pH = 7.50in phosphate-buffered medium.

Temperature (°C)	30	35	40
^{4} k$_{obs}$s^{-1}	3.60	5.75	8.61

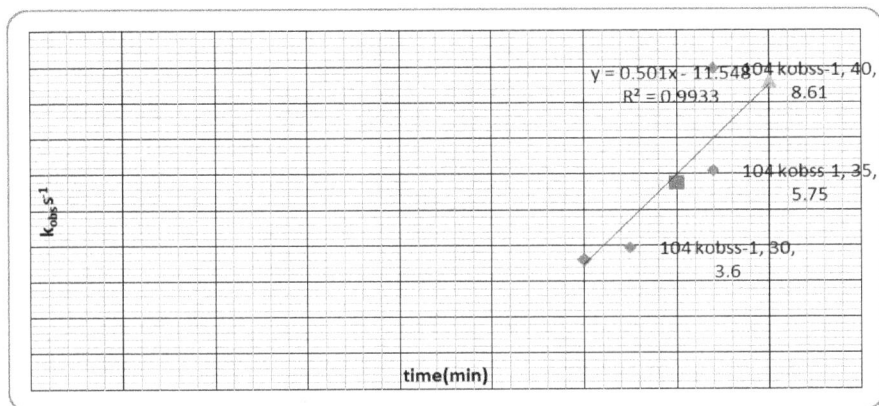

Fig.6.Effect of temperature at $[S(IV)] = 2x10^{-3}$mol dm^{-3},$[CoO] =$ 0.1g L^{-1},$[Resorcinol] = 4x10^{-6}$moldm^{-3},time= 30°C and pH = 7.50

Discussion

In an aqueous solution SO_2 is present in four forms HSO_3^-, $SO_2.H_2O$, SO_3^{2-} and $S_2O_5^{2-}$ Governed by the following equations.

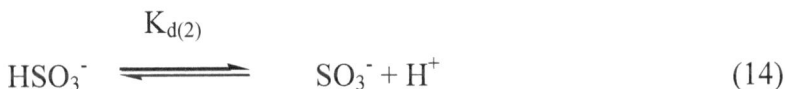

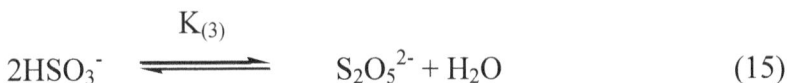

$$SO_2(g) + H_2O \overset{K_H}{\rightleftharpoons} SO_2.H_2O(aq.) \qquad (12)$$

$$SO_2.H_2O(aq.) \overset{K_{d(1)}}{\rightleftharpoons} HSO_3^- + H^+ \qquad (13)$$

$$HSO_3^- \overset{K_{d(2)}}{\rightleftharpoons} SO_3^- + H^+ \qquad (14)$$

$$2HSO_3^- \overset{K_{(3)}}{\rightleftharpoons} S_2O_5^{2-} + H_2O \qquad (15)$$

K_H is Henry's and $K_{d(1)}$,$K_{d(2)}$ are acid dissociation constants, $K_{(3)}$ is the formation constant for $S_2O_5^{2-}$ at 25°C the values are $K_H = 1.23$ mol L^{-1} atm^{-1}, $K_{d(1)} = 1.4x10^{-2}$, $K_{d(2)} = 6.24x10^{-8}$ and $K_{(3)} = 7.6x10^{-2}$. At this experiment, the SO_3^{2-} would be predominantly present in the pH range of 7.50-8.50. We have only assumed SO_3^{2-} species to be reactive in the subsequent because the rate of reaction is almost pH-independent. In several heterogeneous aqueous phase autoxidation processes of S(IV) catalysed by transition metal oxides, the

45

formation of surficial complexes via the adsorption of S(IV) and O_2 on the particle surface and the oxidation of S(IV) via the participation of multiple oxidation states have been postulated.

The dependence of oxygen in the current investigation reveals that the creation of surficial complex by adsorption of O_2 on the particle surface of CoO occurs in a quick step.

The addition of resorcinol, like ethanol, slows down the rate of catalysed reactions of CoO in alkaline media, according to Gupta *et al.*,(1991)[44]. This suggests the presence of oxy sulphur free radicals such as SO_3^-, SO_4^-, and SO_5^- in a radical mechanism. The inhibition is produced by inhibitors that scavenge SO_4^-, such as benzene and ethanol.

According to Begum *et al.*,(2018)[45] a radical mechanism is at work in reactions when the inhibition value is between 10^3-10^5. The value of the inhibitory parameter-B was determined to be 1.83×10^3 mol^{-1}dm^3 in this investigation, which is within the same range. In the presence of resorcinol, this strongly agreed with the radical mechanism for the CoO–catalysed reaction.

Based on findings, including resorcinol, the following radical mechanism is hypothesized, which is similar to that described by Gupta *et al.*, (1999), Sameena *et al.*,(2018)[45] and Mudgal *et al.*,(2008)[48] in the ethanol inhibition of the CoO catalysed reaction.

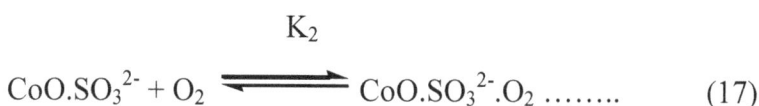

$$CoO + SO_3^{2-} \underset{}{\overset{K_1}{\rightleftharpoons}} CoO.SO_3^{2-} \quad \text{............} \quad (16)$$

$$CoO.SO_3^{2-} + O_2 \overset{K_2}{\rightleftharpoons} CoO.SO_3^{2-}.O_2 \quad \text{........} \quad (17)$$

$$CoO.SO_3^{2-}.O_2 \overset{k_1}{\longrightarrow} CoO + SO_3^{-\bullet} + O_2^- \quad \text{...} \quad (18)$$

$$SO_3^{-\bullet} + O_2 \overset{k_2}{\longrightarrow} SO_5^{-\bullet} \quad \text{.................} \quad (19)$$

$$SO_5^{-\bullet} + SO_3^{2-} \overset{k_3}{\longrightarrow} SO_5^{2-} + SO_3^{-\bullet} \quad \text{.............} \quad (20)$$

$$SO_5^{-\bullet} + SO_3^{2-} \xrightarrow{k_4} SO_4^{-\bullet} + SO_4^{2-} \ldots \qquad (21)$$

$$SO_5^{2-} + SO_3^{2-} \xrightarrow{k_5} 2SO_4^{2-} \ldots \qquad (22)$$

$$SO_4^{-\bullet} + SO_3^{2-} \xrightarrow{k_6} SO_4^{2-} + SO_3^{-\bullet} \ldots\ldots\ldots \qquad (23)$$

$$SO_4^{-\bullet} + X \xrightarrow{k_7} \text{Nonchain product} \ldots\ldots\ldots \qquad (24)$$

$$SO_4^{-\bullet} + \text{Resorcinol} \xrightarrow{k_8} \text{Nonchain product} \ldots \qquad (25)$$

O_2^{-}, which is likewise known to react slowly with sulphur (IV), has no part in the mechanism. It may disproportionately create H_2O_2 and O_2 or impurities may scavenge it. By setting $d[SO_3^{-}]/dt$, $d[SO_4^{-}]/dt$, and $[SO_5^{-}]/dt$ to zero and assuming the steady-state approximation and long-chain hypothesis. The rate of commencement can be shown to be equal to the termination rate.

$$k_1[CoO(SO_3^{2-})(O_2)] = \{k_7[X] + k_8[\text{Resorcinol}]\}[SO_4^{-}] \quad (26)$$

Since the reaction is entirely stopped in the existence of Resorcinol at 1×10^{-3} mol dm^{-3}, the steps (18) and (22) appear to be unimportant. The contribution of propagation reaction (Eq. 21) plays a significant role in the CoO catalyzed reaction. The reaction is halted in the occurrence of a large amount ofResorcinol concentration, even though the autoxidation reaction should have occurred even in the occurrence of a high Resorcinol amount. As a result, we decided to disregard the step (Eq. 21) and merely assume the reaction rate indicated by the equation- (27).

$$--d[S(IV)]/dt = R_{cat} = k_6[SO_4^{-\bullet}][SO_3^{2-}] \qquad (27)$$

By substituting the value of $(SO_4^{-\bullet})$ we get

$$R_{cat} = \frac{k_6 \, k_1 \, [CoO.SO_3^{2-}.O_2][SO_3^{2-}]}{k_7[X] + k_8[\text{Resorcinol}]} \qquad (28$$

From equilibrium Eq.13 and Eq.14

$$R_{cat} = \frac{k_6 \, K_1 K_2 \, [CoO][S(IV)][O_2]}{\{1+k_1[S(IV)]k_7[X] +k_8 \, [Resorcinol]\}} \qquad (29)$$

At fixed O_2, replacing $k_6 \, K_1 \, K_2[O_2]$ by k^1 we get

$$R_{cat} = \frac{k^1 \, [CoO][S(IV)]}{\{1+k_1[S(IV)]k_7[X] +k_8 \, [Resorcinol]\}} \qquad (30)$$

Since we observed that reaction rate clear first order in [S(IV)], The value of $k_1[S(IV)]<<1$ so the above rate law can be reduced to

$$R_{cat} = \frac{k^1 \, [CoO][S(IV)]}{k_7[X] +k_8 \, [Resorcinol]\}} \qquad (31)$$

The inhibition constant-B has been calculated to be 1.83×10^3 $mol^{-1}dm^3$. As a result, it's concluded that resorcinol serves as a free radical scavenger in the CoO-catalysed autoxidation of aqueous sulfur dioxide in an alkaline medium and that a free radical mechanism is at work in this system[47,48].

Conclusion

Resorcinol was reported to act as an inhibitor in CoO catalysed SO_2 autoxidation in an alkaline medium, and a free radical mechanism was hypothesized based on the observed rate law.

$$-d[S(IV)]/dt = (k_1+k_2[CoO])[S(IV)]/1 + [Resorcinol]$$

The rate constants and order of the reactions were determined using the experimental data. The reaction order in SO_2 was first-order in both the presence and absence of resorcinol. The influence of pH on SO_2 oxidation was tested in the presence of CoO and resorcinol, and it was observed that the rate of SO_2 oxidation was independent of the pH change during the process. The apparent empirical energy of activation for the reaction is **68.55 KJ mol^{-1}** when a graph of logk v/s 1/T is plotted. Our findings suggest that the resorcinol used in this study turns as an inhibitor rather than a catalyst for SO_2 autoxidation.

The inhibition factors (B) for uncatalysed and CoO catalysed autoxidation of SO_2 in the existence of resorcinol are 1.9×10^3 mol^{-1} dm^3 and 1.83×10^3 mol^{-1} dm^3, respectively, which are

consistent with previous findings of inhibition factors in the 10^3- 10^5 range.

References :

1. Brandt C, van Eldik VR (1995) Transition metal catalyzed oxidation of aqueous sulfur (IV) oxides. Atmospheric relevant process and mechanisms. Chem Rhem Rev 95:119-190.

2. Hemann H (2003) Kinetics of aqueous–phase reactions relevant to atmospheric chemistry. Chem Rev 103:4691-4716.

3. Gupta, K.S.(2012).Aqueous phase atmospheric oxidation of sulfur dioxide by oxygen: role of trace atmospheric constituents metals, volatile organic compounds and ammonia *J.Indianchem. Soc.,89*: 713- 724.

4. Gupta K.S, Jain U, Singh A, Mehta RK, Manoj SV, Prasad DSN, Sharma A, Parashar P, Bansal SP. Kinetics and mechanism of the osmium(VIII)-catalysed autoxidation of aqueous sulfur dioxide in acidic and alkaline media. *Journal of the Indian Chemical Society .2004;81(12):1083-92.*

5. Acker K, Moller D, WieprechiW, Auel R, Kalass D, and Tscherwenka W, 2001, Nitrous and nitric acid measurements inside and outside of clouds at mt. Brocken Water Air and Soil Pollution,130, 331-336.

6. Berresheim, H., & Jaeschke, W. (1986). Study of metal aerosol systems as a sink for atmospheric SO2. *Journal of atmospheric chemistry, 4*(3), 311-334.

7. Prasad DSN, Mehta RK, Parashar P, Madnawat PV, Rani A, Singh U, Manoj SV, Bansal SP, Gupta KS. Kinetics of surface-catalyzed autoxidation of aqueous sulfur dioxide in cobalt (III) oxide suspensions. Journal of the Indian Chemical Society. 2003;80(4):391-4.

8. Bhargava R, Prasad DS, Rani A, Bhargava P, Jain U, Gupta KS. Kinetics of autoxidation of aqueous sulfur dioxide in suspensions of nickel (III) oxide. Transition Metal Chemistry. 1992 Jun1;17(3):238-41.

9. Prasad DSN, Rani A, Gupta KS. Surface-catalyzed autoxidation of sulfur (IV) in aqueous silica and copper (II) oxide suspensions. Environmental science& technology. 1992 Jul;26(7):1361-8.

10. Gupta KS, Singh R, Saxena D, Manoj SV, Sharma M. Role of manganese dioxide in the autoxidation of sulfur (IV) in oxic and anoxic suspensions *Ind. J. Chem.*1999, 38A,1129- 1138.

11. Manoj SV, Mishra CD, Sharma M, Rani A, Jain R, Bansal SP, Gupta KS. Iron, manganese, and copper concentrations in wet precipitations and kinetics of the oxidation of SO_2 in rainwater at two urban sites, Jaipur and Kota, in western India. Atmospheric Environment. 2000 Aug 2;34(26):4479-86.

12. Ghosh MK, Rajput SK. Kinetics and Mechanism of Lanthanum (III) Catalysed Oxidation of Rwd3fD-ribose by Cerium (IV) in Aqueous Acidic Medium. Asian Journal of Research in Chemistry. 2012;5(10):1271-7.

13. Manoj, S. V., Singh, R., Sharma, M., & Gupta, K. S. (2000). Kinetics and mechanism of heterogeneous cadmium sulfide and homogeneous manganese (II) catalysed oxidation of sulfur (IV) by dioxygen in acetate buffered medium.

14. Bäckström, H. L. (1934). Der Kettenmechanismus bei der Autoxydation von Aldehyden. *Zeitschrift für physikalische Chemie*, *25*(1), 99-121.

15. Warneck, P., & Ziajka, J. (1995). Reaction Mechanism of the Iron (III)- Catalyzed Autoxidation of Bisulfite in Aqueous Solution: Steady State Description for Benzene as Radical Scavenger. *Berichte der Bunsengesellschaft für physikalische Chemie*, *99*(1), 59-65.

16. Ziajka, J., & Pasiuk-Bronikowska, W. (2003). Autoxidation of sulfur dioxide in the presence of alcohols under conditions related to the tropospheric aqueous phase. *Atmospheric Environment*, *37*(28), 3913-3922.
17. Connick, R. E., & Zhang, Y. X. (1996). Kinetics and mechanism of the oxidation of HSO3-by O_2. 2. the manganese (II)-catalyzed reaction. *Inorganic Chemistry*, *35*(16), 4613-4621.
18. Connick, R. E., Zhang, Y. X., Lee, S., Adamic, R., & Chieng, P. (1995). Kinetics and mechanism of the oxidation of HSO3-by O2. 1. the uncatalyzed reaction. *Inorganic Chemistry*, *34*(18), 4543-4553.
19. Kuo, D. T., Kirk, D. W., & Jia, C. Q. (2006). The chemistry of aqueous S (IV)-Fe-O2 system: state of the art. *Journal of Sulfur Chemistry*, *27*(5), 461-530.
20. Brandt, C., & Van Eldik, R. (1995). Transition metal-catalyzed oxidation of sulfur (IV) oxides. Atmospheric-relevant processes and mechanisms. *Chemical Reviews*, *95*(1), 119-190.
21. Grgić, I., Podkrajšek, B., Barzaghi, P., & Herrmann, H. (2007). Scavenging of SO4− radical anions by mono-and dicarboxylic acids in the Mn (II)-catalyzed S (IV) oxidation in aqueous solution. *Atmospheric Environment*, *41*(39), 9187-9194.
22. Prasad, D. S. N., Rani, A., Madnawat, P. V. S., Bhargava, R., & Gupta, K. S. (1991). Kinetics of surface-catalyzed oxidation of sulfur (IV) by dioxygen in aqueous suspensions of cobalt (II) oxide. *Journal of molecular catalysis*, *69*(3), 393-405.Barker, J. R. (1995). *Progress and problems in atmospheric chemistry* (Vol. 3). World Scientific.
23. Bigelow S. L.,1988, Catalytic effects in the oxidation of sodium sulfite by air oxygen , *Zeitschriftfuerphysikalische Chemie,26,493-532.*
24. Alyea, H. N., & Bäckström, H. L. (1929). The inhibitive action of alcohols on the oxidation of sodium sulfite. *Journal of the American Chemical Society*, *51*(1), 90-109.
25. Hussain, F., Begam, S., Sharma, A. K., & Prasad, D. S. N. (2018). Effect of isopropyl alcohol on the autoxidation of S (IV) catalyzed by Co2O3 in alkaline medium. *Bull. Pure Appl. Sci. 37 (1): 9, 18.*

26. Ziajka J, Pasiuk-Bronikowska W (2003) Autoxidation of sulfur dioxide in the presence of alcohols under conditions related to the tropospheric aqueous phase. Atmos Environ 37:3913–3922.

27. Ghosh, M. K., & Rajput, S. K. (2012). Kinetics and Mechanism of Lanthanum (III) Catalysed Oxidation of D-ribose by Cerium (IV) in Aqueous Acidic Medium. *Asian Journal of Research in Chemistry*, *5*(10), 1271-1277.

28. Wang, L., Xing, L., Liu, J., Qi, T., Zhang, S., Ma, Y., & Ning, P. (2021). Construction of lattice-confined Co-MCM-48 for boosting sulfite oxidation in wet desulfuration. *Chemical Engineering Journal*, *407*, 127210.

29. Meena, V., Dayal, Y., Saxena, D., Rani, A., Chandel, C.P.& Gupta, K.S., (2016). The influence of diesel-truck exhaust particles on the kinetics of the atmospheric oxidation of dissolved sulfur dioxide by oxygen. Environ SciPollut Res., 23(17):17380-92.

30. HUIE, R. E., & SIECK, L. W. (1999). 3 SO, Radical Monoanions—Reactions. *S-Centered Radicals*, *1*, 63.

31. Liu, J., Wang, H., Wang, L., Xing, L., Zhang, S., Xiao, H., & Ma, Y. (2019). The defect-engineered cobalt-based solid catalyst for high-efficiency oxidation of sulfite. *Chemical Engineering Science*, *197*, 1-10.

32. Wilkosz, I., & Mainka, A. (2008). Mn (II)-catalysed S (IV) oxidation and its inhibition by acetic acid in acidic aqueous solutions. *Journal of atmospheric chemistry*, *60*(1), 1-17.

33. Schöne, L., Schindelka, J., Szeremeta, E., Schaefer, T., Hoffmann, D., Rudzinski, K. J., ... & Herrmann, H. (2014). Atmospheric aqueous phase radical chemistry of the isoprene oxidation products methacrolein, methyl vinyl ketone, methacrylic acid, and acrylic acid–kinetics and product studies. *Physical Chemistry Chemical Physics*, *16*(13), 6257-6272.

34. Podkrajšek, B., Grgić, I., Turšič, J., & Berčič, G. (2006). Influence of atmospheric carboxylic acids on catalytic oxidation

of sulfur (IV). *Journal of Atmospheric Chemistry*, *54*(2), 103-120...

35. Sharma, A. K., Sharma, R., & Prasad, D. S. N. (2017). Kinetics of isoamyl alcohol and aniline inhibited uncatalysed and Ag (I) catalysed autoxidation of S (IV) in an acidic medium. *Asian Journal of Research in Chemistry*, *10*(3), 251-258.

36. Hussain, F. A. I. Y. A. Z., Begam, S. A. M. E. E. N. A., Sharma, A. K., & Prasad, D. S. N. (2018). Co_2O_3 catalyzed oxidation of SO_2 in aqueous solution differing effect of benzamide in alkaline medium. *Chem. Sci. Trans*, *7*(4), 600-609.

37. Sharma, A. K., Parasher, P., Sharma, R., & SN Prasad, D. (2017). Ag (I) Catalyzed Oxidation of SO_2 in Aqueous Solution Differing Effect of Benzoate Ions in Acidic Medium. *Current Physical Chemistry*, *7*(4), 338-347.

38. Sharma, A. K., Sharma, R., Prasad, D. S. N., & Parashar, P. (2016). The Inhibitive action of Aniline on the autoxidation of sodium sulfite in acidic medium. *J. Anal. Pharm. Res*, *17*(5), 14-23.

39. Sharma, A. K., Sharma, R., & Prasad, D. S. N. (2017). The effect of atmospheric aromatic amides on the Ag (I) catalyzed S (IV) autoxidation in an aqueous solution. *the Experiment*, *40*(1), 2354-2363.

40. Sharma, A. K., Sharma, R., & Prasad, D. S. N. (2017). Role of organics in atmospheric catalytic autoxidation of aqueous sulfur dioxide in acidic medium. *Malaysian Journal of Chemistry*, *19*(1), 1-12.23.

41. L. Wang, Y. Ma, W. Zhang, Q., Li, Y., Zhao, Z. Zhang, *J. Hazard. Mater,***2013**, 258-259

42. Dhayal, Y., Chandel, C. P. S., & Gupta, K. S. (2014). Role of some organic inhibitors on the oxidation of dissolved sulfur dioxide by oxygen in rainwater medium. *Environmental Science and Pollution Research*, *21*(5), 3474-3483.

43. Meena, V. K., Dhayal, Y., Saxena, D., Rani, A., Chandel, C. P., & Gupta, K. S. (2016). The influence of diesel—truck exhaust particles on the kinetics of the atmospheric oxidation of dissolved sulfur dioxide by oxygen. *Environmental Science and Pollution Research, 23*(17), 17380-17392.

44. Prasad, D.S.N., Rani, A., Madnavat, P.V.S., Bhargava, R. &Gupta, K.S.(1991). Kinetics of surface catalyzed oxidation of sulfur(IV) by dioxygen in aqueous suspensions of cobalt(II) oxide.*J. Mol. Catal., 69*:395-405.

45. Begam S, Hussain F, Singh J, Sharma AK, Prasad DS. Kinetics of sodium sulfite oxidation catalyzed by Co_2O_3 and inhibited by ethylene glycol. Asian Journal of Research in Chemistry. 2018 Jun 30;11(3):610-6

46. Sharma, A.K., Sharma, R.&Prasad, D.S.N.(2018). Effect of Aliphatic Mono Carboxylic acids and alcohols on Ag(I) Catalysed oxidation of SO_2 in aqueous solution, J. Mat. Env. Sci.,9(6): 1829-1837.

47. Gupta, K.S., Singh, R., Saxena, D., Manoj, S.V.& Sharma, M.,(1999). Role of manganese dioxide in the autoxidation of sulfur (IV) in oxic and anoxic suspensions. *Ind. J .Chem.,38A*:1129-1138.

48. Mudgal, P. K., Sharma, A. K., Mishra, C. D., Bansal, S. P., & Gupta, K. S. (2008). Kinetics of ammonia and ammonium ion inhibition of the atmospheric oxidation of aqueous sulfur dioxide by oxygen. *Journal of atmospheric chemistry, 61*(1), 31-55.

49. Sharma, A.K., Sharma, R., Prasad, D.S.N. &Parashar, P.(2016). The Inhibitive action of Aniline on the autoxidation of sodium sulfite in acidic medium.*J.Anal.Pharm.Res.,17*(5):14-23.

50. Gupta, K.S.(2012).Aqueous phase atmospheric oxidation of sulfur dioxide by oxygen: role of trace atmospheric

constituents metals, volatile organic compounds, and ammonia *J.Indian Chem. Soc.,89*: 713- 724.

1. Department of Chemistry,
Government College Kota, Kota,Rajasthan, India.
2. Department of Chemistry,
Government P.G. College, Jhalawar, Rajasthan, India.
(Corresponding author: D.S.N. Prasa)
email : dsnp308@gmail.com

6. Latest Management Practices in Relation to Sustainable Development

Nandni Joshi

Dr. Ghanshyam Saini

Abstract :

"Development that meets with the needs of the present generation without compromising the ability of future generations to meet their own needs"

The necessity of prioritizing new management practices related with sustainable developmentas for no it is the foremost requirement of all the businesses. The dimensions that areincluding in work criteria are Economic, Social and Environmental Objectives that have sub dimensions Peace and Security, Cultural, Political and Institutional/Administrative arrangements.Agenda 21 called for all countries to develop sustainable development strategies. For new strategies to be in effect there are needs to be real commitment. In all countries, government at all levels; the private sector, and civil society, that should be must work together in partnership, in transparent ways which enable genuine stakeholder participation. There are necessary mechanisms and processes need to be coordinated to enable continuous improvement and learning. It is important to set out principles and ideas on process and methods, along with the suggestions of how it can be used. Principles are based on the practises of current and past observations, drawing direct from the experience of in both developed and developing countries. Discussion need to be followed for the nature and challenges of sustainable development and the requirement for strategic responses to them.

Keywords : Sustainability, Sustainable Development, SDG, Sustainable development Goals

Introduction :

Sustainable development always encourages us to conserve and enhance our resources, by accordingly changing the manners in which develop and use technologies. All countries are capable in meeting their basic needs of employment, food, energy, water and sanitation.

There are four main types of sustainability are human, Social, Economic and Environmental. It is important to specify which kind of sustainability the one is dealing with as they are very different and vast in dealing so can't be fused all together, although some overlap to certain extent.

There are three types of Sustainability Development are :

- **Economic Viability :**

A project is economically viable if the economic benefits of the project exceed its economic costs, when analysed for society as a whole.The economic costs of the project are not the same as its financial costs-Externalities and environmental impacts should be considered.

The major method for assessment of economic viability of a project is a **Cost-Benefit Analysis (CBA).** Cost and benefits are shown as far as possible in monetary terms so that they can be compared on equal level.

- **Environmental Protection :**
-

Environmental protection is the practice of protecting natural environment by individuals, organizations and governments.Its objectives are to conserve natural resources and the existing natural environment and, where possible, to repair damage and reverse trends.

Environmental protection is important to save lives.

World hunger, global warming, increasing natural disasters, polluted air, water and soil, pesticide use in the fields, Species extinction, and crop failures - we must not believe that we, as the only living beings on a sick planet, remain healthy. In nature, everything is interrelated. Five major environmental problems that world is facing every year are :

- Ozone Depletion, Greenhouse Effect and Global Warming

- Loss of Biodiversity
- Disposal of Wastes
- Deforestation
- Desertification

Benefits of Embracing Sustainability and Green Manufacturing:

"Going green" is not the same thing as sustainability, albeit they are related. Although the terms are often used interchangeably, green is more frequently associated with a singular product or process.

Sustainability is typically high associated with an organization"s holistic approach; it will put entire logistics and production process into considerations.

In the manufacturing industries it is advantageous to focus on both green and sustainability along with that targeted improvements can be more beneficial for your company and looking at the "bigger picture" maximizes the perks of environmental factors.

There are five benefits of Embracing Sustainability and Green Manufacturing:

1. Reduce Energy-Related Costs :

The prime concerns of manufacturers are of Energy and Water costs. If focus can be shifted on improvements then it can be reduce. Often these improvements are realized as annual savings as opposed to quicker, short-term cost reductions.

Switching the energy-efficient lighting and adjust lighting level according to the production schedule it will reduce your long term electrical costs. Regular inspection of equipment is also beneficial.

For example, air compressor leaks can be a waste of energy and increase expenses. Changing how you package your products and supplies can provide cost reductions and free up space at your facility. Solar and wind energy, along with energy efficient equipment and machinery, will greatly reduce monthly utility bills. Implementing strategies such as recycling and going paperless will also save on supply costs. Sustainability can improve your bottom-line.

2. Attract New Customers and Increase Sales :

Sustainable and Green practices can make the company more marketable. Consumers are more aware about the environment and continuous improvements will strengthen your reputation. Highlighting your initiatives to the public will help to attract a whole new audience or customers that will increase your sale. For manufacturers it is important to seek government contracts where green manufacturing standard are oftena factor.

In the current scenarios it is very common to enable buyers to easily promote or criticize companies for their green practices, or lack of thereof.

3. Tax Incentives :

There are a variety of tax credits and rebates on both the federal and state level for manufacturers who proactively implement more sustainable improvements.

4. Boost Workforce Morale and Innovations :

Sustainable improvements are a collaborative effort. Employees work together can identify and implement green and sustainable initiative; it fosters a culture of team work and continuous improvements. Employees can work with more dedication whenthey have a sense of pride in their company.

By internally communicating the importance of changes and the impact they are having business and environment, manufacturers will positively influence their corporate culture.

5. Societal Impact :

In addition to Increase Company"s profitability, tour action can make a real difference as it is shown in the efforts done by employees. By implementing changes, you will have a smaller carbon footprint and reduce the numbers of toxins released into the atmosphere. Future generations ultimately benefits from improved air and water quality, fewer landfills and more renewable energy sources.

Major Features of Sustainable Development :

1. Sustained rise in Real per Capita Income and Economic Welfare :

From the time things are more in favor of Sustainable development there should be a major rise in real per capita income and economic welfare overtime.

2. Rational use of the Natural Resources :

Sustainable development never meant that natural resources should not be used at all in any circumstances it simply means it can be used in a manner that they are not excessively exploited.

3. No Reduction in the Ability of Future Generation to meet their own needs :

The aim of sustainable development aims at making of a natural resources and environments for asking or raising the standard the existing standard of living in such a way as not to reduce ability of the future generation to meet their own needs.

4. No increase in Pollution :

Sustainable development eliminates all those activities which are in order to maintain existing high standard of living, prove deter mental to natural resources and environment.

According to the concept one should be keep in view from undertaking such activities as may increase pollution and decrease quality of life of future generations.

Recent Practices of Managing Sustainable Development :

When you want to reduce your footprint you have to do continuous effort that won"t happen overnight. Going green can make you person who will make better choices while performing day to day activities, so add up a smallest sustainable practices canadd up. The key to success is to turning those practices into consistent habits.

Below are few sustainable practices that can become habits to make your lifestylegreener:

1. Reuse Paper and Plastic Bags for Shopping :

Unless you"re completely unaware of the recycling efforts that have been going on for several decades, as we know about the push to reuse paper and plastic bags. Many campaigns have been launched to encourage people about the recycle bags as well by school students on road rally, by college students by road show etc.

In fact reuse and recycling of paper and plastic bags is on e of the best things that you can do for the environment. Getting plastic bags from the grocery shops or frofarmer market at the time of shopping you can store it and use it next time.

2. Opt for Paperless Documents :

The next time that you receive a paper bill in the mail, print movie ticket or purchase a newspaper, think about the tress that were cut down to make them treesthat were cut down to make them. Trees are very major part of the environment as they remove carbon dioxide from the air by which we get oxygen.

This is responsibility of each and every person to reduce the need to cut down the tree by getting paperless utility bills and e-tickets and by reading the news online. To save trees and improving quality of air choosing paperless alternatives can prevent clutter.

3. Opt for Paperless Documents :

The next time that you receive a paper bill in the mail, print movie ticket or purchase a newspaper, think about the tress that were cut down to make them treesthat were cut down to make them. Trees are very major part of the environment as they remove carbon dioxide from the air by which we get oxygen.

This is responsibility of each and every person to reduce the need to cut down the tree by getting paperless utility bills and e-tickets and by reading the news online. To save trees and improving quality of air choosing paperless alternatives can prevent clutter.

4. Opt for Paperless Documents :

The next time that you receive a paper bill in the mail, print movie ticket or purchase a newspaper, think about the tress that were cut down to make them treesthat were cut down to make them. Trees are very major part of the environment as they remove carbon dioxide from the air by which we get oxygen.

This is responsibility of each and every person to reduce the need to cut down the tree by getting paperless utility bills and e-tickets and by reading the news online. To save trees and improving quality of air choosing paperless alternatives can prevent clutter.

5. Avoid Disposable Kitchen Items :

Even in kitchen there are so many ways to reduce waste and become moresustainable.

Instead of using single-use paper towel can use towel of cloth that is washable andcan be reuse for long period of time.

By avoid tissue paper to wrap lunch in Tiffin can use cloth tissue that can be washon daily basis and reuse.

Same with plates avoid using paper plates or plastic plates and silverware instead of single-use paper, plastic and Styrofoam alternatives.

Rather than buying filtered water in bottle, improve filtration system at you replace and if have habit to bring water with you it is important to carry non plastic bottle that can be washed and filled.

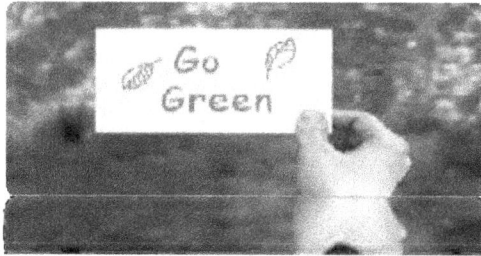

Sustainable Development Goals :

The Sustainable development Goals is a collection of 17 Global goals designed by the UN to be a blueprint to achieve a better and more sustainable future for all. The world I currently facing so many serious natural resources and environmental challenges: Like Global climate change, Freshwater depletion, Ocean Over- fishing, Deforestation, water and air pollution and the struggle to feed a planet of billions. India ranked 63rd in the Global Sustainability Index and is the world"s third-largest energy consumer and greenhouse gas emitter.

With a view to the environment, sustainability is about managing and protecting Earth"s natural resources, ecosystems, climate, and atmosphere so that current generations and future generations will live a decent life and millions of other species with whom we share the planet will also be benefitted.

According to UN, The Sustainable Development Goals (SDGs) are the world"s shared plan to end severe [poverty, reduce inequality, and protect planet by 2030.

Eliminate Poverty
1. Erase Hunger
2. Establish Good Health and Well-Being
3. Provide Quality Education
4. Enforce Gender Equality
5. Improve Clean Water and Sanitation
6. Grow Affordable and Clean Energy
7. Create Decent Work and Economic Growth
8. Increase Industry, Innovation, and Infrastructure
9. Reduce Inequality
10. Mobilize Sustainable Cities and Communities
11. Influence Responsible Consumption and Production
12. Organize Climate Action
13. Develop Life below Water
14. Advance Life on Land
15. Guarantee Peace, Justice, and Strong Institutions
16. Build Partnerships for the Goals

The four objectives of sustainable development are :
- **Stable economic growth-**
The eradication of poverty and hunger to ensuring a healthy life.
- **Conservation of natural resources –**
Achieve universal access to basic services such as water, sanitation, andsustainable energy.
- **Social progress and equality –**
Reduce inequalities in the world, especially gender inequalities. Supporting the generation by the development of opportunities through inclusive education anddecent work. Foster innovation and resilient infrastructures by creating communities and cities capable of producing and consuming sustainably.
- **Environmental protection –**
Caring for the environment by combating climate change and protecting oceansand terrestrial ecosystems.
India as a nation is entrepreneurial and the apex of the changes. With Indian being world"s youngest country its youth needs to be engaged in early and action to create and sustain long term momentum that can see its targets through and drive.
More than 70 & of the world population lives in the cities. Cities

already consume 80% of global material and energy supplies and produces 75 % of all carbon emissions.

"No matter how complex global problems may seem, it is we ourselves who have given rise to them. They cannot be beyond our power to resolve"

Conclusions :

Immediate steps need to be taken to contribute in Sustainable Development :

1. Sign the W.A.S.H pledge
2. Provide a healthy Workplace
3. Review your supply chain and implement sustainability practices.
4. Give projects to the Sustainability Development Goals (SDGs)
5. Invest in Renewable Energy
6. Encourage „Recycle, Reduce and Reuse"
7. Support Education of the future generation –Locally or Globally
8. Reward the Responsible behaviour
9. Give Paid Volunteer Days
10. Keep environment clean and healthy

Governments of all countries must ensure more shares for the education about cleaning and sustaining of natural resources and must ensure that each and every citizen are responsible and ready to take responsibility in sustainable development. Also, proper resources and full-fledged infrastructure must be provided as well.

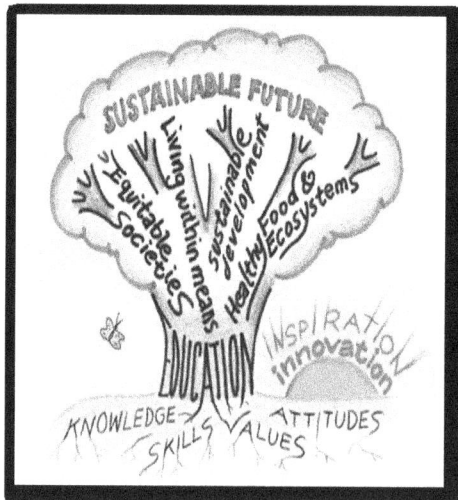

References :
1. Sustainable Development Solutions Network. (2013). *An Action Agenda for Sustainable Development. Report for the UN Secretary- General.* Paris, France and New York, USA: SDSN.
2. The United Nations. (2015). *Transforming our world: the 2030 Agenda for Sustainable Development.*
3. Organisation for Economic Co-operation and Development. (2006). *Good Practices in the National Sustainable Development Strategies of OECD Countries.*
4. Sustainable Development Solutions Network and Institute for Sustainable Development and International Relations. (2014). *Pathways to Deep Decarbonization.* New York: SDSN, IDDRI.
5. Sustainable Development Solutions Network. (2015). *Indicators and a Monitoring Framework for the Sustainable Development Goals: Launching a data revolution for the SDGs. A report for the Leadership Council of the Sustainable Development Solutions Network.* Revised working draft (version 7).
6. Espey, J. (2015). *Data for Development: A Needs Assessment for SDG Monitoring and Statistical Capacity Development.* Sustainable Development Solutions Network. Available at http://unsdsn.org/wp- content/uploads/2015/04/Data-for-Development-Full-Report.pdf.
7. Kroll, C., (2015) *Sustainable Development Goals: Are the rich countries ready?* Sustainable Governance Indicators, SDSN and Berelsmann Stiftung. Gutersloh: Berelsmann Stiftung.
8. McFadden, L., Priest, S., Green, C. (2010). *INTRODUCING INSTITUTIONAL MAPPING: A GUIDE FOR SPICOSA SCIENTISTS.* Flood Hazard Research Centre, Middlesex University, London. Available at http://www.coastal-saf.eu/design-step/support/introducing_institutional_mapping.pdf.
9. Organisation for Economic Co-operation and Development. (2015). *Peer reviews of DAC members.* Website. Available at http://www.oecd.org/dac/peer-reviews/
10. Sustainable Development Solutions Network. (2013). *An Action Agenda for Sustainable Development. Report for the UN*

Secretary- General. Paris, France and New York, USA: SDSN. Available at: http://unsdsn.org/wp-content/ uploads/ 2013/06/140505-An-Action-Agenda-for-Sustainable Development.pdf.

Research Scholar,
Research Supervisor,
Department of Management,
Lords University, Alwar

7. Physico-Chemical Analysis of Lentic Fresh Water Ecosystem During Summer Season : Kaylana Lake, Jodhpur, Rajasthan

Arvind Chouhan

Abstract

Physico-chemical status is one of the main influential factors for ecological biodiversity. The life diversity of any water body can be considered a major key factor in determining the portability of water. Kaylana Lake has the greatest importance for Jodhpur city. With the seasonal survey, the specific status of Physico-chemical characteristics and zooplankton diversity in Kaylana Lake have been studied through different weather cycles (2021) across the four regions.

With moderately alkaline water (pH 7.10), alkalinity (103.67 mg/L) and other limnological parameters showed low mean values including chloride (18.36 mg/L), TDS (161 mg/L), and hardness (94 mg/L). The average dissolved water oxygen levels were 5.76 mg/l while average nitrate and sulphate levels were 31.29 mg/l and 126 mg/l respectively. The results of water and soil. The results of parameters indicate that the water in Kaylana Lake is eutrophic.

1. Introduction

Water is an unavoidable thing in life. A Physico-chemical status of an aquatic body is directly proportional to the biological production of that water body. Physico-chemical status of any water body depends upon the climate of the encompassing area and therefore the soil texture of the water body. The life within the water body directly depends upon the Physico-chemical status of the water body.

The seasonal variation in Physico-chemical parameters like temperature, dissolved oxygen, COD, BOD, nitrate, phosphate, TDS, turbidity, etc. of water may provide countable information of water on its quality impacts on the productivity and biodiversity of the reservoir.

To assess the tropic structure of a lake it's important to review the first productivity of the lake. Aiyaz, *et al.*, (2010) studied the diversity of algal flora in Wular Lake, Kashmir, and showed that there was a correlation between conductivity, carbon dioxide, hardness, and nitrate of water with a diversity of algal flora1[1]. A Physico-chemical study by Golmarvi, D., *et al.*, (2016) at Anali International Wetland (Iran) showed the highest numbers of zooplankton were recorded in the summer months and the lowest in winter [2]. Sumathi, M., *et al.*, (2019) in their study conclude that eutrophication in aquatic ecosystems is controlled by either nitrate or phosphate which acts as the limiting factor for plant growth [3]. A bacterial eutrophic study by Ji, B., *et al.*, (2020) at 27 global freshwater ecosystems indicated that the supply of nitrogen and phosphorus from agricultural lands, industrial and domestic wastewaters and aquaculture is the evident cause of the increase in plankton [4].

Choudhary, S., et al., (2021) in their study on Anasagar Lake, Ajmer, Rajasthan concluded that Anthropological activities are responsible for a higher concentration of heavy metals, and the outcome of this in hypereutrophic conditions [5]. A Physico-chemical study by Ray, J.G., et al., (2021) at freshwater bodies (Kerala, India) showed total nitrogen (p<0.0), dissolved oxygen (p<0.05) played a crucial role in algal blooms [6]. Assessing the seasonal pattern of plankton by Panikkar, P., et al., (2022) at various reservoirs of Karnataka state of India showed the dominance of *Mycocystis sp.* in most of the reservoirs was due to high silicate content. It is an indication of a eutrophic condition [7].

The seasonal variation in Physico-chemical parameters like phosphate, nitrate, TDS, BOD, COD, pH, nitrate, turbidity, etc. of water may provide enumerable information on water and its quality impacts on the productivity and biodiversity of the reservoir.

The food chain of the lake ecosystem is comprising zooplankton, phytoplankton as well as secondary and tertiary consumers. Kaylana Lake provides water to the city dwellers. So, the study of Physico-chemical characteristics of Kaylana Lake has high importance, the study of their tropic status may help in optimum utilization, therefore the present investigation is an attempt to study of Physico-chemical parameter and their relationship, phytoplankton and zooplankton status in Kaylana Lake, Jodhpur (Rajasthan) during the period.

2. Materials and Methods

2.1. Study Area

Kaylana lake received water from the surrounding hill area and through Rajeev Gandhi lift Canal a tributary of IGNP (Indira Gandhi Nahar Pariyojna). The lake has importance in the tourism of the city and provides annual drinking and other water needs for the localized.

Fig-1. Kaylana Lake with sites (Courtesy Geo earth)

Location : 26. 17 $^{\circ}$ N, 72. 58 $^{\circ}$ E

City : Jodhpur

State : Rajasthan

Country : India

Max. Depth : 45-50 ft.

2.2. Study Period

May 2022 to June 2022 (Summer season)

2.3. Methodology

Water samples were collected from marked three sampling regions during the peak of the season. Water samples were collected in clean and rinsed polyethylene sampling bottles from the surface and bottom area of the respective site; were brought to the research laboratory for Physico-chemical analysis.

The important Physico-chemical parameters of water include, Turbidity (NTU), Total Alkalinity (mg/l), Chemical Oxygen Demand (COD), Biological Oxygen Demand (BOD), Nitrate (mg/l), water transparency, pH value, Calcium (mg/l), Chloride (mg/l), Fluoride (mg/l), Total Hardness (mg/l), were analyzed by the methods as per IS 3025 and APHA 22nd Edt.

3. Result and Discussion

3.1. Physico-chemical Analysis

Table-1. Physico-chemical parameters of Surface water of Kaylana Lake

S.N.	Parameter	Site 1	Site 2	Site 3	Average	WHO Parameter
1	Biological Oxygen (mg/L)	29.4	22.73	28.4	26.84	<5
2	Calcium (as Ca), mg/L	58.5	55.29	5.55	39.78	60
3	Chemical Oxygen (mg/l)	8.18	7.45	9.1	8.24	250
4	Chloride (as Cl), mg/L	107.22	101.43	116.43	108.36	250
5	Colour, Hazen	0.5	0.62	0.97	0.69	5
6	Fluoride (as F), (mg/L)	0.30	0.30	0.30	0.30	1
7	Iron (as Fe, (mg/L)	0.025	0.022	0.03	0.026	0.3
8	Magnesium (as Mg) (mg/L)	20.2	17.66	21.8	19.87	<30
9	Nitrate (as	33.2	31.55	31.35	32.03	10

	NO3), (mg/L)					
10	pH value	7.11	7.09	7.10	7.10	6.5-8.5
11.	Turbidity, NTU	0.8	0.82	0.96	0.86	5
12	Sulphate (as SO4), mg/L	119.3	123.5	129.4	124.06	500
13	Total Alkalinity, mg/L	101	96	111	103.67	200
14	Total Dissolved Solids (mg/L)	139	147	197	161	300
15	Total Hardness (mg/L)	86	107	89	94	120

According to the study, Kaylana Lake was characterized by a low level of total dissolved solids (TDS) of 139 mg/L, at site 1, 147 mg/L at site 2, and 197 mg/L at site 3. During the study period, the highest value of alkalinity was found at site 3. The average pH of Kaylana Lake was 7.10, which is slightly basic. The average value of total hardness during the study was 94 mg/L with upper surface water. This increase in total hardness during the summer period is due to the high rate of photosynthesis. In the summer season, the highest value of Biological Oxygen Demand (BOD) was found at site 1. The notable thing was the average value of Biological Oxygen and Nitrate was much higher than the WHO permissible limit.

In the present study, the value of fluoride shows similarities by an average value of at all three sites. According to WHO (1997), the permissible limit for fluoride in drinking water is 1.0 mg/L. No pesticide residue was found in the water sample as there is any agricultural area nearby.

Physio-chemical parameters (Top Surface Water)

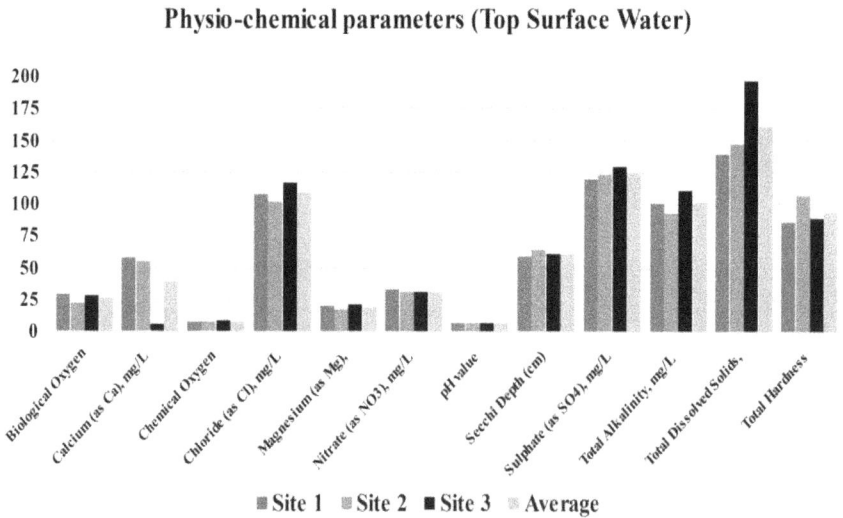

Fig-1. Graphical Analysis of Physico-chemical parameters (Top Surface Water)

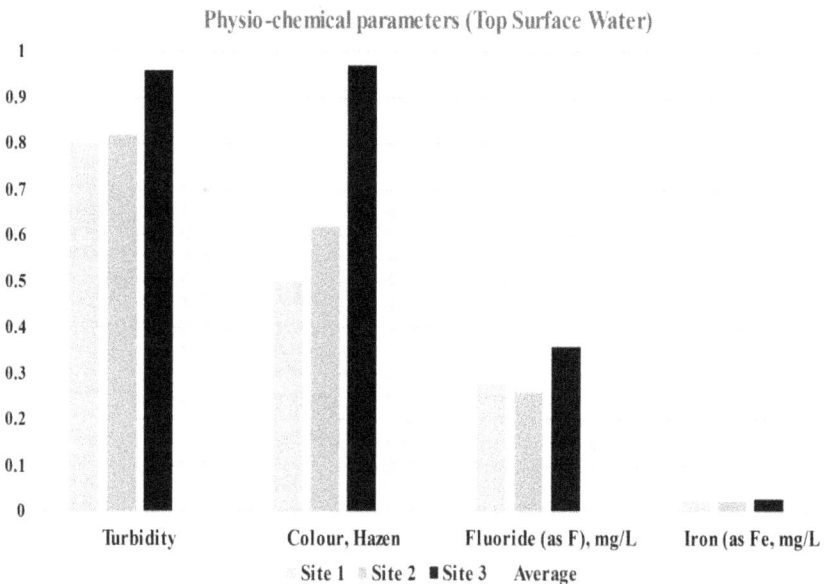

Fig-2. Graphical Analysis of Physico-chemical parameters (Top Surface Water)

Comparison with Lakhotiya Talav of Pali

The value of almost all parameters was close to Kaylana Lake of Jodhpur. The Lakhotiya Talav is also a eutrophic water body.

S.N.	Parameter	Site 1	Site 2	Site 3	Average
1	Biological Oxygen (mg/L)	45	43.6	42.8	43.80
2	Calcium (as Ca), mg/L	42	49.75	53.5	48.12
3	Chemical Oxygen (mg/l)	8.19	7.45	9.8	8.48
4	Chloride (as Cl), mg/L	109.22	104.2	116.43	109.95
5	Colour, Hazen	0.56	0.59	0.79	0.65
6	Fluoride (as F), (mg/L)	0.5	0.4	0.5	0.47
7	Iron (as Fe, (mg/L)	0.028	0.029	0.03	0.03
8	Magnesium (as Mg) (mg/L)	19.8	18.6	21.8	20.07
9	Nitrate (as NO_3), (mg/L)	33.2	32.4	31.35	32.32
10	pH value	7.1	7.09	7.1	7.10
11	Turbidity, NTU	0.86	0.89	0.94	0.90
12	Sulphate (as SO4), mg/L	126.3	124.3	129.4	126.67
13	Total Alkalinity, mg/L	104	103	111	106.00
14	Total Dissolved Solids (mg/L)	158	178	196	177.33
15	Total Hardness (mg/L)	91	103	97	97.00

Hulyal, et al., (2009) in a study on Physico-chemical factors of Almatti reservoir of Bijapur (Karnataka) indicate that there is a positive correlation between Dinophytes density and total alkalinity, total hardness, EC, calcium carbonate [8]. In the Physico-chemical study of Atyal pond in Kolhapur, Maharashtra, Sawanth, et al., (2010) reported that the pond is rich in nutrients and becomes eutrophic [9]. Vass, K.K., et al., (2015) in their study reached on conclusion that in inland aquatic ecosystems, Phosphorus is the most limiting nutrient element [10]. In the limnological study of Jaisamand Lake (Rajasthan), Balali, et al., (2016) concluded that the presence of essential nutrients in the adequate amount needed for primary producers [11].

Conclusion

The ecosystem of anyplace depends on location, fauna, and flora there. Biodiversity also plays a vital role in human welfare like food for good health, security, social relationship, life and freedom of choice, etc. The current study has relevancy to the Physico-chemical study of Kaylana Lake, Jodhpur, Rajasthan.

Acknowledgment

The author is extremely thankful to SPCGC, Ajmer for providing the requisite facilities.

References

[1]. Aiyaz, R., Mir, A., Wangones, A. R., Yoursef and Wanyanes (2010). Diversity Index of Algal Flora in Water Lake Kashmir. Nature Envi. and Pol Tech. 9 (2):293-298.

[2]. Golmarvi, D., Kapourchali, M. F., Moradi, A. M., Fatemi, M., and Nadoshan, R. M. (2016). Influence of Physico-chemical Factors, Zooplankton Species Biodiversity, and Seasonal Abundance in Anzli International Wetland, Iran. *Open Journal of Marine Science, 7(1), 91-99.*

[3]. Sumathi, M., & Vasudevan, N. (2019). Role of Phosphate in Eutrophication of water bodies and its Remediation. *Journal of Chennai Academy of Sciences, 1, 65-86.*

[4]. Ji, B., Liang, J., and Chen, R. (2020). Bacterial Eutrophic Index for Potential Water Quality Evaluation of a Freshwater Ecosystem. *Environmental Science and Pollution Research,* 27(26), 32449-32455.

[5]. Choudhary, S., Sharma, S., Sharma, B., and Upadhyay, B. (2021). Water Quality Analysis of Anasagar Lake, Ajmer, Rajasthan. *Asian Journal of Advances in Research, 13-20.*

[6]. Ray, J. G., Santhakumaran, P., and Kookal, S. (2021). Phytoplankton Communities of Eutrophic Freshwater Bodies (Kerala, India) in Relation to the Physico-chemical Water Quality Parameters. *Environment, Development and Sustainability, 23 (1), 259-290.*

[7]. Panikkar, P., Saha, A., Prusty, A. K., Sarkar, U. K., and Das, B. K. (2022). Assessing Hydro geo-chemistry, Water Quality Index (WQI), and Seasonal Pattern of Plankton Community in Different small and Medium Reservoirs of Karnataka, *India. Arabian Journal of Geosciences, 15(1), 1-17.*

[8]. Hulyal, S. B., and Kaliwal, B. B. (2009). Dynamics of

Phytoplankton in Relation to Physico-chemical Factors of Almatti Reservoir of Bijapur District, Karnataka State. *Environmental monitoring and Assessment, 153(1), 45-59.*

[9]. Sawanth, R. S., Telare, A. B., Desai, P. D., and Desai, J. S. (2010). Variations in Hydro Biological Characteristics of Atyal Pond in Gondhinglaj Tahasil. District-Kolhapur, Maharashtra. *Nature Env. And Poln Tech 9 (2).*

[10]. Vass, K. K., Wangeneo, A., Samanta, S., Adhikari, S., and Muralidhar, M. (2015). Phosphorus Dynamics, eutrophication and fisheries in the aquatic ecosystems in India. Current Science, 1306-1314.

[11]. Balali, V.K., Sharma, L.L., and Ujjania, N.C., (2016). Limnological Study of Jaismand Lake, India and its Suitability for Aquaculture and Fisheries. *International Journal of Applied and Pure Science and Agriculture Volume 02, Issue 1, January 2016.*

Assistant Professor (Zoology),
Government College, Luni (Jodhpur) and
Research Scholar, SPCGC, Ajmer
email : chouhan.arvind9@gmail.com,

8. Medicinal Trees of Sariska Tiger Reserve : An Ethnobotanical and Pharmacological Review

Dr.Ved Prakash Gupta

The Sariska Tiger Project is situated in Alwar district in the north-eastern part of Rajasthan (27°4' to 28°4' N and 76°7' to 76°13' E). The hills surround a fertile valley and plateau, which are covered by dense forests. After the independence of India, it was declared a reserve forest by the government of Rajasthan in 1955. In view of the protection of its rich biodiversity, it was declared the "Tiger Project" by the Government of India and Rajasthan state in 1979. The Sariska Tiger Project covered an area of about 800 km2. According to the criteria for the classification of forests in India given by Champion and Seth (1968), the Sariska forest is a tropical dry deciduous thorn forest. The sariska forest is rich in plant species diversity and has about 403 plant species (Parmar 1985).

Medicinal plants, including trees, have been used for centuries by traditional healers to treat various illnesses and ailments. These plants contain natural compounds that have therapeutic properties such as anti-inflammatory, anti-bacterial, anti-viral, anti-fungal, and analgesic properties. And can be used in the development of modern medicine. Trees, in particular, are an important source of medicinal plants due to their large size and the vast array of compounds they contain. Many prescription drugs contain active ingredients derived from medicinal plants, and many other plants are used for Ayurvedic and homoeopathic remedies. Different cultures have contributed to the development of various medicinal plants, but there are some that remain popular throughout the world. Medicinal plants may be used to supplement modern treatments or act as alternatives for certain health conditions. Many of the plant species found in the Sariska Reserve are also economically valuable, both for their traditional uses and for their potential use in pharmaceuticals. The long history of use of medicinal plants has provided valuable clues to their efficacy and safety, though more research is always needed to understand and verify their pharmacological properties. The data was collected through a combination of literature reviews and field surveys. Relevant studies and research papers were identified The field surveys were conducted in the Sariska Tiger Reserve to collect information from local communities about the traditional medicinal uses of these tree species and interaction with the forest officials and local people revealed that there are a number of tree medicinal plants in Sariska Tiger Reserve. Local people directly use various plant products and their organ extracts for treatment of various diseases. This chapter gives an account of common tree medicinal plants found in Sariska Tiger Reserve, along with their family, local name and medicinal uses.

Acacia Catechu Mimosaceae "Kala Khair"

The heartwood of the tree Is used in traditional medicine by the locals for its numerous health benefits. The wood of this plant contains high amounts of tannins, which makes it useful in the treatment of diarrhoea, dysentery, and other gastrointestinal disorders. A water solution of its wood is also used as a mouthwash or gargle for the treatment of sore throats and other oral infections.The root of this plant is used to treat skin conditions such as eczema, acne, and psoriasis. The bark of this plant is also used to treat leucoderma. The wood also has antimicrobial and anti-inflammatory properties, which help soothe and heal the skin. Acacia catechu has been studied for its potential anticancer properties. Some studies have shown that the wood extract can inhibit the growth of cancer cells and induce apoptosis (cell death) in cancer cells (Rashid, M. H., et al. 2015).

Anogeissus Pendula Crassulaceae "Safed Dhok"

Anogeissus pendula bark has substantial anti-inflammatory potential and is used to treat a variety of inflammatory disorders. Bark promotes wound-healing activities as well. This plant's wood is used to cure diseases caused by bacteria, viruses, and fungi. Wood includes flavonoids, tannins, and phenolic chemicals, which have high antioxidant activity and protect the body from free radicals and oxidative stress (Alvi, I. U. et al., 2019). Urticaria is treated with fruit.

Balanites Aegyptiaca Balanitaceae "Hingot"

Balanites aegyptiaca fruit pulp and seed oil are used to treat a variety of skin conditions, including psoriasis, eczema, and acne. To reduce inflammation and improve healing, seed oil is administered topically to the affected area (Hussain, M.S., et al. 2014).The pulp can be consumed raw, cooked, or boiled in water to form a tea to cure gastrointestinal ailments such as constipation, diarrhoea, and dysentery. The pulp of the fruit Is also used to treat respiratory issues such as cough, bronchitis, and asthma.This plant's root bark is used to cure fever and malaria. The bark is boiled with water, and the resulting decoction is drunk as tea. Bark is used to treat dog bites and piles.

LanneaCoromandelica Anacardiaceae "Gurjan"

The leaves of this plant are crushed and boiled in water are used to treat respiratory problems such as cough, asthma, and bronchitis. Leaves also used in chronic rheumatism.The bark Is used to treat digestive problems such as diarrhea, dysentery, and stomach pain bark is also used to treat fever and malaria and various skin problems such as eczema, psoriasis, and dermatitis by local community.The bark and leaves of Lannea coromandelica are used to promote wound healing. The leaves are crushed and applied topically to the affected area, while the bark is boiled in water to make a decoction that is used as a wash or poultice (Kumar, A et al. 2019)

Mallotus Philippensis Euphorbiaceae. "Rohni/Roli"

The powdered seeds of this plant are used to treat skin conditions such as eczema, psoriasis, and itching. The powder is combined with water or oil to form a paste that is applied topically to the affected area. The plant and fruit extracts can lower blood glucose levels and enhance insulin sensitivity, which may aid in the management of diabetes. Fruit gland and hair are purgatives, anthelmintics, and used to cure tapeworm infestation. The plant extract has the ability to suppress the growth of harmful microorganisms such as Staphylococcus aureus, Escherichia coli, and Pseudomonas aeruginosa. (Kalaichelvan, V.K. et al., 2011)

Mitragyna Parvifolia Rubiaceae "Kalam/Kratom"

Leaves are the most commonly used for medicinal purposes. The leaves are believed to have pain-relieving, mood-enhancing, and energy-boosting properties. leaves of this plant contain alkaloids such as mitragynine and 7-hydroxymitragynine, which are believed to use to relieve chronic pain, headaches, and muscle pain. Its analgesic properties are due to the interaction of alkaloids with the mu-opioid receptor in the central nervous system (CNS) (Hassan et al., 2019). The bark of this tree is used to make a decoction that is believed to have antipyretic (fever-reducing) properties. Roots are used to treat dysentery and diarrhea. They are boiled in water and the decoction is consumed Seeds are used to treat stomach problems such as constipation and indigestion. They are eaten raw or crushed and mixed with water. The stem of Kratom is used to make a poultice that is applied to wounds to promote healing.

Sterculia Uurens Sterculiaceae "Katira"

The gum resin of Sterculia urens is used to treat respiratory problems such as cough and asthma (Singh, B. et al., 2011). It is mixed with honey and consumed orally. The bark of this plant is used for its astringent properties. It is used to treat diarrhoea, dysentery, and other gastrointestinal disorders (Kulkarni, Y. A. et al., 2013). The bark is powdered and mixed with water or milk to make a decoction. The leaves are used to treat skin diseases such as eczema and psoriasis. The leaves are ground into a paste and applied topically to the affected area. The seeds are used for their anti-inflammatory properties. They are ground into a paste and applied to the joints to relieve pain and inflammation caused by arthritis. The fruit is used for its laxative properties. It is consumed raw or roasted to relieve constipation.

Syzygium Cumini Myrtaceae "Jamun"

The fruit of Syzygium cumini has been used to manage diabetes due to its hypoglycemic properties (Ahmed, F et al., 2017). The fruit is also rich in antioxidants, which can help protect against oxidative stress and inflammation. The bark has astringent and anti-diarrheal properties used to treat gastrointestinal disorders such as diarrhoea and dysentery. The bark is also rich in tannins, which can help reduce inflammation and improve wound healing. The leaves of Syzygium cumini have been traditionally used to treat various ailments such as wounds, ulcers, and skin infections. They are believed to possess antibacterial and anti-inflammatory properties, which can help in the management of these conditions. The leaves are also rich in flavonoids and other phytochemicals, which can help protect against oxidative stress and inflammation (Rao CV, et al., 2011).

Terminalia Arjuna Combretaceae

Local communities utilise *Terminalia arjuna* bark to cure cardiac ailments such as chest discomfort, palpitations, and irregular heartbeat. Terminalia arjuna tree bark is used for its cardio-protective qualities. It contains arjunolic acid, arjunic acid, and flavonoids, which have been found to lower blood pressure, lower cholesterol, and improve cardiac function (Pardhe BD, et al. 2012). The bark is also used to treat arthritis and rheumatism due to its anti-inflammatory and analgesic effects. It is also employed in the treatment of digestive diseases such as diarrhoea, dysentery, and abdominal pain. The bark is also used to treat wounds and as an astringent. Leaves are used in traditional medicine for their anti-inflammatory and wound-healing qualities. They are also used to treat respiratory conditions such as asthma, bronchitis, and coughing. Fruits are high in vitamin C and antioxidants, making them good for overall health and well-being.

Terminalia Bellirica Combretaceae "Baheda"

Local people use fruit and fruit walls to treat respiratory problems such as asthma and bronchitis. Cough, sore throat, and headache (Rahman MM, et al., 2013). It is also employed in the treatment of digestive diseases such as constipation, diarrhoea, and dysentery. In Ayurveda, fruit is used to make trifala churn. The bark is used for its anti-inflammatory and astringent qualities. It is used to treat skin conditions, wounds, and bleeding problems. Terminalia bellirica leaves are used to cure fever, cough, and cold. They are also employed as anti-inflammatory and antioxidant agents.

Conclusion

Tree medicinal plants found in the Sariska Tiger Reserve have significant therapeutic properties that have been utilized by local communities for centuries. The plants contain a diverse range of secondary metabolites, such as flavonoids, alkaloids, tannins, and terpenoids, which exhibit numerous pharmacological activities such as antioxidant, antimicrobial, antidiabetic, anti-inflammatory, and anticancer effects. Scientific studies have validated the medicinal properties of these plants, highlighting their potential as sources of novel drugs for various diseases. these medicinal plants represent an essential resource for the local communities of Sariska Tiger Reserve and have the potential to offer significant benefits to the broader community. However, overexploitation, habitat destruction, and unsustainable harvesting practices have posed a significant threat to the survival of these medicinal plants. Conservation efforts are essential to preserve these species and ensure their sustainable use. Community-based approaches that involve the active participation of local communities can play a crucial role in the conservation and sustainable management of these plants. The use of modern biotechnological tools can also aid in the conservation and sustainable utilization of these medicinal plants.

Referances
Ahmed F, Urooj A. Traditional uses, medicinal properties, and phytopharmacology of *Syzygium cumini:* A review." Journal of Pharmacognosy and Phytochemistry. 2017;6(3):335-342.
Alvi IU, Parveen S, Khan MS, et al. Phytochemical screening and in-vitro antioxidant activity of *Anogeissus pendula* leaves. Int J Pharm Sci Res 2019;10:4313–20.
Bandari MM. flora of the Indian desert. MPS Repress. Jodhpur 1990.
Champion, H.G. and Seth, S.K., 1968 A revised survey of the forest types of India. Government of India Press, Delhi, pp. 404.
Choudhary, S., & Jain, S.K. (2014). Ethnomedicinal and Ethnobotanical Uses of Plants in Sariska Wildlife Sanctuary and Its Surrounding Areas, Rajasthan, India. International Journal of Advanced Research, 2(10), 245-259.
Das A, Datta A, Bhattacharya S, Sengupta S, and Banerji A. The use of *Terminalia arjuna* in the treatment of cardiovascular disorders: A review. Journal of Ethnopharmacology. 2017;197:157–172
Dhiman, A.K., & Dhiman, P. (2010). Ethnobotanical and phytochemical study of medicinal plants of Sariska Wildlife Sanctuary, Rajasthan, India. Journal of Applied Pharmaceutical Science, 3(6), 189–195
Hassan, Z., Muzaimi, M., Navaratnam, V., Yusoff, N.H.M.,

Suhaimi, F.W., Vadivelu, R., Vicknasingam, B.K., Amato, D., von Hörsten, S., Ismail, N.I.W. and Jayabalan, N. (2019). From Kratom to Mitragynine and its derivatives: physiological and behavioural effects related to use, abuse, and addiction. Neuroscience & Biobehavioral Reviews, 98, pp. 537–559.

Hussain MS, Fareed S, Ansari SH, et al. Anti-inflammatory activity of *Balanites aegyptiaca* fruit extract. J Ethnopharmacol 2014;154:523–7.

Jain, S.K. (1991). Ethnobotany of the tribals of Rajasthan, India. Journal of Economic and Taxonomic Botany, 15, 799-812.

Kalaichelvan VK, Sathish S, Ramkumar VS, and Muralidharan P. In vitro antimicrobial activity of *Mallotus philippensis* against bacterial pathogens. J Med Plants Res. 2011;5(2):249-254.

Kirtikar, K.R., & Basu, B.D. (1935). Indian medicinal plants Dehra Dun: International Book Distributors.

Kulkarni YA, Garud MS. Traditional knowledge on medicinal plants used by the village people of Hukkeri taluk, Belagavi district, Karnataka, India. Journal of Medicinal Plant Research. 2013;7(44):3248-3254.

Kumar A, Kumar A, Kumar V, et al. Evaluation of wound-healing potential of *Lannea coromandelica* using an in vivo murine model. Drug Dev Res. 2019 Dec;80(8):1103-1113.

Naik VN. Identification of common Indian medicinal plants, Scientific Publishers (India), Jodhpur, 2004; 81-7233-373-0. 6.

Pardhe BD, Mahajan SG. An Overview of *Terminalia arjuna*- A Herbal Drug for Cardiac Disorders. Journal of Pharmaceutical Science and Technology. 2012;4(4):201-205.

Parmar, P.J., 1985. A contribution to the flora of Sariska Tiger Reserve, Alwar District, Rajasthan. Bull. Bot. Surv. India 27(1-4) : 29–40.

Rao CV, et al. *Syzygium cumini* (L.) Skeels: A review of its chemical, pharmacological, and ethnomedicinal properties. Journal of Pharmacy Research. 2011;4(11):4043-4046.

Rahman MM, Faruque MO, Hasan MR, et al. Antipyretic activity of *Terminalia bellirica* fruit. International Journal of Pharmacy and Pharmaceutical Sciences. 2013;5(3):695-699.

Rajput MS, Sutar NG, and Khairnar MR. In vitro antibacterial activity of *Anogeissus pendula* Edgew bark against gram negative bacteria. J Ayurveda Integr Med 2013;4:183-5.

Rashid, M. H., Inafuku, M., Sugimoto, C., & Kawanishi, S. (2015). Potential anticancer properties of bioactive compounds of *Gymnema sylvestre* and *Acacia catechu.* Journal of Traditional and Complementary Medicine, 5(3), 144–148

Saikia, P., Ryakala, V. K., Sharma, P., Goswami, P., & Bora, U. (2011). *Acacia catechu* ethnomedicine, phytochemistry, and pharmacology: a review Journal of Ethnopharmacology, 136(3), 390-410.

Shetty BV, Pandey RP. Flora of Tonk district, Botanical Survey of India. Calcutta 1983.

Shetty BV, Singh V. Flora of Rajasthan, I Botanical survey of India, Calcutta 1987.

Shetty BV, Singh V.Flora of Rajasthan, II Botanical survey of India, Calcutta, 1991.

Shetty BV, Singh V. Flora of Rajasthan, III Botanical Survey of India, Calcutta, 1993.

Singh B, Kumar A, Kumar V, et al., *Sterculia urens*: An Overview of its Chemical, Pharmacological, and Ethnomedicinal Properties Journal of Medicinal Plant Research. 2011;5(6):901–905.

Singh, R.K., & Sharma, R. (2006). Ethnomedicinal study of plants used by the Bhoxa community in the buffer zone of Sariska Tiger Reserve, India Journal of Ethnopharmacology, 107(2), 230-233.

Assistant Professor,
R.R.Government College,Alwar,
Rajasthan.

9. Climate Change is a Challenge for Sustainable Development

Mahesh Kumar Nitharwal

Abtract

Climate action and sustainable development are inextricable. Climate change presents a new type of challenge for development. Climate change is a threat multiplier. It loudens existing warnings, aggravating problems for the economy, environment and society. Climate change is the most significant challenge to achieving sustainable development, and it threatens to drag millions of people. Climate change is not just a long-term issue. It is happening today, and it entails uncertainties for policy makers trying to shape the future. Policy makers all over the world are facing similar challenges. While we certainly know that the climate will change, there is great uncertainty as to what the local or regional impacts will be and what will be the impacts on societies and economies. Coupled with this is often great disagreement among policy makers about underlying assumptions and priorities for action. Many decisions to be made today have long-term consequences and are sensitive to climate conditions – water, energy, agriculture, fisheries and forests, and disasters risk management. The links between climate change and sustainable development are strong. Poor and developing countries, particularly least developed countries, will be among those most adversely affected and least able to cope with the anticipated shocks to their social, economic and natural systems. India is committed to sustainable development with equal emphasis on its three dimensions - social, economic, and environmental. Be it national or global, environmental decline and global warming occurred gradually over decades and centuries, picking up pace with time. We must remember that the clock is now alarming on the needed global action to combat and contain this decay. This action should be fair, just and equitable for all countries so that the future we want will be a future in which there is ecological and economic space for sustainable development for all.

Keywords : Climate change, Global crisis, Environment, Sustainable.

Introduction :

Over the past few decades climate change has emerged as a real threat to the Earth. Not only India but countries all over world are facing a severe menace resulting due to these changes. Hence it is global phenomenon. Vigorous topographical changes are seen at rapid rate as its ill effects are constantly appearing near future. Some Islands may even disappear from the map; the level at which glaciers are melting and sea level is rising, increasing the flow of rivers in North India. The northern parts of the country will receive more rain than the eastern part. Cloudburst is becoming common, in view of that, in the near future, a terrible situation can be seen. Urbanization and Deforestation are serious matter of concern. Due to the increasing human population and the indiscriminate exploitation of natural resources for their needs and due to human activities, the increase in the concentration of carbon dioxide in the troposphere and ozone duplication (GHGs) in the stratosphere is one of the main reasons for global warming and climate change. Uninterrupted human activities cause adverse effect on environmental balance. Due to climate change, natural disasters like floods, droughts and storms are seen every day, as well as the effect of climate change can be seen on the livability, health and economy of the globe[1-3]. Climatic change is a composite issue and is a permanent change in the nature of average weather which could also be caused by natural and human activities. Indistinguishably it is related to the community, civilization or compositely humankind. Not only can it be felt over a large area but its effect is visible all over the world.

Causes of Climatic Changes[4-6]

Natural Causes :

1. **Greenhouse Gases**

The main driver of climate change is the greenhouse effect. Some gases in the Earth's atmosphere act a bit like the glass in a greenhouse, trapping the sun's heat and stopping it from leaking back into space and causing global warming. Many of these greenhouse gases occur naturally, but human activities are increasing the concentrations of some of them in the atmosphere, in particular:

- A. carbon dioxide (CO_2)
- B. methane
- C. nitrous oxide
- D. fluorinated gases

CO_2 produced by human activities is the largest contributor to global warming. Methane is a more powerful greenhouse gas than CO_2, but it has a shorter atmospheric lifetime. Nitrous oxide, like CO_2, is a long-lived greenhouse gas that accumulates in the atmosphere over decades to centuries. Non-greenhouse gas pollutants, including aerosols like soot, have different warming and cooling effects and are also associated with other issues such as poor air quality.

2. Causes for Rising Emissions

- A. Fossil fuels, burning of coal, oil and gas produces carbon dioxide and nitrous oxide accounting of 75 percent of greenhouse emissions.
- B. DEforestration- Cutting down forests to create pastures and farms loses the beneficial effect and the carbon stored in the trees is released into that the atmosphere, adding to the greenhouse effect.Trees help to regulate the climate by absorbing CO_2 from the atmosphere.
- C. producing food causes emission of greenhouse gases. Increasing livestock farming produce large amounts of methane when they digest their food.
- D. Fertilisers containing nitrogen produce nitrous oxide emissions are also major contributor the above said theme.

3. Changes in the Earth's Orbit and Rotation

Changes in the earth's orbit around the sun and its axis of rotation (tilt and wobble of earth's axis) have cooling or heating effect on Earth's climate.

4. Volcanic Activity

Volcanoes can impact in climate. Major explosive volcanic eruptions releases large quantities of volcanic gases droplets and aerosols. Some explosive volcano eruptions can throw particles (e.g., SO_2) into the upper atmosphere, where they can reflect enough sunlight back to space to cool the surface of the planet for several years and has a potential of global warming.

5. Reflectivity or Absorption of the Sun's Energy

Activities such as agriculture, road construction, and deforestation can change the reflectivity of the earth's surface, leading to local warming or cooling. This effect is observed in heat islands, which are urban centers that are warmer than the surrounding, less populated areas. One reason that these areas are warmer is that buildings, pavement, and roofs tend to reflect less sunlight than natural surfaces. While deforestation can increase the earth's reflectivity globally by replacing dark trees with lighter surfaces such as crops, the net effect of all land-use changes appears to be a small cooling.

Manmade Causes

1. Greenhouse Gas Emission

Greenhouse gas emission is said to be the largest man-made climate swapper so far. Humans are now producing large amounts of greenhouse gasses on such a level that it has upset energy balance. Some of these greenhouse gases are long-lived like carbon dioxide and nitrous oxide, so the damage they cause is obvious. However, short-lived substances like methane still affect the energy balance as they are very potent and there are so many of them. Moreover, human activity continues to release them into the atmosphere.

2. Fossil Fuel Usage

Fossil fuel are made from decomposing plants and animals. Their burning produces carbon dioxide that is the primary greenhouse gas forcer of climate change. In itself it is not a particularly warming gas, but the amount that we are emitting into the atmosphere makes it the most damaging. These gases trap heat in atmosphere and causes global warming.

3. Black Carbon

It has emerged as major global climate change contributor next to CO_2. Another by-product of fossil fuels is black carbon, which is produced when fossil fuels, biofuels, and biomass are not properly combusted and emit soot. It enters the atmosphere as fine particles (aerosols) and absorbs large amounts of heat and infrared radiation.

4. Industrial Production & Farming

Emissions from factories contribute directly to the greenhouse effect while runoff waste alters the chemical make-up of water and air. Chemical pesticides, herbicides and fungicides used in industrial farming also wreak havoc to the atmosphere. Livestock farming also releases large amounts of methane into the air, driving up the amount of greenhouse gases already in the atmosphere.

5. Agriculture

Agriculture accounts for 14% of total greenhouse gas emissions, and with the need for more agriculture to provide for our ever-growing needs, its impact is growing rapidly. The main agricultural contributors to climate forcers include carbon released from farmland soil by inappropriate farming and grazing practices

6. Deforestation

Vast swatches of primary forests are being wiped out to make way for unsustainable farming, urbanization or for logging and the production of paper goods. Trees absorb carbon dioxide from the atmosphere, so as more trees are cut down, the level of carbon dioxide in the air will increase. In short, deforestation affects climate in a big way.

7. Urbanization

As our populations increase and our cities reach maximum capacity, we start to expand them in what is called urban sprawl. This decreases the amount of vegetation available to absorb carbon dioxide.

Effects of Climatic Change (In India)[7-10]

India is ranked fourth among the list of countries most affected by climatic changes. Some of its outcomes in the country are:-

1. India is an agricultural country where 60% of agriculture depends on rainfall and it hosts 33% of the world & climate change will have significant impact on the food and nutritional security of the country.

2. India ranks 13th in the list of countries vulnerable to climate change 40°C was touched mainly due to climate change, says Awadh Avantika Goswami Deputy Program Manager Climate Change CSE and it was when 2021 was the year of La- Nino, the Pacific current known to bring cooler temperatures globally Indian meteorologists have informed that global warming has reduced this effect of La-nino. According to the researchers of CSE , there will be more evaporation of water from the water bodies of rising summer, which will have a serious impact on water security and increase the moisture in the soil due to increase in heat. There will be a shortage of water and irrigation will be required for agriculture. More heat will increase the use of water from drinking and right to fighting fire in forest buildings.

3. Greenhouse gas emissions are third largest in the world and main source is coal. This is an alarm for increasing pollution in the country.

4. We have seen devastating forest fires not only in India but in many parts of the world, which will increase due to increase in temperature.

5. The number of rainy days in India is decreasing every year, with an average of 100 hours of rain per year, but the days on water security and increase the moisture in the soil due to increase in heat. Heat wave frequency and power are increasing because of climatic change. There will be a shortage of water and irrigation will be required for agriculture. More heat will increase the use of water from drinking and right to fighting fire in forest buildings. We have seen devastating forest fires not only in India but in many parts of the world, which will increase due to increase in temperature.

6. The number of rainy days in India is decreasing every year, with an average of 100 hours of rain per year, but the days of extreme rainfall are increasing.

Conclusion :

Impacts of climatic changes are already being observed across the world. But its severity is so pronounced that that even if greenhouse emissions are reduced drastically the effects will take considerable time to lower the devastating nature. The potential affects are for all sectors of human and natural systems. The magnitude and rate of impacts changes considerably. So, every country should act proactively to anticipate the impacts of these climatic changes. We should prepare ourselves to reduce their effects and react as the impact arrives. An anticipatory adaptation should be adapted as a desirable risk management strategy. Such adaptation strategy offers reduction in costs across different levels of government sectors and economy ensuring a wide range of mutually supportive services.

References
1. Arto-Blanco M., Meira-Cartea P.A., Gutiérrez-Pérez J, (2017), Climate literacy among university students in Mexico and Spain: influence of scientific and popular culture in the representation of the causes of climate change, *Int. J. Global Warming*, 12(3/4),448- 467.
2. Warner K., Hamza, M., Oliver-Smith A., (2010), Climate change, environmental degradation and migration, *Nat Hazards*, 55, 689–715.
3. Goldberga M.H., Lindenb S.V., Maibachc E., and Leiserowit A, (2019), Discussing global warming leads to greater acceptance of climate science, *Environmental Sciences*, 116(30), 14804–14805.
4. Fakana S.T., (2020), Causes of climate change, *Global Journal of Science Frontier Research*, XX(II),71-121.
5. Hegerl G. C., Brönnimann S., Cowan T., Friedman A.R. ,Hawkins E., Iles C., Müller W., Schurer A. and Undorf S., (2019), Causes of climate change over the historical record, *Environmental Research Letters*, 14 (123006), 1-25.
6. Kakaki S., (2013), Climate Change: Its Causes, Effects and Control, *Journal of Educational and Social Research*, 3(10), 73-77.
7. Zhang N, Yu, K. and Chen, Z. (2017), How does urbanization affect carbon dioxide emissions? A cross country panel data analysis, *Energy Policy*, 107, 678-687.
8. Heshmati H.M., (2020), Impact of Climate Change on Life, *Environment Change and Sustainability*, 1-20.
9. Balasubramanian M and Birundha V.D., (2012), Climate Change and its Impact on India, *The IUP Journal of Environmental Sciences*, VI(1), 31-46.
10. Sathaye J., Shukla P.R. and Ravindranath N.H., (2006), climate change, sustainable development and india: global and national concerns, *Current science*, 90(3), 314-317.

Assistant Professor
Government College Baran
email : maheshchoudhary1987jul@gmail.co

10. Climatic Changes Threatens Sustainable Development

Dr. Sonlata Bargotya

Abstract

Environmental sustainability means reducing our impact on the environment and adopting practices that use natural resources sustainably. Climate change and Sustainable development are inextricably linked with each other. Climate change currently is a serious concern and dangerous risks to humanity. Assessing the effects of climate change on environmental sustainability is the foremost task of present scientific outlook. Sustainability constitutes a major problem that many countries are experiencing like industrial pollution, degradation of land as well as natural disasters caused by the global warming. The ideology of sustainability that is being practiced and implemented is becoming increasingly important as water resources, species and biodiversity is declining day by day. Climate change in conjunction with socio-economic conditions can increase vulnerability in both developed and developing countries. This can threaten the environmental sustainability and lead to many adverse effects to the nature and fauna. Simultaneously environmental sustainability is good environmental management and a strong focus on the needs of future generations. This includes energy use, greenhouse gas emissions, ozone depletion, water use, waste reduction and management, and use of materials. Now a day's Environment Sustainability refers to balancing environmental and ecological concerns with social and economic aspects of development in other words 'triple bottom line' approach, which encompasses of the three pillars of program sustainability – environmental, social and economic. Mitigating climate change, addressing waste and pollution, and ensuring environmental sustainability are among the world's most pressing issues.

Keyword : Environment, Climate, Sustainability, Greenhouse gas.

Introduction :

The connection between Sustainability and Climatic changes stems from the fact that development is correlated to climatic variations both having common elements leads to Synergy of provocation. Sustainable development is defined as "the development that meets the needs of the present without compromising the ability of the future generation to meet their own needs sustainable development is not compromising with the economic growth or slumping economic growth for the sake of environment". It is an inevitable component for maintaining environmental quality. Therefore, maintaining ecological balance is inhabitable part of sustainable development. Thus, we can address a Synergy between sustainable development and climatic changes projected global climatic changes[1]. With respect to India global climate change models predicts that the current changes are human induced climatic changes and if the present situation persists the global temperature in is likely to rise by nearly 5 degree centigrade or even more by the end of 21st century.

Greenhouse effect and global warming is expected to continually increase by the end of century this will a uniformly increase the temperature rise across the planet. Some part of the world will experience the coldest and hotness at extreme this is interrelated influence the rainfall patterns.

Projected Climatic Changes in India[2-7]-

The uninterrupted human activities are creating reversible climatic changes including climatic events like heavy rainfall, droughts and heat wave. India is the country that is primarily a agricultural nation has deadly threatened by unstoppable menace of climatic changes. The portfolio of climatic models predicts profile of rising temperature and changing rainfall patterns across the country. Being a developing country, India is facing unpredictable challenges there by affecting the overall progress of the country.

1. Warming of Oceans :

Indian Ocean is warming at a higher rate than either ocean. This indirectly increases heat flux and flooding which will be irreversible effect of climatic change. Warming of ocean will definitely lead to rise in the sea levels contributing to severe coastal flooding in low lying areas. This will be an irreversible effect of climate change.

2. Changes in Rainfall Pattern :
Changes in rainfall recent variations in hydrological cycle pattern are a direct fall out of global warming and climatic change. The disturbed differential warming rate over land and ocean is creating a susceptibility to Indian land to drought and flooded events. This current rainfall distribution changes across the country will impact the water resources and food security and disturbed ecological systems. Oceans and seas are rising all over the world. Hence, coastal ecosystem will be disturbed by sea level rise and temperature elevation. Major risk is for the heavily populated delta regions due to increase flooding. This directly displace thousands of people and damages their occupation mainly aquaculture industries.

3. Drought :
Among the aforesaid natural disasters drought is also most disasters hazard as it disturbs numerous human societies. In other words, monsoon rainfall deficiency is a major tool for drought evaluation. Drought is often linked with desertification but desertification is not synonyms with drought. Desertification is simply degradation of land in arid, semi arid and dry sub-humid areas. It is crawling of death on the land. It is a major threat to agriculture productivity. Desertification due to human activities like removal of vegetation from land deforestation and uncontrolled grazing of by animals' agriculture system developed by green revolution has boosten up the process.

4. Tropical Cyclone :
The devastating natural calamity in world is tropical cyclone. They originate over ocean in tropical areas and move towards the coastal areas bringing a wide skill destruction caused by storms, vigorous winds and excessive heavy rainfall. In India, tropical cyclone originates over Bay of Bengal, Arabian sea, Indian ocean. Cyclones carry high very high wind velocity and heavy rainfall hitting the countryside coastal States. Prominently East coast is more prone to tropical cyclone from then to West coast. These lead to destruction of life and property also destroy vegetation erosion of beaches number of death and sever damage to life and property.

Effect on Monsoon :

To meet agricultural and water needs India is totally dependent on Monsoonal season. Significant changes in monsoon patterns have been noted by researchers. IIT scientists warn that India will experience a decline in summer rainfall by the 2050s. Since maximum percent of total annual rainfall in India is summer rainfall, it is crucial for Indian agriculture, this could have a devastating effect on the Indian economy, and on food security.

5. Increased Temperature :

Scientists report that surface air temperatures over India are going up at the rate of 0.4°C per hundred years, particularly during the post-monsoon and winter season. Predictions are that mean winter temperatures will increase by as much as 3.2°C in the 2050s, and 4.5°C by the 2080s. Summer temperatures will increase by 2.2°C in the 2050s and 3.2°C in the 2080s. Extreme temperatures and heat spells have already become common over Northern India, often causing loss of human life.

6. Effect on Agriculture :

Increased temperatures and changed rainfall patterns will impact agricultural production. Even a minute change in temperature 1degree centigrade effects the crop cycle by 5-20 percent. Higher temperatures reduce the total duration of a crop cycle by inducing early flowering, thus shortening the 'grain fill' period. The shorter the crop cycle, the lower the yield per unit area. Increased temperature also mean increased evaporation and transpiration rates. With no rainfall to compensate, yields will be reduced. Rise in surface temperature will create more conducive conditions for pest infection, which is already a major constraint in achieving higher crop production in India, and hence loss of crop.

7. Effect on Forests :

Increase in temperatures will result in shifts of lower altitude tropical and subtropical forests to higher altitude temperate forest regions, resulting in the extinction of some temperate vegetation types. This could potentially result in species extinction and decline in biodiversity. Increased dry spells could also place dry and moist deciduous forests at increased risk from forest fires.

Conclusion :

The climate change is the biggest Challenge of present century. It is a tedious task for entire world and serious risk for humanity. If the disasters effects are ignored ones at the local level it will be proved to fatal problems at global level tomorrow. Such a devastating challenges is more pronounce challenge for developing countries like India. As India is seeking to be a global power it has to deal with climatic changes at global issue. In critical terms foresightedness is required to see how much it has already impacted in the country and how much it will impact in forthcoming future. Therefore, country should approach its policies towards adaptation and mitigation. It is also about enhancing capability to protecting and responding to natural events.

References :

1. Venkatesan M., Gopalakrishnan S., Gnanasekaran D. (2013). "Growth of literature on climate change research: A Scientometric study". Journal of Advances in Library and Information Science, 2(4), 236-242.

2. Krishnan R., Sanjay J., Gnanaseelan C., Mujumdar M., Kulkarni A., Chakraborty, S., (2020). Introduction to Climate Change Over the Indian Region. In Assessment of Climate Change over the Indian Region. Springer, Singapore.

3. Yan D., Xie S. P., (2008), Geophysical Research Letters, Role Of Atmospheric Adjustments In The Tropical Indian Ocean Warming during The 20th Century In Climate Models, 35, 1-5.

4. Panagariya A., (2009), Columbia University and Brookings Institution, Climate Change and India: Implications and Policy Options, India policy forum, 2009–10. 73-161.

5. Sharma M., Singh R., Kathuria A., (2022), Climate Change and the Indian Economy – A Review, Current World Environment, 17(1), 20-31.

6. Husain U., Javed S., (2019), Impact of Climate Change on Agriculture and Indian Economy: A Quantitative Research Perspective from 1980 to 2016, Industrial Engineering & Management, 8(2). 1-4.
7. Srinivasan J., (2019), Impact of Climate Change on India, India in warming world: Integrating climatic change and development, Oxford Academics, 31-44.

Assistant Professor,
Department of Chemistry
Government College, Tonk (Rajasthan)
email : b.sonlata@gmail.com

11. Dumping of Toxic Products in Oceans

Dr Ranjeet Singh Budania*
Dr Neetu Yadav**

Abstract

The ocean covers two-thirds of the surface of the Earth, it is surprisingly vulnerable to human influences such as <u>overfishing</u>, pollution from run-off, and dumping of waste from human activity. This kind of pollution can have serious economic and health impacts by killing marine life and damaging habitats and ecosystems. Toxins from pesticides, fertilizers, and other chemicals used on farms contaminate nearby rivers that flow into the ocean, which can cause extensive loss of marine life in bays and estuaries leading to the creation of dead zones. The dumping of industrial, nuclear and other waste into oceans was legal until the early 1970's when it became regulated; however, dumping still occurs illegally everywhere.

Litter items such as 6-pack ring packaging and microfilament fishing lines can entrap pelicans and other seabirds, and ultimately strangle or starve the birds. Whales, dolphins, and other marine mammals are at risk through ingestion or entanglement of plastic refuse. Plastic bags are mistakenly ingested by sea turtles as jelly fish, a common food item. For example, the world's largest living turtle, the leatherback, is found off our Atlantic and Pacific coasts. With a shell as long as 2.5 metres, it can weigh up to 900 kilograms. You wouldn't think much could get in this giant's way. However, common plastic debris is causing leatherbacks terrible trouble. They mistake plastic bags, balloons or containers for jellyfish—their favourite food. Once swallowed, the plastic clogs the turtles' intestines, causing them to die. Leatherbacks are already endangered worldwide because humans hunt the adult turtles and their eggs for food. They certainly don't need to deal with another deadly menace like plastic debris. When animals get tangled, the debris causes cuts and infection. Seabirds, turtles, dolphins, and seals get exhausted from trailing nets behind them. These creatures can slowly strangle, suffocate, or die from infection. Recent studies in Alaska show that, each year, as many as 30,000 northern fur seals get entangled in plastic debris and die. Marine debris can also damage boat engines by clogging intake valves and ports and becoming tangled around propellers. Although some claim the risk to human health is small, the long-term effects of nuclear dumping are not known, and some estimate up to 1,000 deaths in the next 10,000 years as a result of evaporated nuclear waste.

Keywords : toxic, wastes, debris, plastic, nuclear, fishing, pesticides, fertilizers

Introduction

Plastic is a synthetic organic polymer made from petroleum with properties ideally suited for a wide variety of applications including: packaging, building and construction, household and sports equipment, vehicles, electronics and agriculture. Over 300 million tons of plastic are produced every year, half of which is used to create single-use items such as shopping bags, cups and straws. If discarded improperly, plastic waste can harm the environment and biodiversity.Microplastics have been found in tap water, beer, salt and are present in all samples collected in the world's oceans, including the Arctic. Several chemicals used in the production of plastic materials are known to be carcinogenic and to interfere with the body's endocrine system, causing developmental, reproductive, neurological, and immune disorders in both humans and wildlife. Recently, microplastics were found in human placentas but more research is needed to determine if this is a widespread problem.[1,2]

Toxic contaminants also accumulate on the surface of plastic as a result of prolonged exposure to seawater. When marine organisms ingest plastic debris, these contaminants enter their digestive systems, and over time accumulate in the food web. The transfer of contaminants between marine species and humans through consumption of seafood has been identified as a health hazard, and research is ongoing.

Plastic Pollution

Plastic waste damages the aesthetic value of tourist destinations, leading to decreased income from tourism. It also generates major economic costs related to the cleaning and maintenance of the sites. The build-up of plastic litter on beaches can have a negative impact on a country's economy, wildlife, and the physical and

100

psychological wellbeing of people. The UN 2030 Agenda for Sustainable Development calls for action to 'Conserve and sustainably use the oceans, seas and marine resources' (Goal 14) and 'By 2025, prevent and significantly reduce marine pollution of all

kinds, particularly from land-based activities, including marine debris and nutrient pollution' [3,4]

Observations

Radioactive wastes and oil pollution were the first two types of marine pollution to receive international attention.

In response to the extremely dangerous nature of nuclear waste materials, controls have been established relatively quickly compared to other forms of marine pollution.

Gulf Oil Spill

The international community has recognized the importance of minimizing environmental damage from radioactive wastes. This recognition is particularly crucial in view of the inevitable increase in the amount of these wastes. Several countries have a significant reliance on nuclear power and have future commitments to nuclear energy programs.' As of 1983, there were 277 nuclear power plants in operation around the world and 241 units under construction or on order.2 Nuclear power has been considered a viable energy source especially for developing nations, such as Pakistan, that neither possess energy resources such as oil or coal,3 nor are able to finance the importation of these commodities.[5,6]

Textile Dyes Pollution

The developing nations see nuclear power as their most desirable alternative for rapid economic growth. Coal and solar energy are often mentioned as alternative sources but they do not compare favorably to nuclear power in terms of practical and environmental considerations. Efficient, low-cost solar collection systems have not yet been implemented and energy storage continues to be a problem. Substantial reliance on coal would result in large amounts of carbon dioxide being released into the atmosphere. This could eventually lead to undesirable changes in climate due to the "greenhouse effect." 4 Therefore, nuclear power could become a major worldwide source of energy.[7,8]

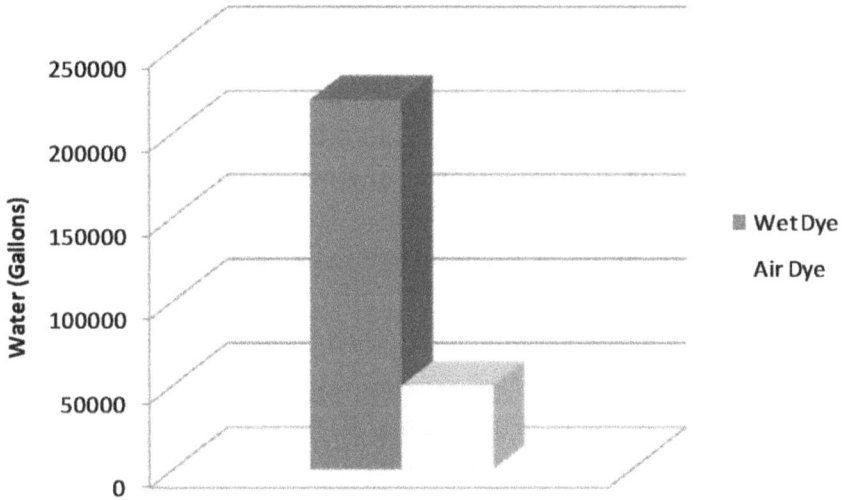

Textile Dyeing Industry-an Environmental Hazard

The textile dyes significantly compromise the aesthetic quality of water bodies, increase biochemical and chemical oxygen demand (BOD and COD), impair photosynthesis, inhibit plant growth, enter the food chain, provide recalcitrance and bioaccumulation, and may promote toxicity, mutagenicity and carcinogenicity. In spite of this, the bioremediation of textile dyes, that is, the transformation or mineralization of these contaminants by the enzymatic action of plant, bacteria, extremophiles and fungi biomasses is fully possible. Another option is the adsorption. Despite some disadvantages, the bioremediation is essentially positive and can be progressively enhanced by modern biotechnological techniques that are related to the generation of more degrading and more resistant engineered organisms. This is a sustainable solution that provides a fundamental and innovative contribution to conventional physicochemical treatments. The resources of environmental biotechnology can, therefore, be used as tangible technological solutions for the treatment of textile dye effluents and are related to the ethical imperative of ensuring the minimum necessary for a quality life for the humankind.[9,10]

Microalgae attached to microplastics are assumed to be more easily captured by filter feeders than free microplastics in the water column [11,12]. After microplastics are assimilated into the organism they accumulate in the gut, translocate into other tissues or are excreted, depending on the size, shape and composition of the particles. For example, fish fed with langoustines (*Nephrops norvegicus*) containing polypropylene filaments were found to ingest but not to excrete the microplastic strands, further corroborating the potential for trophic transfer and ecological impacts

Discussion

The chemicals found in plastic marine litter can be classified in the following four categories of origin:

- Chemicals intentionally added during the production process (additives such as flame retardants, plasticizers, antioxidants, UV stabilisers, and pigments);
- Unintentional chemicals coming from the production processes, including monomers (e.g. vinyl chloride, BPA, etc.)which may also originate from UV radiation onto the plastic waste—and catalysts, normally present in traces (ppm);
- Chemicals coming from the recycling of plastic waste; and finally,
- Hydrophobic chemicals adsorbed from environmental pollution onto the surface of the plastics.[13,14]

Chemical Pollution Effect
Marine scientists say they have found what they believe to be as many as 25,000 barrels possibly containing DDT dumped off the southern California coast near Catalina Island, where a massive underwater toxic waste site dating back to the second world war has long been suspected.[15]

Results
The wastes that are dumped into the oceans tend to have toxic substances, which soak in all the oceanic oxygen. This leads to a marked depletion of oxygen available to mammals and other fishes causing them to die in their natural habitat

Cargo Spill
• Cargo ships both accidentally and deliberately discharge crude oil into the ocean. As far as ocean pollution goes, this is one of the primary causes.
• Other reasons for marine pollution are the dumping of industrial waste. These products contain toxins including mercury, PCBs, PAHs, and radioactive material, all of which pollute the ocean.
• Heavy rains and floods wash trash and debris into the waters.[17]

Sri Lankans face upto Unmeasurable Cost of Cargo Ship Disaster
• Human waste and sewage water that has been partially treated or untreated goes into the ocean. This is called "garbage dumping" and is one of the world's leading causes of ocean pollution.
• Automobiles emit carbon dioxide due to fossil fuels being burned. This leads to air pollution. The carbon dioxide in the air reaches the ocean and becomes acid rain which then pollutes the water.
• Oil spills are dangerous for marine life and can affect coral reefs that thrive in the ocean. In fact they can greatly affect the life cycle. The gills of fish can be clogged by spilled oil which can block off respiration. If sunlight is blocked, marine plants will die because it affects photosynthesis and its process.[18]

Sewage Dumping
- These toxins not only affect the marine life, but they affect humans as well. For example, let's say the fish are contaminated, if someone were to catch a fish and eat it, they could get food poisoning.
- If garbage is dumped into the ocean, the oxygen in the water could be depleted. This results in poor health for marine life due to lack of oxygen. Animals such as seals, dolphins, penguins, sharks, whales, and herring could all die.
- Bottles and other plastics including bags can suffocate or choke sea creatures. Thinking they are food, they may eat them. Plastic items are one of the major causes of death among turtles. They think plastic bags look like jellyfish and try to eat them.[19]

The effects of ocean dumping are due to our carelessness. Roughly two thirds of the world's marine lives have been threatened with chemicals we throw down the drain every day such as house hold cleaners. It may do you good to remember that marine life is a part of our food chain. Not only do we eat fish and other marine life, but so do other animals. Underwater creatures are a main food source for other fish and bears.

There's a lot we can do to save our oceans. The best place to start is to keep them clean and not throw anything into them. It's also a good idea to keep the beaches clean. Garbage on the beach can easily end up in the water. Another thing we can do is to stop pouring chemicals down the drain such as paint or oil. Stop using toxic household products and don't overwater our lawns, in other words, conserve water.

Now that you know the cause and effects of ocean dumping, you'll be able to understand that it's just something you shouldn't do. You never know how much water is worth, until you have none. It's best to remember the causes, consider the animals and always keep them in the back of your mind. If we work together we can stop the effects of ocean dumping for good.

Conclusion

Solutions and Management to Ocean Dumping

1. Management and Minimization of Waste Dumping at the Port

Ocean dumping challenges compound day after day. Regardless, the waste substances that are disposed of in the oceans can be controlled through effective management and minimization efforts. Primarily, efforts should focus on controlling and monitoring cargo activity at the port while limiting the amount of waste substances dumped into the ocean from the ships.

Moreover, by taking effective management and minimization strategies at the ports, cargo sweeping activity that releases slag and iron ore pellets can be controlled to reduce the possibilities of ocean dumping.[20]

Reuse of Plastic Waste
2. Education and Awareness Creation
The initiation of campaigns aimed at stopping ocean dumping can go a long way in educating people and creating awareness on the hard facts regarding the problem. Most people are unaware of the dangers of ocean dumping simply because they are not enlightened about its repercussions.

For instance, for a long time, some people have held on the belief that dumping in the ocean eliminates the toxicity of the trash. In truth, this misconception is merely due to a lack of awareness creation. So, the lack of education and awareness on the dumper's part is to blame for ocean dumping. However, environmental networks like "*Stop Ocean Dumping*" campaigns can tremendously aid in addressing the problem.

3. Regulations and Laws
Regulations and laws account for the most effective tool for addressing the issues surrounding ocean dumping. As much as laws are put in place, further implementation of the laws is important. It's not just enough to enact laws and regulations to mitigate the ocean dumping problems.

Clean up Projects
Rather, responsible parties, people and organizations must seriously assume their responsibility to deal with the common problems. Bans should center on convicting industries, institutions and people that engage in ocean dumping activities.
A great example is the Ocean Ban Act of 1988 intended to put an end to industrial sewage sludge and waste dumping at sea in the US. Other prominent effective acts in history include the Ocean Dumping Act (ODA) and Clear Water Act (CWA) initiated by the US to deal with ocean dumping problems. In other words, the enactment and use of appropriate laws and regulations against ocean dumping can do wonders in mitigating the problem.
4. Organizing a Cleanup
In order to prevent or reduce ocean dumping, it is essential that we all do our part in cleaning up the mess. And, in order to make that happen, a clean up drive could be organized to clear the shoreline.
If the shore can be properly cleaned off the mess, ocean dumping rates can be reduced manifolds. While the small wastes can be picked up by hand, agencies could be hired in order to clean the heavier mess on the shoreline. A clean shore could easily ensure a cleaner ocean.

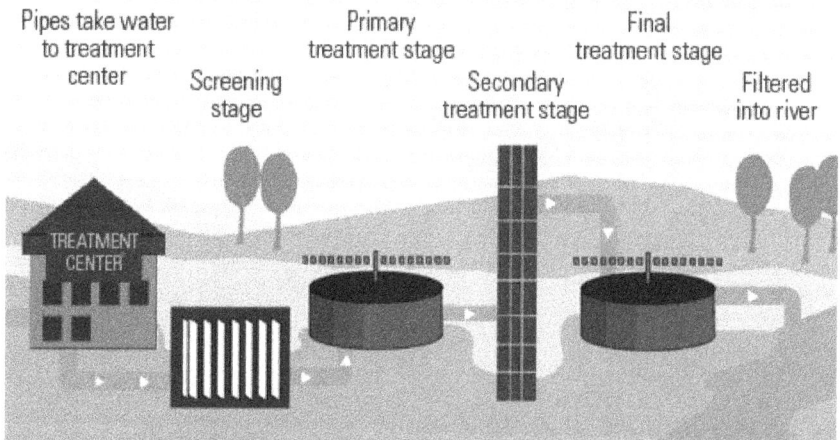

| Pipes take water to treatment center | Screening stage | Primary treatment stage | Secondary treatment stage | Final treatment stage | Filtered into river |

Sewage Treatment Plants
5. Securing Items on the Boats
Often, it has been seen that the small boats on which the fishermen

sail in the oceans can be a cause of the ocean dumping problem. It happens because the materials that they carry on the boat are often not properly secured.This gives the wind a chance to blow things off the boat. Also, if the waves are big, the turbulence could also have the same effect or even adverse. In order to prevent any event of this sort, it is better to ensure that everything on the boat is properly secured.

Wastewater treatment plants
6. Raise Your Voice against the Wrong
Everyone needs to do their bit in saving the ocean. So if anyone is seen throwing things into the ocean or even if they are seen littering the shoreline, it is essential that they are stopped from doing the same. It is important to openly raise our voices against such an act. This could help in reducing ocean dumping.[21]

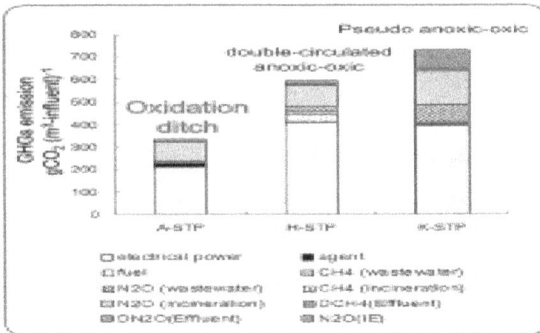

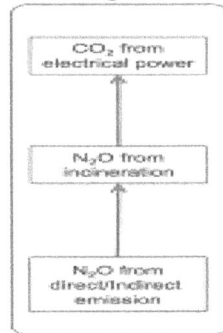

References
1. Pavlov, V.K.; Stanovoyà, V.V. The Problem of Transfer of Radionuclide Pollution by Sea Ice. Mar. Pollut. Bull. 2001, 42, 319–323. [CrossRef]
2. Waller, C.L.; Griffiths, H.J.; Waluda, C.M.; Thorpe, S.E.; Loaiza, I.; Moreno, B.; Pacherres, C.O.; Hughes, K.A. Microplastics in the Antarctic marine system: An emerging area of research. Sci. Total Environ. 2017, 598, 220–227. [CrossRef] [PubMed]
3. Lusher, A.L.; Tirelli, V.; O'Connor, I.; Officer, R. Microplastics in Arctic polar waters: The first reported values of particles in surface and sub-surface samples. Sci. Rep. 2015, 5, 14947. [CrossRef]
4. Huang, D.; Lin, J.; Du, J.; Yu, T. The detection of Fukushima-derived radiocesium in the Bering Sea and Arctic Ocean six years after the nuclear accident. Environ. Pollut. 2020, 256, 113386. [CrossRef]
5. Horton, A.A.; Barnes, D.K.A. Microplastic pollution in a rapidly changing world: Implications for remote and vulnerable marine ecosystems. Sci. Total Environ. 2020, 738, 140349. [CrossRef] [PubMed]
6. Sjoblom, K.-L.; Linsley, G. Sea disposal of radioactive wastes: The London Convention 1972. IAEA Bull. 1994, 2, 12–16.
7. IAEA. Inventory of Radioactive Material Resulting from Historical Dumping, Accidents and Losses at Sea; International Atomic Energy Agency: Vienna, Austria, 2015.
8. Hu, Q.-H.; Weng, J.-Q.; Wang, J.-S. Sources of anthropogenic radionuclides in the environment: A review. J. Environ. Radioact. 2010, 101, 426–437. [CrossRef]
9. Lebreton, L.; Slat, B.; Ferrari, F.; Sainte-Rose, B.; Aitken, J.; Marthouse, R.; Hajbane, S.; Cunsolo, S.; Schwarz, A.; Levivier, A.; et al. Evidence that the Great Pacific Garbage Patch is rapidly accumulating plastic. Sci. Rep. 2018, 8, 1–15. [CrossRef]
10. Jakacki, J.; Andrzejewski, J.; Przyborska, A.; Muzyka, M.; Gordon, D.; Nawała, J.; Popiel, S.; Golenko, M.; Zhurbas, V.; Paka, V. High resolution model for assessment of contamination by chemical warfare agents dumped in the Baltic Sea. Mar. Environ. Res. 2020, 161, 105079. [CrossRef]

11. Stock, F.; Kochleus, C.; Bänsch-Baltruschat, B.; Brennholt, N.; Reifferscheid, G. Sampling techniques and preparation methods for microplastic analyses in the aquatic environment—A review. TrAC Trends Anal. Chem. 2019, 113, 84–92. [CrossRef]

12. Martínez-Vicente, V.; Clark, J.R.; Corradi, P.; Aliani, S.; Arias, M.; Bochow, M.; Bonnery, G.; Cole, M.; Cózar, A.; Donnelly, R.; et al. Measuring Marine Plastic Debris from Space: Initial Assessment of Observation Requirements. Remote Sens. 2019, 11, 2443. [CrossRef]

13. Raha, U.K.; Kumar, B.R.; Sarkar, S.K. Policy Framework for Mitigating Land-based Marine Plastic Pollution in the Gangetic Delta Region of Bay of Bengal—A review. J. Clean. Prod. 2021, 278, 123409. [CrossRef]

14. Mitrano, D.M.; Wohlleben, W. Microplastic regulation should be more precise to incentivize both innovation and environmental safety. Nat. Commun. 2020, 5324. [CrossRef] [PubMed]

15. Du, Z.; Zhu, H.; Zhou, Q.; Wong, Y.D. Challenges and solutions for ship recycling in China. Ocean Eng. 2017, 137, 429–439. [CrossRef]

16. Yu, Y.; Zhou, D.; Li, Z.; Zhu, C. Advancement and Challenges of Microplastic Pollution in the Aquatic Environment: A Review. Water Air Soil Pollut. 2018, 229, 1–18. [CrossRef]

17. Cole, M.; Lindeque, P.; Halsband, C.; Galloway, T.S. Microplastics as contaminants in the marine environment: A review. Mar. Pollut. Bull. 2011, 62, 2588–2597. [CrossRef]

18. Barría, C.; Brandts, I.; Tort, L.; Oliveira, M.; Teles, M. Effect of nanoplastics on fish health and performance: A review. Mar. Pollut. Bull. 2019, 151, 110791. [CrossRef]

19. Wang, W.; Ge, J.; Yu, X. Bioavailability and toxicity of microplastics to fish species: A review. Ecotoxicol. Environ. Saf. 2020, 189, 109913. [CrossRef]

20. Bishop, G.; Styles, D.; Lens, P.N.L. Recycling of European plastic is a pathway for plastic debris in the ocean. Environ. Int. 2020, 142, 105893. [CrossRef]

21. Prata, J.C.; Silva, A.L.P.; da Costa, J.P.; Mouneyrac, C.; Walker, T.R.; Duarte, A.C.; Rocha-Santos, T. Solutions and

Integrated Strategies for the Control and Mitigation of Plastic and Microplastic Pollution. Int. J. Environ. Res. Public Health 2019, 16, 2411. [CrossRef]

*Assistant Professor
Department of Geography
Seth RL Saharia Government PG College kaladera Jaipur
**Assistant Professor
Department of Geography
Seth RL Saharia Government PG College kaladera Jaipur

12. Photocatalytic Degradation and Microbial Studies of Copper (II) Mustard Urea Complex with Light Intensity Effect

Vandana Sukhadia

Abstract

Photocatalytic degradation has been considered to be a regimented and rapid process for degradation for Copper (II) Mustard Urea complex. Photocatalytic degradation has concerned in scientific commune all over the world owing to its several applications in environment, energy, waste water treatment, pollution control, green chemistry, etc. Copper (II) Mustard Urea complex has been synthesized and considered through FT-IR, NMR, ESR studies. This article recalls and demonstrates the photocatalytic degradation of Copper (II) Mustard Urea complex by heterogeneous photocatalytic process using ZnO as semiconductor. Reaction rate is preferred at the similar time as the photocatalytic activity, which has been governed by a number of factors .The degradation was conceded out spectrophotometrically in non- aqueous and non polar solvent benzene. Photo-degradation of Copper soap complex varies with light intensity and also affect rate of degradation in different manner. Total degradation was calculated and compared with respect to percent degradation.

Keywords : Copper (II) Mustard Urea complex, Zinc oxide as semiconductor, Photocatalytic degradation, Non-aqueous media, light intensity.

Introduction

Photocatalysis is the acceleration of a photoreaction in the subsistence of catalyst. In catalyzed photolysis, light is captivated by an adsorbed subtract. Photocalysis has become one of the most precious approaches to degrade extremely poisonous naturally produce compounds, like cyanotoxins that cannot be isolated through conventional treatment process [1].

Photocatalytic degradation has been measured to be a well-organized and rapid process for degradation of Copper soap derived from edible and non edible oils. Heterogeneous photocatalysis on semiconductor surfaces has concerned a lot of attention due to application like water disinfection, degradation and complete mineralization of organic contaminants in waste water and purification and water splitting for hydrogen production [1-3]. ZnO nano particles are also predictable to be one of the multifunctional inorganic nanoparticles with effective anti bacterial activity. ZnO nano structures exhibits high catalytic efficiency, strong adsorption ability and Au used more and more frequently in the manufacture of sunscreen [4].

In comparable to this initial participation from photo electro-chemistry, photocatalysis acquire precious role from other chemical sub disciplines and grow to be a main regulation owing to joint enhancement of scientist arising from different fields: photochemistry, electrochemistry, analytical chemistry, surface science, electronics and catalysis also [5]. Photocatalytic techniques may create to be sooner and more inexpensive than the conventional techniques of treating pollutant.

Current study involves the degradation of complex derived from Copper (II) Mustard soap with Urea ligand. From the analytical data the stoichiometry of complex has been noticed to be 1:1 (metal: ligand). Magnetic moment studies propose the dimeric nature of complex.[6]

Shape and Structure of Micelles :

A micelle is an aggregate of surfactant molecules dispersed in a liquid colloid. The aggregation method depends, on the amphiphilic species and the state of the system in they are dissolved. Hartley proposed that micelles are spherical with the charge groups situated at the miceller surface [6], whereas, Mc Bain recommended that lamellar and spherical forms coexist [7]. X-ray studies by Harkins *et al* [8].Then suggested the sandwich or lamellar model. Later, Debye and Anacker proposed that micelles are rod shaped rather than spherical or disk like [9].

As shown in Figure-1 Micelles of ionic surfactants are aggregates composed of a compressive core surrounded by a less compressive surface structure [10] and with a rather fluid environment (of viscosity 8-17 centipoise (cP) for solubilized nitrobenzene in SDS and cetyltrimethylammonium bromide micelles) [11]. Copper ion attached to micelles have essentially the same hydration shell near the micellar surface as in bulk phase and do not penetrate into the non polar part of the micelles [12] so the volume change caused by the binding of divalent metal ions to micelles is very small [13].

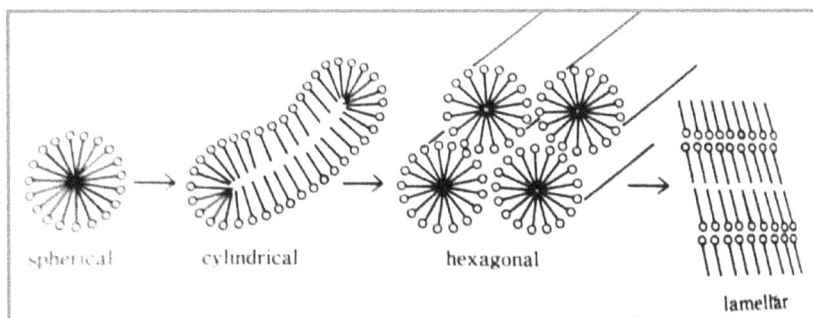

Figure-1 Change in micelle shape and structure with changing surfactant concentration.

Materials and Methods

Initially Copper(II) Mustard soap is equipped by direct metathesis of corresponding potassium hydroxide with oils to get soap with minor excess of requisite amount of Copper sulphate at 50-55°C [14]. Once washing with hot distilled water and alcohol, the sample was dried at 60-80°C and recrystallized with hot benzene.

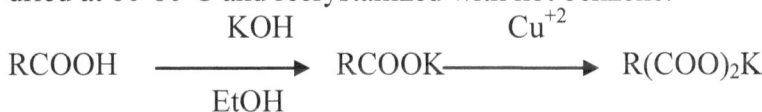

$$RCOOH \xrightarrow[\text{EtOH}]{KOH} RCOOK \xrightarrow{Cu^{+2}} R(COO)_2K$$

The synthesized soap derived from edible oil was refluxed with ligand Urea in 1:1 ratio using benzene as solvent for one hour. It was subsequently filtered hot, dried, recrystallized and purified in hot benzene. The complex is dark green and soluble in benzene. Physical parameters are recorded on the basis of its elemental analysis, 1:1 (metal:ligand) type of stoichiometry has been suggested.

Table 1. Fatty acid composition of oil used for Copper soap/complex synthesis [15]

Name of oil	% Fatty acids					
Composition	16:0	18:0	18:1	18:2	18:3	Other acids

| Mustard oil | 2 | 1 | 25 | 18 | 10 | $(C_{20}-C_{41}\%)$ |

Table 2. The composition and physical data of complex

Name of Complex	Colour	M.P . C°	Yeild %	Metal Content		S.V.	S.E.	Average Molecular Weight
				Obs.	Cal.			
Copper Mustard Urea CMU	Dark green	68	92	8.46	8.35	-	-	759.724

CMU- Copper Mustard Urea complex,

S.V-Saponification value,

S.E- Saponification equivalent

Different amount of catalyst were taken varied from .01, .02, .03, .04, .05 & .06 gm to study the effect of these on the degradation at the same complex solution.

Photocatalytic degradation of CMU complex was recorded at lambda maximum 680nm. Irradiation was carried out in covered glass bottles for the protection of evaporation of solvent with a 200 W tungsten lamp. A water strain was used to keep away from thermal degradation .Concentration of soap complex remains constant during experiment to know the effect of catalyst with the help of solar meter (CEL India Model SM 201). Absorption of light is recorded by U.V. visible spectrophotometer (SYSTRONIC MODEL 106) at different intervals of time.

Result and Discussion

Photocatalytic degradation of Copper Mustard Urea complex was recorded at λ_{max} 680 nm .A plot of 2+ logs O.D. (absorbance) versus time was linear and follows pseudo first order kinetics. Rate of the reaction was calculated using the following expression:

K=2.303x slope

Percent- Degradation of Cmu Complex :

Photocatalytic degradation of CMU complex was carried out by using ZnO as semiconductor under light .Complex degradation was initially identified by color change. Initially the color of complex was dark green- blue which was gradually fades to light green after 2 h. Further light green was disappears slowly and solution becomes almost colorless after completion 18 h light exposure.

Percentage of complex degradation was estimated by the following equation [16].

$$\% \text{ degradation} = A_o - A_t/A_o * 100$$

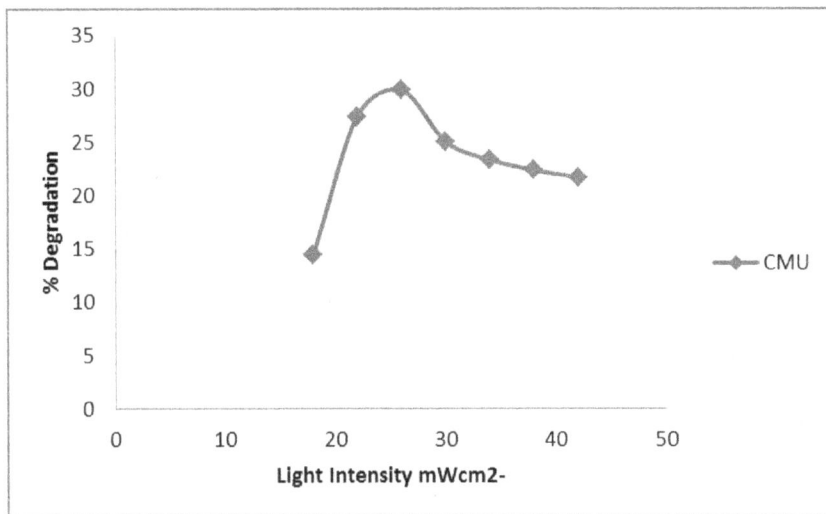

Figure-2 Effect of Light Intensity on Percent Degradation
Effect of light intensity

Photocatalytic degradation of CMU complex was also affected by light intensity. The light intensity was varied from 18, 22, 26, 30, 34 and 42 mW cm^{-2} to 42 mWcm^{-2}. The results are tabulated in Table 3 and presented in Figure-3

The data indicates that the rate of photocatalytic degradation of CMU complex was found to highest at 30 mWcm^{-2}. Further increase in light intensity resulted decrease in the rate of degradation. Value of K1>>K2 shows that the rate of degradation of unsaturated segment is much higher than that of the saturated segment at light intensity 30 mWcm^{-2} as the number of photon striking per unit area of ZnO powder increase with increase in the light intensity, there is a corresponding increase in the rate of photocatalytic degradation of

119

complex . The rate of photocatalytic degradation was found to decrease with further increase in light intensity due to thermal effect. [17, 18, 19]

Solvent   -Benzene,

Amount of ZnO   -0.02 gm,

 [CMU complex]   -Concentration of Copper Mustard Urea Complex,

 Concentration of Complex
in gm mole /lit   - 0.0008M.

Table 3 Effect of Light Intensity on Copper Mustard Urea Complex

Light Intensity $(mWcm^{-2})$	$K_1x10^{-5} sec^{-1}$	$K_2x10^{-5} sec^{-1}$	$K_3x10^{-5} sec^{-1}$
18	10.03	9.06	13.28
22	12.7	10.2	10.7
26	14.4	9.06	5.09
30	21.9	14.4	17.8
34	17.8	13.6	10.2
38	12.5	12.5	12.28
42	17.1	10.5	6.88

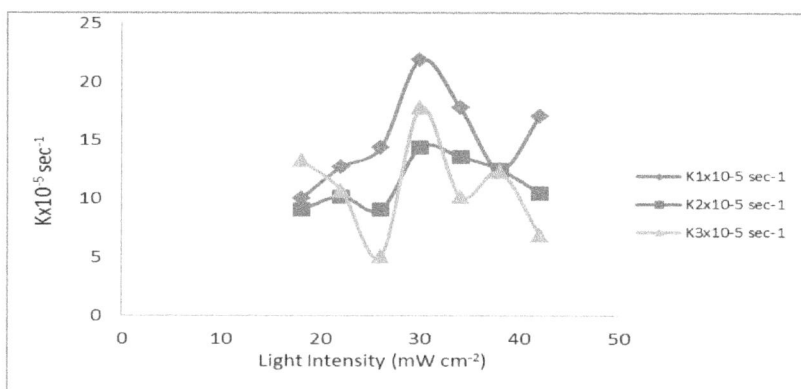

Figure-3 Effect of Light Intensity on Copper Mustard Urea Complex.

Application of The Study
Photodregradation has been considered in a lot of reaction of biological, synthetic and industrial significance here energy received from Sun can be better utilized for converting the pollutants into less toxic or just about harmless materials. Photo degradation plays a vital role in specific phenomena such as foaming, wetting, detergency, emulsification, fungicides etc. The study will endow with much information towards green , safe and sound chemistry.

Conclusion
Current study suggests that the rate of photocatalytic degradation of Copper soap complexes increases by increasing quantity of catalyst at a definite limit and then decreases which may be due to increase in aggregation of macromolecules in solution which decreases the probability and the rate of degradation including various steps of metal ligand breaking, unsaturated segment and saturated segment bond breaking of complex respectively. Rate of degradation increases with increasing amount of semiconductor at some extent and further decreases.

References
1. Hoffemann, M. R., Martin, S. T., Choi, W. Y and Bahemam, D. W., (1995). Environmental Applications of Semiconductor Photocatalysis, *Chem. Rev.*, 95, 69-96. doi: 10.1021/cr00033a004.
2. Mills, A. and Le Hunte, S., (1997) .An overview of semiconductor photocatalysis. *J. Photochem Photobiol A: Chem,* 108, 1-98. http://dx.doi.org/10.1016/S1010-6030 (97)00118-4
3. Tryk, D. A., Fujishima, A. and Honda, K. (2000). Recent topics in photoelectrochemistry: achievements and future prospects Author, *Electrochem, Acta,* 45, 2363-2376. http://dx.doi.org/10.1016/S0013-4686(00)00337-6
4. Ankamwar, B., Choudhary, M., (2005). Gold nano triangles biologically synthesized using Tamrind leaf extract and potential application in vapour sensing, *Synthesis and reactivity in Inorganic and Metal-Organic Chemistry,* 35, 19-26.

5. Herrmann, J. M., (2012). Titania-based true heterogeneous photocatalysis, *Environ Sci Pollut Res*, 3655-3665.

6. Hartley, G. S., (1936). *Aqueous solution of Parrafin Chain Salts*, Hermann, Paris.

7. McBain, J. W., (1944). Colloid Chemistry, Theoritical and applied J.Alexander,ed), Reinhold, New York.

8. Bloor, D. M., Gormally, J. and Wyn- Jones, E. (1915). *J.Chem. Soc., Faraday Trans.*, 180.

9. Baumuller, W., Hoffman Ulbricht, H. W., Tondre, C. ,and Zana, R. (1978). Solution chemistry of surfactant, *J. Colloid Interface Sci .*, 64, 418.

10. Mehta, V. P., Talesara, P. R., Sharma, R., Gangwal, A.,and Bhutra, R. (2002).Surface tension studies of ternary system: Copper soap plus benzene plus methanol at 313K, *Indian Journal of Chem. Sec. A,* 41, A(6), 1173-1176.

11. Sharma, R., Tak, P., Saxena, M. , Bhutra, R.and Ojha, K. G.(2008). Synthesis and Characterization of Antifungal Agents Containing Copper(II) Soaps and Derived from Mustard and Soyabean Oil, *Tenside surf. Det.*,45 (2)87-92. doi.org/10.3139/113.100366

12. Sharma, A., Sharma,V., Mathur, R. P.and Ameta, S. C.(2001). Degradation kinetics of Copper(II) soap derived from pongamia pinnata in presence of irradiating semiconductor ZnO, *Poll. Res.*, 20(3), 419-423.

13. Mattoon, R. H., Stearn, R. S., Harkins, W. D., (1974). Fluorinated Surfactants and Repellents, *J.Phys. Chem.*, 15, 209.

14. Debye P., Anacker, E.W., (1951). Micelle Shape from Dissymmetry Measurements. *J. Phys. Colloid chem.,* 55, 644.

15. Stark, R. V., Kasakevich, M. L., Granger, J. W ,(1982). *Molecularmotio of micellar solute;A carbon 13 NMR relaxation study, J. Phys Chem.*, 86, 335.

16. Vanaja, M., Paulkumar, K., Baburaja, M., Rajesh Kumar, S., Gnanajobitha, G. , Malarkodi, C., Sivakavinesan, M., Annadurai, G.,(2015). *Bioinorganic chemistry and applications*.

17.Sachdeva, D., Parashar, B. , Bhardwaj, S., Punjabi, P. B. , Sharma, V. K., (2010). Use of *Pure and N, S-Codoped Bimetallic* Cerium Cadmium Oxide Nanoparticles as

Photocatalyst for the Photodegradation of Fast Green, *Int. J. Chem. Sci.*, 8(2), 1321-1328.

18. Ameta, R. , Vardia, J., Punjabi, P. B., Ameta, S. C.,(2006). *Indian J. Chem. Tech.,* 114-116.

19. Upadhyay,R., Sharma, O. P, Jaker, S., Sharma, R. K., Sharma, M. K., (2013). Photocatalytic degradation of Azure B using Copper hexacyanoferrate as semiconductor, *Int. J. Chem. Sci.,* 331-340.

Assistant Professor,
Department of Chemistry,
S.D. Govt. College, Beawar (Raj.), India
Email : vandana.vandana.sukhadia@gmail.com

13. Chemical Toxicity Caused by Textile Dyeing Process

Dr. Renu Bala

Abstract

The aim of this paper is to analyse chemical toxicity caused by textile dyeing process. The process of applying colour to fibre, stock, yarn, fabric is called dyeing. Environment suffers greatly from pollution caused by coloured effluent released from textile dyeing units, affecting the ground water and soil. Dyes are generally synthetic aromatic compounds, some may be embodied with heavy metals in their structure. The waste water from textile industry caused serious environmental hazards. Presence of sulpher, napthol, VAT dyes, nitrates, acetic acid, soaps, and heavy metals like copper, arsenic, lead, cadmium, mercury, nickel, cobalt and some auxiliary chemicals make effluent toxic. The waste water from textile plant is classified as most polluting of all the industrial sector, considering the volume generated and effluent composition.

Keywords : Effluent, hazard, toxicity, carcinogenic.

Introduction

Since times immemorial, human has been fascinated by colours. He had discovered various ways of extracting the colouring materials from a number of plant sources for application to his own articles and to brighten his colours.

Dyes usage was started in 2600 BC in China followed by 715 BC, wool dyeing established as craft in Rome. India has a rich tradition in dyes and coloured fabrics. Probably, the earliest known dyes were indigo (a blue dye) and alizarin (a red dye), were obtained from plants. Most of the natural dyes have been replaced today by synthetic dyes, which can produce desired shades, not available in natural dyes. Today, almost all the dyes which are being used, are synthetic dyes.

Synthetic Dyes

As soon as synthetic organic chemistry was introduced, so did the manufacture and use of synthetic dyes. William H. Perkin is considered as founder of synthetic dyes [14].

In 1865, he prepared the first synthetic dye called Perkins Mauve or Mauveine. Synthetic dyes are organic compounds used for imparting colour to textile, paper, leather, plastic reasonably permanent fashion or permanent manner.

Chemistry of Colour

Colour have a wonderful chemistry of their own. Dissimilar to most organic compounds, dyes molecules possess colour because –

(i) they absorb light in visible spectrum (400-700 nm), its colour will be that of light reflected i.e. complimentary to that absorbed.

(ii) have at least one chromophore (colour bearing group).

(iii)have a conjugated system i.e. a structure having alternating double and single bond.

(iv)exhibit resonance of electrons which is stabilizing force in organic compounds.

If any of these property is lacking from the molecular structure, the colour is lost. Apart from this, most dyes contain groups known as auxochromes (colour helpers). In general, chromophors gives the dye molecule its particular colour while the auxochrome increases the intensity of colour, make the dye molecule more water soluble, and improve the color fastness properties of dyed or printed fibre.

Chemical toxicity and environmental hazards

Chemical toxicity is the ability of a chemical molecule or compound [9] to damage susceptibles sites or cells in the human body or in other living biological system including plants, animals or even ecosystem.

Chemical toxicity is very dangerous for human health as it may cause several types of severe disease, after prolonged intake, chronic disease [7] in human beings due to their consumption may include cardiovascular disorders, carcinogenicity, neurological problems and brain disorder. These elements may be any one or in combination of cadmium, lead, mercury, copper, arsenic, fluoride, nitrate, chromium etc.

Textile effluents [9] consists of several synthetic dyes and toxic chemicals containing acids, sulphur, napthol, nitrates, H_2O_2, surfactant dispersing agents and toxic heavy metals, such as Cu, Cr, Cd, Zn, Ni, As and Pb.

Textile effluents has high pH value and high TDS. Because of use of

common salt, level of TDS increases and when, salt content increases, it contaminates water and make it unsuitable for domestic, industrial and agricultural use.
The efforts of producing dye with long-lasting colouring comes at the cost of highly stable and inert organic structure. Dye effluent is considered to be one of the most harmful effluents, being carcinogenic to human and aquatic life. It is also responsible for the eutrophication and nonesthetic pollution.[15]
The dye effluent restricts sunlight penetration in contaminated water bodies. Long persistence of dye molecules in water bodies increased chemical oxygen demand (COD) also causes foul odor. Hazardous effects of dye [15] on human life dysfunction of central nervous system (CNS), kidney, reproductive system, brain, liver etc.

Conclusion

Effluent water coming out of textile industries require treatment before it is discharged to either water bodies or in open space. Untreated textile effluents are becoming the cause of many environmental problems, which is a matter of great concern. This is required under Water (Prevention and Control of Pollution) Act, 1974. The economic benefits from the textile industries are drawn by the handful of industrialists but ecological adverse impacts are experienced by innocent and poor people.
In order to protect human health, WHO, USEPA and BIS have given some standard values for chemicals in water. Some techniques to remove harmful chemical from water are bioremediation[6], phytoremediation, adsorption, ion-exchange, photocatalysis etc. Adsorption based water treatment has been found better for drinking water treatment and phytoremedial for on-site treatment of water soil.

References
1. An overview of effluent treatment for the removal of pollutant dyes, Yadav Sarita et al, Asian Journal Research in Chemistry, 2012.
2. Synthetic textile dyes : constitution, dying process and environmental impacts, Saini Rummi Devi et al, Asian Journal of Research in Chemistry, 2018.

3. Pollution due to synthetic dyes toxicity and carcinogeneity studies and remediation Ratna, Padhi B.S., International Journal of Environmental Sciences, Vol.3, Issue 3, 2012.
4. Environmental hazard in textile dyeing waste water from local textile industry, Fahum Uddin, Cellulose 28, 10715-10739, 2021, review paper.
5. Bhardwaj V., Pausa K., Gaurav S. (2014) Toxicity of heavy metals pollutants in textile mills effluent, Int. J. Sci. Eng. Res. 5(7) : 664.
6. The molecular basis of chemical toxicity, J.D. McKinney, 1985 cited by 29.
7. Chemical water contaminants : Potential risk to human health and possible remediation, Vinod Kumar Chaudhary, Akansha Patel, in contamination of water, 2021.
8. APHA 1995 standard methods for the examination of water and waste water, American Public Health Association, Washington D.C.
9. https://www.sciencedirect.com.
10. Nupur Mathur, Pradeep Bhatnagar, Journal of Environmental Biology 28(1), 123-126, 2007.
11. Bhatt, S.R. and Gokhale, S.V., 1984, Pollution control in textile and allied industries of Indian mazingua, pp.40.
12. De, A.K., 1987, Environmental Chemistry, Wiley Eastern Limited, New Delhi.
13. Carriere, J. Lones, J.P. and Broadbent, A.P. Deolouni Zalion of 'Textile Dye Solutions' Ozone S.C. Energy.
14. Nikhil Yogesh Upadhye, Dept. of Textiles, DKTE's Textile and Engineering Institute, Ichalkaranji, India.
15. Shailesh A. Ghodke, Irina Potoroko, 'Advanced Engineered Nanomaterials for the Treatment of Waste Water', in Handbook of Nanomaterials for Industrial Applications, 2018.

Associate Professor,
Department of Chemistry,
Government Girls College, Chomu, Jaipur
email : drrenubalachemistry@gmail.com

14. Effect of Sublethal Dose of Ethion on the Detoxification Enzymes in the Liver of Albino Rat

[1]Dr. Sachi Devi. P,
[2]Dr. D. Aruna Kumari ,
[3]Dr.U. Srineetha

Abstract

Ethion[$(O,O,O',O'$-tetraethyl S,S'-methylene s(phosphorodithioate))] an organophosphorous (OP) insecticide was introduced seven decades ago for use on plants and animals as an insecticide, acaricide and ovicide. The aim of present study was to investigate the sublethal effect of ethion on the detoxification enzymes in the liver of *Albino rats*. Adult male *Albino rats* of Wistar strain were orally administered ethion ($1/5^{th}$ of LD_{50} *i.e.* 42mg/kg body weight) for 30 days with an interval of 48h. Animals were randomly divided into four groups. The first group served as control. Second group of animals was treated with ethion for 10 days, third and fourth groups of animals were administered for 20 days and 30 days respectively. Antioxidant enzymes namely Catalase (CAT), Superoxide dismutase (SOD), Glutathione Peroxidase (GPx) and Glutathione Reductase (GR) are the first line of defense against oxidative stress. Pesticide exposure caused inhibition of antioxidant enzymes namely SOD, CAT, GPx and GR in the liver. Decrease in the activities of these enzymes changes the redox status of the cells. Results of the present study clearly showed days and exposure frequency-dependent decrease in the activities of CAT, SOD, GPx, GR in in the liver. The severity of the damage was also assessed by histopathological studies. The histological observations of the liver in the Ethion exposed *Albino rats* reveal central vein congestion (CVC), Dilated sinusoids (DS), Nuclear Degenerative Change(NDC), sinusoidal Hemorrhage (SH), Focal Necrotic Areas(FNA) and Amyloid Precipitation(AP). The results of the present study suggest that Ethion adversely affects liver functions leading to its physiological impairment.

Keywords: *Albino rats*, Ethion, Liver, Catalase (CAT), Superoxide dismutase(SOD), Glutathion Peroxidase (GPx) and Glutathione

Reductase (GR), Histopathological Changes.

Introduction

Organophosphorus (OP) compounds have been widely used for a few decades in agriculture for crop protection and pest control, thousands of these compounds have been screened and over one hundred of them have been marketed for these purposes (Mogda *et al.*,2009). OP pesticides are often used indiscriminately resulting in detrimental exposure to humans and other nontarget species. Currently OP compounds are the most frequently used pesticides worldwide (Heudorf *et al.*, 2006). All vital organs like liver, kidney, heart, nervous and reproductive systems are seriously impaired under OP exposure (FerahSayim, 2007). Ethion [(*O,O,O',O'*-tetraethyl *S,S'*-methylene bis(phosphorodithioate))] an OP compound was introduced in 1956 for use on plants and animals as an insecticide, acaricide and ovicide. Ethion, is a major environmental contaminant in many parts of the world and poses a significant threat to environmental and public health. Among many OP compounds Ethion is one of the substances that were approved for use in agricultural crops. Ethion is an insecticide that is used in a variety of forms and in several oil solutions and combinations with other chemicals. As a result, the acute toxicity values vary considerably. Ethion poisoning has been reported in workers harvesting grapes and peaches. Liver is the major organ which is targeted by OP compounds. Hence, in the present investigation the liver toxicity was studied under OP stress. The commonly used methods for detecting organ specific effects related to OP exposure are clinical biochemistry tests and histopathological evaluations. Hence, in the present study, we have examined various detoxification enzymes in the liver of Ethion exposed *Albino rats*. Bhatti *et al.* (2011) reported that *in vivo* administration of Ethion results in oxidative damage to erythrocyte membranes in the rats. There are many clinical reports on impaired liver caused by acute organophosphorus compound poisoning, however, there is limited literature pertaining to Ethion toxicity in the liver of rats. Hence in the present investigation various parameters were evaluated in the liver of Ethion exposed *Albino rats*. The present study clearly indicates that Ethion exposure seriously impairs detoxification mechanism in the liver of *Albino rats.*

Materials and Methods

Test Chemical

Ethion (92.5%) pure in crystalline form was obtained from Hyderabad chemical limited, Hyderabad, A.P. India.

Animal and Experimental Design

The protocol was approved by the Institutional Animal Ethics Committee, S.V. University (Regd. NO. 438/01c/CPCSEA). Male adult *Albino rats* of 7 weeks old and aged 200 ± 20g. was obtained from Indian Institute of Science (I.I.Sc.), Bengaluru. They were housed in an ambient temperature $28 \pm 2°C$ in a 12 h light/dark cycle and a minimum humidity of 40%.The animals had free access to commercial pellet diet supplied by SaiDurga Feeds and Foods, Bengaluru, India and water *ad libitum.* All the male healthy adult male *Albino rats* were randomly divided into four groups having six rats per group. The first group animals were considered as control animals. Second group of animals was treated with ethion via oral gavage ($1/5^{th}$ of LD_{50} *i.e.* 42mg/kg body weight) for 10 days, third and fourth groups of animals were administered for 20 and 30 days with an interval of 48h respectively.

Biochemical Estimations

The activity of SOD was assayed by the reduction of nitro blue tetrazolium. Here the Superoxide was produced by riboflavin mediated photochemical reaction system. Superoxide dismutase activity was determined according to the method of **Beachamp and Fridovich (1971).** Se-Dependent Glutathione Peroxidase was determined by a modified version **Flohe and Gunzler (1984)** at $37°C$. GR activity was determined by a slightly modified method of **Carlberg and Mannervik (1985)** at $37°C$. Catalase activity was measured by a slightly modified version of **Aebi (1984)** at room temperature.

Histopathological Studies

For light microscopic examination, samples of liver from the control and Ethion administered rats were fixed in Buoin's fluid. After a routine processing, paraffin – embedded tissue samples were sectioned at 3–5μm thickness and stained with Mayer's haematoxylin and eosin.

Statistical Treatment

The data was subjected to One way Analysis of Variance (ANOVA) and post ANOVA tests (S-N-K test) using SPSS (ver. 21) in the personal computer and $p < 0.01$ was considered as statistically significant.

Results

Biochemical changes

The results are presented in the Table 1. From the results it is evident that the activity of all the detoxification enzymes in the liver studied in the present investigation showed a decrement when compared to their respective controls. The decrease was maximum in 30 days exposed animals when compared to 10 and 20 days exposed animals.

Histopathological changes

Histopathological studies of ethion exposed animals reveal marked pathological changes in liver which include moderate to severe infiltration of inflammatory cells, mild congestion, dilated sinusoids, Nuclear Degenerative Change (NDC), sinusoidal Hemorrhage (SH), Focal Necrotic Areas (FNA), Amyloid Precipitation (AP) and other degenerative changes in hepatocytes.

Table 1: Changes in the activity levels of various detoxification enzymes in the liver of *Albino rat* exposed to sub lethal dose of Ethion.

Liver	Control	10 days	20 days	30 days	F value
Superoxide Dismutase	3.425	3.023	2.354	1.386	26.220[*]
(superoxide anions reduced/mg	0.560	0.809	0.450	0.476	
protein/h.)		(-11.73)	(-31.27)	(-59.53)	
Glutathione Peroxidase	2.690	2.368	2.022	1.564	30.007[*]
(μmoles of NADPH oxidized /mg	0.219	0.212	0.463	0.107	
protein/h.)		(-11.97)	(-24.83)	(-41.85)	
Glutathione Reductase	1.585	1.306	1.023	0.676	34.127[*]
(μmoles of NADPH oxidized /mg	0.078	0.0608	0.074	0.052	
protein/h.)		(-17.60)	(-35.45)	(-57.35)	
Catalase	1.539	1.193	0.815	0.410	57.806[*]
(μmoles of H_2O_2 decomposed/mg	0.330	0.581	0.219	0.1905	
protein/h.)		(-22.48)	(-47.04)	(-73.35)	

Values are expressed in Mean ± SD of six individual observations. Values in parenthesis indicate % change cover control. [*]P < 0.01

Discussion

Free radicals play an important role in a number of biological processes, some of which are necessary for life. Free radicals have also been implicated in certain cell signalling processes. However, because of their reactivity these same free radicals can participate in unwanted side reactions resulting in cell damage. It has been well indicated that the exposure to organophosphorus pesticides induce oxidative stress in *vivo* models. The enzymes associated with antioxidant defense are reported to be altered as a result of organophosphorus exposure, and the lipid peroxidation was found as the most common molecular mechanism of action of organo phosphorus pesticides.

Free radicals and ROS can readily react with biomolecules, starting a chain reaction of free radical formation. It leads to oxidative stress and disrupts the balance between ROS production and antioxidant homeostasis. In order to stop this chain reaction, a newly formed radical must either react with another free radical, eliminating the unpaired electrons or react with a free radical scavenger a chain breaking or primary antioxidant (Nordberg and Arner, 2001). Low levels of ROS are vital for many cell signaling events and are essential for proper cell functions, this imbalance can result in cell dysfunction and destruction resulting in tissue injury.

Xenobiotics comprise important sources of ROS, which are produced in the cells during normal metabolic processes involving oxygen. ROS are released during a number of metabolic reactions like cellular respiration, processes of biosynthesis and biodegra- dation, biotransformation of xenobiotics and during phagocytosis. There are about 60 enzymatic reactions that use O_2 as a substrate where ROS are formed. However, the concentration of ROS may be significantly increased by exposure to different environmental toxins produced from the industry, agriculture, tobacco smoke, or pollution accidents. Excessive ROS generation leads to damage of cellular components and a condition known as 'oxidative stress' is generated. Lipids, proteins and nucleic acid are sensitive targets of ROS. The cells have various mechanisms to combat oxidative stress and repair damaged macromolecules. The primary defense is offered by enzymatic antioxidants which have been shown to scavenge

ROS.

The balance between activation and detoxification of organophosphorus pesticides determines their risk to humans. Antioxidants may exert their activity by several mechanisms, like by suppressing the production of active species by reducing hydro peroxides and H_2O_2, by sequestering metal ions, termination of chain reaction by scavenging active free radicals and also caused repairing and/or clearing damage of cell. Biosynthesis of other antioxidants or defense enzymes is also induced by some antioxidants. (**Tiwari, 2001**). Therefore, antioxidants synthesized in body or supplied from outside like phytoconstituents plays important role to protect the body from free radical induced injury.

Free radicals occur continuously in all cells as part of normal function. Oxygen free radicals are detrimental to the integrity of biological tissue and mediate their injury. The mechanism of damage involves lipid peroxidation, which destroys cell structures, lipids, proteins and nucleic acids. They cause damage to cell membranes with the release of intracellular components, leading to further tissue damage. (**Poli *et al.*, 2004**). Antioxidant enzymes and nonenzymatic defense system minimizes the harmful effect of ROS by various antioxidant mechanism. Oxidative stress is a harmful condition that occurs when there is an excess of ROS and/or a decrease in antioxidant levels, this may caused tissue damage by physical, chemical, psychological factors that lead to tissue injury in mammals. It is hypothesized that ROS may play a role in organophosphorus induced tissues injury as these compounds have been shown to increase production of ROS in target tissues. Pesticide exposure alone or in combination, caused inhibition of antioxidant enzymes namely SOD, CAT, GPx and GR in all the rat tissues examined.

Antioxidant enzymes namely CAT, SOD, GPx and GR are the first line of defense against oxidative stress. Decrease in the activities of these enzymes changes the redox status of the cells. Results of the present study clearly showed days and exposure frequency-dependent decrease in the activities of CAT, SOD, GPx, GR in liver of rat. CAT seems to be maximally susceptible to inhibition by Ethion. Technical monographs suggest that the hydrolysis of ester bonds of organophosphorus compound plays an important role in the detoxification of these compounds. (**Miguel A Sogorb and Eugenio Vilanova, 2002**).

Ethion affects various enzymatic antioxidants such as Superoxide dismutase (SOD), Catalase, GPX & GR. All the enzyme activities in the present study decreased as compared to their respective controls. This indicates the failure of anti-oxidant defense system. The SOD was assayed to observe the levels of detoxification of superoxide anion radicals. With the increase in the time duration of the administration of pesticide, the SOD activity levels decreased. Ethion induced oxidative stress resulted in tissue damage and in depletion of SOD activity levels.

Catalase activity was estimated to assess the H_2O_2 reduction potential of tissue. The depleted Catalase activity levels was more in 30 days administered groups which indicate the potentials of organophosphorus compounds in inducing oxidative stress. GPX is a member of a family of peroxidase enzymes whose function is to detoxify peroxides in the cell. Glutathione peroxidase is considered as the major detoxification enzyme for H_2O_2. The GPX enzymes play a critical role in protecting the cell from free radical damage, particularly Lipid peroxidation. The activity of glutathione peroxidase is significantly reduced in all tissues.

The oxidized form of glutathione disulfide (GSSG) is reduced to GSH by the enzyme Glutathione Reductase (GR), which uses NADPH as a co-factor. In tissues GR activity is for lower than GSH-Px activity. All the values have shown a decreasing trend in antioxidant enzymatic activity.

References

1. Ben Amara, I., Soudani, A. Troudi, H. Bouaziz, T. Boudawara and Zeghal, N. 2011. Antioxidant effect of vitamin E and selenium on hepatoxicity induced by dimethoate in female adult rats. Ecotoxicol. Environ Saf, 74:811-819.
2. Bergmeyer, H.V (1965). In: Methods of enzymatic analysis Ed. H.V. Bergmeyer Academic Press, New York, 401.

3. Bhatti, G.K, Kiran, R and Sandhir, R. (2011) Alterations in Ca^{2+} homeostasis and oxidative damage induced by ethion in erythrocytes of Wistar rats: ameliorative effect of vitamin E. Environ ToxicolPharmacol. 31(3):378-86.
4. Bhatti, G.K, Kiran, R and Sandhir, R. (2010). Modulation of ethion-induced hepatotoxicity and oxidative stress by vitamin E supplementation in male Wistar rats. Pesticide Biochemistry and Physiology. 20(3): 119-26.
5. Colowick, S.P and Kaplan (1957). In Methods of Enzymology. Academic Press, New York, 501.
6. Eraslan, G, Kanbur, M. and Silici, S (2009). Effect of carbyl on some biochemical changes in rats. The ameliorative effect of bee pollen. Food Chem. Toxicol., 47: 86-91.
7. FerahSayim (2007). Dimethoate induced biochemical and histopathological changes in the liver of rats. Experimental and Toxicologic Pathology 59: 237-243.
8. Garba, S.H, Adelaiye, A.B and Mshelia, L.Y. 2007. Histopathological and biochemical changes in rat kidney following exposure to pyrethroid based mosquito coil. J. Appl. Sci. Res. 3: 1788-1793.
9. Heudorf U, Butte W, Schulz C, Angeref J (2006). Reference values for metabolites of pyrethroid and organophosphorous insecticides in urine for human bio monitoring in environmental medicine. Int. J. Hyg. Environ Health, 209: 293-9.
10. Lee Y.L. and Lardy A.A. (1965). Influence of thyroid hormones on L-glycerophosphate dehydrogenases in various organs of the rat. J. Biol. Chem. 240: 1427-1430.
11. Lowry, O.H, Rosenbrough, N.J and Randall R.J (1951). Protein measurement with the Folinphenol reagent. J. Bio. Chem. 193: 265-275.
12. Mogda, K.M Afaf AI El-Kashoury M.A and Rashed, KM, *Nature and Science*, 2009, 7, 2, 1-15.
13. Moore S and Stein W.H (1954). A modified Ninhydrin reagent for the photometric determination of amino acids and related compounds. J. Bio. Chem. 221: 907-913.
14. Natelson, S (1971). Total cholesterol procedure on free fatty acids in serum. In: Techniques of clinical biochemistry III Edn.

Charles. C. Thomas Publishers, spring field Illinois, USA pp. 263-268.

15. Ncibi, S. Othman, M.B, Akacha, A. Kriffi, M.N and Zougi, L (2008). OpuntiaFicusindica extract protects against Chlorpyrifos induced damage on mice liver. Food Chem. Toxicol. 46: 797-802.

16. Singh, N.N, Das V.K and Singh, S (1996). Effect of Aldrin on carbohydrates, protein and ionic metabolism of fresh water catfish Heteropneustes fossils. Bull. Of Env. Cont. and Toxicol.57: 204-210.

17. Saafi, E.B, Louedi, M. Elfeki, A, Zakhama, A, Najjar, M.F, Hammami, M and Achour, L (2011). Protective effect of date palm fruit extract (*Phodactylifera L*) on Dimethoate induced oxidative stress in rat liver. Exp. Toxicol. Pathol. 63: 433-441.

18. Yahya, S, Al-Awthan, Mohammed, A Al-Douis, Gamal, H, El-Sokkary and Esam (2012). Dimethoate induced oxidative stress and morphological changes in the liver of guinea pig and the protective effect of vitamin C and E. Asian J. Biol. Sc. 5(1): 9-19.

[*1]S.K. R & S.K.R Govt. College for Women(A), Kadapa, A.P
sachidevipureti@gmail.com
[2]Government College (A), Anantapur, A.P
dr.arunaprasad11@gmail.com
[3]Government College for Men (A), Kadapa,
A.P srineetha.ummadi@gmail.com

15. पर्यावरण संरक्षण का गांधीवादी दृष्टिकोण

राजेश गुप्ता

पर्यावरण सुरक्षा गांधीवादी कार्यक्रमों का प्रत्यक्ष एजेंडा नहीं था, लेकिन उनके अधिकांश विचारों को सीधे तौर पर पर्यावरण संरक्षण से जोड़ा जा सकता है। हरित क्रांति, गहन पर्यावरण आंदोलन आदि ने गांधीवादी विचारधारा के प्रति कृतज्ञता स्वीकार की। आश्रम संकल्प (जिन्हें गांधी जी के ग्यारह संकल्पों के रूप में जाना जाता है) ही वे सिद्धांत हैं जिन्होंने गांधी की पर्यावरण संबंधी विचारधारा की नींव रखी थी। गांधी का स्वदेशी विचार भी प्रकृति के खिलाफ आक्रामक हुए बिना, स्थानीय रूप से उपलब्ध संसाधनों के उपयोग का सुझाव देता है। गांधी ने कृषि और कुटीर उद्योगों पर आधारित एक ग्रामीण सामाजिक व्यवस्था का आह्वान किया। भारत के लिये गांधी की दृष्टि प्राकृतिक संसाधनों के समझदारी भरे उपयोग पर आधारित है, न कि प्रकृति, जंगलों, नदियों की सुंदरता के विनाश पर। उनका प्रसिद्ध कथन "पृथ्वी के पास सभी की जरूरतों को पूरा करने के लिये पर्याप्त संसाधन हैं, लेकिन हर किसी के लालच को नहीं" दुनिया भर के पर्यावरणीय आंदोलनों के लिये एक उपयोगी नारा है।

गाँधी चिन्तन समावेशी विकास का साहित्य है। गाँधी सतत् विकास के लिए अहिंसा एवं पवित्र साधनों पर बल देते है। उनका मानना था जैसा साधन वैसा साध्य' ही समग्र विकास का मूल्य है। गाँधी का विकास से तात्पर्य वस्तुओं का विकास नहीं अपितु मनुष्यों का विकास है। मनुष्य एवं मनुष्येत्तर दोनों का विकास है। यह तभी हो सकता है जब प्राकृतिक संसाधनों का अनुचित दोहन न हो रहा हो। गाँधी मनुष्य जीवन के साथ–साथ समस्त प्राकृतिक जगत की चिन्ता करते हैं। उन्हें विकास के स्त्रोतों के अस्तित्व की चिन्ता है। गाँधी पारम्परिक भारतीय चिंतन की तरह समस्त प्रकृति को पूज्य मानते हैं। गाँधी का सादा जीवन भी पर्यावरण चेतना की अभिव्यक्ति है। मनुष्य प्रकृति का सूक्ष्म अंश है यदि वह इसके विधान को नहीं मानेगा, तो यह मानव को दण्डित करेगी और किया है। गाँधी का चिन्तन इस दृष्टि से प्रकृति विधान का नैतिक दस्तावेज है। जिसमें सामाजिक एवं पर्यावरणीय चेतना का स्पष्ट उल्लेख है।

पर्यावरण प्रदूषण : विकट समस्या :

पर्यावरण प्रदूषण वर्तमान युग की सबसे विकट और सम्भावित समस्या है जिससे मानवीय अस्तित्व खतरनाक स्थिति से गुजरने को बाध्य हो रहा है। हवा, पानी व मिट्टी अपने आप में प्रकृति की ओर से शुद्ध व ग्रहण करने योग्य हैं और जीवन के निर्बाध संवाहक है। ये सभी तत्व अपनी प्राकृतिक अवस्था में रंगहीन, गन्धहीन, स्वादहीन होते है। जब इसमें कोई पदार्थ इस सीमा तक मिल जाता है कि उसके नैसर्गिक गुणों का ह्रास होने लगता है तथा उसके भौतिक, रासायनिक और जैविक गुण बदल जाते हैं। इन विजातीय पदार्थों की वजह से ये अपनी प्राकृ

137

तिक गुणवत्ता को छोड़ देते है जिससे जीवों को क्षति होने लगती है अथवा जब पर्यावरणीय जगत में नकारात्मक परिवर्तन अथवा ह्रास होने लगता है तो इसे प्रदूषण कहा जाता है।

अमेरिकी राष्ट्रीय विज्ञान अकादमी के अनुसार ''प्रदूषण जल, वायु या भूमि के भौतिक, रासायनिक या जैविक गुणों में होने वाला कोई भी अवांछनीय परिवर्तन है जिससे मनुष्य, अन्य जीवों, औद्योगिक प्रक्रियाओं या सांस्कृतिक तत्वों तथा प्राकृतिक संसाधनों को कोई हानि हो या होने की आशंका हो अर्थात प्रकृति को अवयवों में कोई भी विजातीय पदार्थों का मिलना जो जीव सम्पदा को क्षति पहुँचाएं, प्रदूषण के अन्तर्गत आते हैं।'' एम. वाल्टर के अनुसार, ''प्रदूषण पर्यावरण में पायी जाने वाली अवांछित अद्रव्यताएँ है। इन्हें प्रकृति स्वयं शुद्ध नही कर पाती है, इसलिए ये प्रदूषण के अन्तर्गत आती है।

पर्यावरणीय प्रदूषण वर्तमान समय की भयावह समस्या है। आज जितने जहरीले रसायनों का उत्पादन एवं उत्सर्जन हो रहा है, उतना विगत किसी भी संस्कृति और सभ्यता में नहीं हुआ है। परिणामस्वरूप जीवनदायक तत्व जल हवा मिट्टी में प्रदूषण से समस्त पारिस्थितिक तन्त्र कुप्रभावित हुआ है। जल, वायु तथा मिट्टी प्रदूषण से जैव विविधता में नकारात्मक परिवर्तन परिलक्षित होता है। प्रदूषण और संसाधन दहन के दुष्चक्र का दायरा बढ़ता जा रहा है। क्लोरो फ्लोरो कार्बन का एक अणु ओजोन परत के एक लाख अणुओं को नष्ट कर देता है और ओजोन परत में एक प्रतिशत की कमी से पृथ्वी पर 2 प्रतिशत त्वचा कैंसर की वृद्धि हो जाती है।

हरित प्रभाव, प्रदूषण एवं अन्य भौतिक परिवर्तनों से पृथ्वी की जलवायु में परिवर्तन उल्लेखनीय मात्रा में हो रहे हैं। पृथ्वी की जलवायु में परिवर्तन का बहुत बड़ा कारण ग्रीन हाउस गैस (कार्बन डाई ऑक्साइड, जलवाष्प, मीथेन, नाइट्रस ऑक्साइड) की निरन्तर वृद्धि से बहुत ही जल्द भारतीय उपमहाद्वीप की लाखों एकड़ जमीन पानी में समा आयेगी। अकेले बंगलादेश की ही 13 मिलियन आवादी प्रभावित होगी। चावल उत्पादन में 16 प्रतिशत की कमी आ जायेगी। अलनिनो प्रभाव, प्रशान्त महासागर में पैदा होने वाली गर्म जल धाराओं का प्रभाव है जो पूरी दुनिया में उथल–पुथल मचा सकता है। अलनिनो के कारण इण्डोनेशिया में सूखा पड़ा। भारत में भी यह मॉनसून में अस्थिरता का प्रमुख कारण है। मौसम वैज्ञानिकों के हाल के अध्ययन से यह निष्कर्ष सामने आया है कि 'ग्लोबल वार्मिंग' के कारण गरीब और विकासशील देशों की फसलों की पैदावार के ऊपर इसके नकारात्मक प्रभाव देखने को मिलेंगे, वहीं कुछ विकसित देशों को फसलों की पैदावार में इससे वृद्धि होने की सम्भावना है। वैज्ञानिक ग्लोबल वार्मिंग के नये खतरों में धरती पर बढ़ते रेगिस्तान को भी जोड़ रहे हैं। मरूस्थलीकरण का विस्तार इतनी तेजी से हो रहा है कि दुनिया के 110 देशों में रेगिस्तान पाँव फैला चुका है। पिछले कुछ वर्षों में आयोजित पर्यावरण से जुड़े कई अंतरराष्ट्रीय सम्मेलनों में वैज्ञानिकों ने चेतावनी दी है कि वैश्विक तापमान वृद्धि के कारण दुनिया घर के ग्लेशियर तेजी से पिघल

रहे हैं। इससे बंगलादेश और नीदरलैण्ड सहित विश्व के अनेक देशों के तटीय इलाकों के डूबने का खतरा बन गया है।

अंटार्कटिका की तीन बर्फीली परतें दक्षिणवर्ती, दक्षिण लार्सन और प्रिंस गुस्ताव तो पूरी तरह पिघलकर गायब हो चुकी है। प्रत्येक वर्ष 110 अरब टन कार्बन डाई ऑक्साइड धरती से होने वाले समान जैविक प्रक्रियाओं द्वारा वायुमण्डल में पहुँचती है। संयुक्त राष्ट्र पर्यावरण कार्यक्रम के अनुसार उद्योगों, मोटर वाहनों घरेलू उपयोग आदि की ऊर्जा आवश्यकता को पूरा करने के लिए जलाये जा रहे कोयले या पेट्रोल आदि से प्रत्येक वर्ष 5.7 अरब टन कार्बन डाई ऑक्साइड पर्यावरण में पहुँच रही है। इसके अलावा प्रत्येक वर्ष 2 अरब टन से ज्यादा कार्बन डाई ऑक्साइड उष्ण कटिबंधीय जंगलों के विनाश (जलने) से वायुमण्डल में पहुँच रही है। औद्योगिकरण के पूर्व में वायुमण्डल में कार्बन डाई ऑक्साइड की मात्रा 290 पी. पी. एम. या 0.029 प्रतिशत थी जो आज यह चढ़कर 0.38 प्रतिशत हो गयी है। इस प्रकार इसमें 25 प्रतिशत की वृद्धि हुई है। नाइट्रस ऑक्साइड कृषि में उर्वरकों के प्रयोग और कृषि कार्यों में उत्पन्न चीजों के सहने गलने से निकलती है। नाइट्रस ऑक्साइड भी प्रतिवर्ष 0.25 प्रतिशत की दर से बढ़ रही है। इसका प्रत्येक अणु कार्बन डाई ऑक्साइड को तुलना में 250 गुणा अधिक ताप पैदा करता है। मीथेन गैस ग्रीन हाउस प्रभाव पैदा करने वाली गैसो में एक प्रमुख गैस है। यह धान के खेतों, नम भूमि, दलहन भूमि, खनन कार्य, गैस डिलिंग, जैविक पदार्थों के सड़ने आदि से उत्पन्न होती है। इसके अलावा गाय, भैंस, भेड़, बकरी, घोड़ा, ऊँटे, सुअर आदि पशुओं और लकड़ी खाने वाले कीड़ों जैसे दीमक आदि भी इसके स्त्रोत है। यह पिछले कुछ दशकों में 0.9 प्रतिशत की वार्षिक दर से बढ़ रही है। समूचे विश्व से वर्तमान में लगभग 52.5 करोड़ टन मीथेन वायुमण्डल में पहुँच रही है। तापमान बढ़ाने में इसका प्रत्येक अणु कार्बन डाई ऑक्साइड की तुलना में 25 गुना अधिक प्रभावी है।

क्लोरो फ्लोरो कार्बन सिंथेटिक सौगिकों का समूह है। यह यौगिक एयर कण्डीशनरों तथा रेफ्रीजरेटरों में ठण्डा करने, छिड़काव करने वाले यन्त्रों में प्रणोदक के रूप में झाग को फैलाने और इलेक्ट्रॉनों को घटकों की सफाई और आग बुझाने के आधुनिक यन्त्रों में इस्तेमाल होते है। वर्तमान में इसकी खपत में अत्यधिक वृद्धि हुई है और यह 4 प्रतिशत की दर से वायुमण्डल में बढ़ रही है। ओजोन पराबैंगनी विकिरण को सोखकर धरती के जीव–जन्तुओं की रक्षा करती है परन्तु धरती के नजदीक वायुमण्डल में इसका जमाव गर्मी बढ़ाने का कार्य करती है। यह नाइट्रोजन के ऑक्साइड, मीथेन हाइड्रोकार्बन और अन्य कार्बनिक यौगिकों के आपसी क्रिया से बनी है। इन गैसों एवं यौगिकों को बढ़ती मात्रा के कारण ओजोन का क्षय हो रहा है जिससे पृथ्वी के ताप में वृद्धि हो रही है।

विश्व मौसम विज्ञान संगठन के अनुसार ओजोन मण्डल के सुराख का क्षेत्रफल लगभग एक करोड़ वर्ग किलोमीटर अर्थात यूरोप महाद्वीप के क्षेत्रफल के लगभग बराबर है और इसमें लगातार वृद्धि हो रही है। यह छिद्र अंटार्कटिका क्षेत्र

के ऊपर स्थित है। ओजोन परत यह छिद्र सन् 1985 से चिंता का विषय बना हुआ है। नवीनतम शोधों के अनुसार यह छिद्र और बड़ा होता जा रहा है, साथ ही कनाडा, पश्चिमी यूरोप, रूस, इंगलैण्ड के उत्तरी भाग स्केन्डिनेविया, नावें और स्वीडन के ऊपर भी विशाल क्षेत्र बनने की आशंका पैदा हो गयी है। ओजोन परत को नष्ट करने वाले क्लोरो फ्लोरो कार्बन का उपयोग औद्योगिक क्षेत्रों में सबसे अधिक किया जाता है। रेफ्रिजरेटर, एयर कण्डीशनर हेयर डाई, सुगन्ध का छिड़काव, पेन्ट, उर्वरकों के निर्माण, प्लास्टिक पेन तैयार करने एयरोस्पेस इलेक्ट्रॉनिक, ऑप्टिकल तथा फार्मेसी उद्योगों से यह अधिक मात्रा में निकलते है। अणु बम का विस्फोट भी ओजोन परत के लिए घातक है। ओजोन परत में छिद्र होने से मेलोनोमा कैंसर रोग, आँखों में मोतियाबिन्द व अन्य असाध्य दृष्टिदोष, प्रतिरोधक क्षमता में कमी, फसलों के उत्पादन में कमी, मछलियों एवं अन्य समुद्री जीवों के वृद्धि में कमी, अस्थमा एवं अन्य फेफड़े से सम्बन्धी रोगों में वृद्धि हो रही है, जो ज्यादा घातक है। इस प्रकार पर्यावरणीय प्रदूषण जो अंधाधुंध औद्योगीकरण, जनसंख्या में वृद्धि और गलाकाट प्रतियोगिता का परिणाम है जो मनुष्य द्वारा मनुष्यों के लिए घातक बनता जा रहा है।

समस्या निदान हेतु महात्मा गाँधी के सिद्धांतों की महत्ता :

ऐसी विपरीत परिस्थितियों में राष्ट्रपिता महात्मा गाँधी के बताये सिद्धान्त की महत्ता प्रमाणित हो जाती है। गाँधी जी के जीवन का आदर्श ''सरल जीवन तथा उच्च विचार'' है। एक व्यावहारिक आदर्शवादी होने के नाते उनको यह ज्ञात हुआ कि इसी दर्शन में आधुनिक सभ्यता के दोषों के उपचार छुपे हुए हैं। गाँधी जी ने कहा कि सुख और सन्तुष्टि दो मानसिक परिस्थितियाँ है और आवश्यकताओं की वृद्धि की कोई सीमा नहीं है। गाँधी जी ने लिखा है कि ''हम देखते हैं कि मस्तिष्क एक व्याकुल पक्षी है, जितना अधिक इसे मिलता है, उतना ही अधिक यह चाहता है और फिर भी यह असन्तुष्ट रहता है।'' वे आगे कहते हैं कि ''इसलिए हमारे पूर्वजों ने हमारे विचारों को सीमित करने की चेष्टा की थी।'' आधुनिक उद्योगवाद मानवीय मान्यताओं को त्यागकर मनुष्य में आवश्यकताओं को बढ़ाने तथा भौतिक धन प्राप्त करने की इच्छा उत्पन्न करता है। गाँधी जी आधुनिक पूँजीवाद के विरुद्ध थे क्योंकि यह मानव श्रम के शोषण पर आधारित है जिसे गाँधी जो हिंसात्मक समझते हैं। वे वृहद मशीनों के उपयोग के पक्ष में भी नहीं है क्योंकि इनसे बेकारी उत्पन्न होने के साथ पर्यावरणीय प्रदूषण, जिससे आज विश्व आक्रांत है, भी बढ़ते है जो मानव के साथ सम्पूर्ण जीव को नष्ट कर देगा और इसमें कुछ थोड़े हाथों में धन का संकेन्द्रण होता है। इसलिए वे आर्थिक विकेन्द्रीकरण को महत्व देते है।

गाँधी जी बड़े पैमाने पर औद्योगीकरण के कट्टर विरोधी है। मशीनों के उपयोग से मनुष्य आलसी हो जाता है और उसको अपने परिश्रम में कोई रूचि नहीं रहती है। इसका तात्पर्य यह कतई नहीं है कि गाँधी जी मशीनों के उपयोग के विरुद्ध है। उन्होंने स्वयं ही कहा है कि ''वह मशीनों के विरुद्ध नहीं है क्योंकि

वह जानते है कि मनुष्य का शरीर और चरखा भी मशीन है और इस दृष्टि से दाँतों को कुरदने की तिली भी एक मशीन है।'' गांधी जी केवल उस मशीन के विरोधी है जिससे परिश्रम को बचाने की चेष्टा की जाती है और जो प्रदूषण फैलाते है। उन्होंने विकेन्द्रीत अर्थव्यवस्था तथा घरेलू एवं कुटीर उद्योगों का स्थापित करने और उसके विकास का समर्थन किया है। इससे एक ओर, जहाँ कोई बेरोजगार नहीं होगा, न आर्थिक संकेन्द्रण होगा और न उद्योगों की चिमनियों से कार्बन डाई ऑक्साइड, मिथेन, नाइट्रस ऑक्साइड, क्लोरो फ्लोरो कार्बन गैसों में बेतहाशा वृद्धि होगी, और न दूसरी ओर ओजोन परत में छिद्र होगा, न अम्ल वर्षा होगी और न हरित प्रभाव पड़ेगा। गाँधी जी के उद्योग हाथों द्वारा चलाने वाले श्रम प्रधान उद्योग होंगे।

प्रकृति एवं पर्यावरण के विषय में गांधी अपने समय से सौ वर्ष आगे की देखते एवं सोचते थे। गांधी काल में प्रकृति या पर्यावरण संरक्षण के संबंध में न जागरूकता थी और न ही ऐसी कोई अवधारणा थी। कम जनसंख्या एवं प्रचुर प्राकृतिक संसाधन की उपलब्धता के कारण पर्यावरणीय समस्याएं उभर नहीं पायी थीं, परंतु, यह गांधी जैसे महान चिंतक की दूरदृष्टि थी, जो आज प्रकृति या पर्यावरण संरक्षण के जिन समस्याओं से हम जूझ रहे हैं, उन सबके निवारण के उपाय उनके विचारों में दिखते हैं। गांधी का प्रकृति प्रेम अद्भुत एवं अतुलनीय था। प्रकृति को वे संपूर्णता में देखते थे एवं उसे मानव जीवन का एकमात्र आधार मानते थे. उनके अनुसार प्रकृति उन्हें उत्साहित एवं रोमांचित करती थी एवं आनंदातिरेक में पहुंचाती थी।

वे प्रकृति को ऊर्जा एवं प्रेरणा के एकमात्र स्रोत के रूप में देखते थे। वे मानते एवं कहते थे कि उन्होंने   प्रकृति के अलावा किसी दूसरे से प्रेरणा नहीं ली और प्रकृति ने उनके विश्वास के साथ कभी धोखा नहीं किया। बकौल गांधी, प्रकृति पृथ्वी पर सभी जीवों को अपने–अपने दायरे में रहना और जीना सिखाती है। मनुष्य अगर अन्य जीवों की तरह अपने दायरे में रहे और अपने स्वार्थवश दूसरे जीवों का अहित न करे, तो इस पृथ्वी पर हमेशा शांति एवं समरसता रहेगी। उनके अनुसार मनुष्य के तीन तरह के पोषण होते हैं– भोजन, पानी एवं हवा, जो हमें प्रकृति से ही मिलते हैं। इन तीनों चीजों की आवश्यकता एवं उपयोगिता के परिप्रेक्ष्य में वे कहते थे, भोजन के बिना आदमी कुछ दिन तक जिंदा रह सकता है, पानी के बिना बहुत कम दिन जिंदा रह सकता है, परंतु, हवा के बिना वह एक पल भी जिंदा नहीं रह सकता है। ज्यादा परेशानी इसलिए होती है कि वह प्रकृति प्रदत्त इन तीनों चीजों का महत्व और कीमत का सही आकलन नहीं करता है। वे हमेशा तीनों चीजों की शुचिता पर जोर देते थे।

पर्यावरणवाद या प्रकृतिवाद का आज की तरह विकसित अवधरणा अनुपस्थित थी, परंतु प्रकृति एवं पर्यावरण संरक्षण की मूल बातें गांधी के विचारों में स्पष्ट रूप से निरुपित हैं। यह काबिले–गौर है कि सत्य और अहिंसा के संबंध में उनके मौलिक विचार का जुड़ाव भी किसी–न–किसी रूप में पर्यावरण संरक्षण से है।

141

गांधी के विचारों में प्रकृति ही सत्य है, जो मानव जीवन का आधार है। अहिंसा प्रकृति के सभी जीवों के साथ–साथ सहजीविता का ही दूसरा नाम है। गांधी के सत्य और अहिंसा के सिद्धांत पर आधारित मानव व्यवहार एवं कर्मों का स्वाभाविक प्रतिफल एवं निष्कर्ष प्रकृति या पर्यावरण संरक्षण ही होता है। पेड़–पौधे अथवा गैर–मनुष्य जीवों को मनुष्य द्वारा क्षति नहीं पहुंचाना ही तो प्रकृतिवाद का मूल सिद्धांत है। प्रकृति एवं पर्यावरण के संबंध में गांधी के विचारों का उत्कर्ष उनके न्यासधरिता के सिद्धांतों में दिखता है। न्यासधरिता का सिद्धांत गांधी के आत्मा के बहुत करीब था और वे इसे प्राकृतिक एवं भौतिक दोनों संसाधनों के परिप्रेक्ष्य में वांछनीय मानते थे। उनके अनुसार मनुष्य को सिर्फ आवश्यकता के अनुरूप ही अर्थ का उपभोग करना चाहिए एवं उससे अधिक उपलब्धि संपत्ति का उपयोग एक न्यासधारी के रूप में करना चाहिए। न्यासधरिता में किसी संपत्ति का कोई उत्तराधिकारी नहीं होता है, बल्कि वह आमजनों के हित में उपयोग किया जाता है। गांधी ने न्यासधरिता के इस सिद्धांत को प्राकृतिक संसाधनों के संदर्भ में भी उतना ही प्रभावी एवं वांछनीय माना है।

इस संदर्भ में उन्होंने मानव विकास के क्रम में प्रकृति के संरक्षण पर जोर देते हुए कहा कि कोई मानव–पीढ़ी उस समय के उपलब्ध प्राकृतिक संसाधनों का न्यासधारी है। उसे सिर्फ आवश्यकताओं की पूर्ति के लिए अथवा जीविका के न्यूनतम स्तर को बनाये रखने के लिए ही प्राकृतिक संसाधनों का दोहन करना चाहिए। यह भी ख्याल रहे कि जितने प्राकृतिक संसाधनों का हम दोहन करते हैं, उतनी ही मात्रा में उन संसाधनों का पुनर्भरण करना भी हमारा दायित्व होता है। इसलिए अगर हम अपनी स्वाभाविक आवश्यकताओं की पूर्ति के लिए प्राकृतिक संसाधनों का उपभोग करते हैं तो हम आगे आने वाली पीढ़ी को भी एक सुरक्षित प्राकृतिक माहौल सौंप सकते हैं। सही मायने में यही तो आधुनिक पर्यावरणवाद है।

इस रूप में गांधी न सिर्फ पर्यावरणवाद के आदि प्रवर्तक थे, बल्कि उनके विचार ही आज प्रस्फुटित और पुष्पित होकर पर्यावरणवाद का स्वरूप ग्रहण कर रहे हैं। इस प्रकार गाँधी जी के आर्थिक विकेन्द्रीकरण की नीति तथा छोटे–छोटे उद्योगों की स्थापना एवं विकास के सिद्धान्त को अपनाकर मानव सभ्यता पर गहराने वाले प्रदूषण के संकट, जो मनुष्य द्वारा उत्पादित संकट है, से निश्चित रूप से विश्व को निजात दिलाया जा सकता है। इस विद्यमान पर्यावरणीय प्रदूषण के बढ़ते खतरे से बचाने के लिए गाँधी जी के सिद्धान्त, नीति एवं विचारों का महत्व और भी बढ़ जाता है। प्रकृति को गांधीवादी नजरिये से देखने पर वैश्विक तापन जैसी समस्याएँ कम हो सकती हैं, क्योंकि इस समस्या की जड़ उपभोक्तावाद ही है। इस समय पूरा विश्व कोरोना वायरस जैसी महामारी से लड़ रहा है। इस महामारी को पर्यावरण क्षरण, स्वच्छता में कमी तथा उपभोक्तावादी जीवनशैली जैसे कारकों का परिणाम माना जा सकता है। गांधीवादी दृष्टिकोण ने सर्वथा पर्यावरण संरक्षण, स्वच्छता, जरुरत के अनुसार ही उपभोग, आत्मनिर्भरता

तथा ग्रामीण अर्थव्यवस्था पर जोर दिया। इस संकट काल में गांधी के विचारों की महत्ता एक बार फिर स्थापित होती है। इस महामारी ने एक अवसर प्रदान किया है कि हमें अपनी खाद्य श्रृंखला में बदलाव करते हुए गांधीवादी सिद्धांतों को अपनाने की आवश्यकता है।

संदर्भ सूची :

1. सिंह, सवीन्द्र, पर्यावरण भूगोल का स्वरूप, प्रवालिका पब्लिकेशन्स, इलाहाबाद, 2016.
2. शर्मा, एच.एस., शर्मा, एम. एल. एवं मिश्रा, आर. एन. भौतिक भूगोल, पंचशील प्रकाशन, जयपुर 2019.
3. रिपोर्ट, दक्षिण एशिया के हॉटस्पॉट : तापमान और वर्षण में परिवर्तन का जीवन–स्तर पर प्रभाव, विश्व बैंक समूह, 2018.
4. नारायण, सुनीता (पर्यावरणविद), जलवायु परिवर्तन के अवश्यंभावी प्रभाव, बिजनेस स्टैण्डर्ड, दिनांक 14.8.18.
5. सक्सेना, के. जी., जलवायु परिवर्तन और सम्पोषणीय विकास, योजना, प्रकाशन विभाग, दिल्ली, दिसम्बर 2015.
6. गाँधी, हिन्द स्वराज्य, अनुवादक ठाकुरदास नाणावटी, सर्व सेवा संघ प्रकाशन, वाराणसी, 2006.
7. यंग इन्डिया, पत्रिका, (13 अक्टूबर 1921 टैगोर को उत्तर देते हुए)।
8. गाँधी, ग्राम–स्वराज, संग्राहक–हरिप्रसाद व्यास, नवजीवन प्रकाशन मन्दिर, अहमदाबाद, 2013, पृष्ठ– 486. कोठारी रजनी, पॉलिटिक्स इन इंडिया।
9. सिंह, श्री भगवान, महात्मा गाँधी के चिंतन में तुलसीदास, बहुवचन, महात्मा गाँधी अन्तर्राष्ट्रीय हिन्दी विश्वविद्यालय, वर्धा, वर्ष 3, अंक 18, जनवरी–मार्च 2002.
10. गाँधी, हिन्द स्वराज्य, अनुवादक ठाकुरदास नाणावटी, सर्व सेवा संघ प्रकाशन, वाराणसी, 2006.
11. योजना आयोग रिपोर्ट 2006 (डी बंधोपाध्याय कमिटी)।
12. स्वाधीनता सी.पी.एम. की मुख्य पत्रिका, शारदीय विशेषांक, 2004.
13. तिवारी, एस.के., ओद्योगिक विकास और ग्लोबल वार्मिंग, 2017.
14. आर्थिक समीक्षा 2020–21, भारत सरकार।
15. योजना 13. कुरुक्षेत्र 14. इण्डिया टुडे

सहायक आचार्य, राजनीति विज्ञान
बाबू शोभाराम राजकीय कला महाविद्यालय, अलवर
email : rajeshalwar44@gmail.com

16. A Critical study of the Ban on Select Single Use Plastics in India : Challenges & Opportunities towards achieving Sustainable Development Goals

[1]Avdesh Bhardawaj,
[2]Raghav Bhardwaj*,
[3]Sushma Bharadwaj,
[4]Poonam Bhardwaj,
[5]Anurag Singh Chaudhary,
[6]Yadvendra Ahlawat

Abstract

The adverse impacts of littered single use plastic (SUP) items on the environment, including marine, are globally recognized. Government of India notified the Plastic Waste Management Amendment Rules-2021, on 12th August 2021 which bans manufacture, import, stocking, distribution, sale and use of identified single use plastic items, which have low utility and high littering potential, all across the country from July 1, 2022. But this ban is partial and not a blanket one as only a select few items have been prohibited. Although a step in the right direction, more needs to be done. This paper is intended to critically examine this new policy, its pros and cons as well as identify and suggest the challenges and opportunities therein towards achieving sustainable development goals as well as arresting climate change due to it. The methodology adopted here is literature review and virtual telephonic and questionnaire-based interviews conducted with 136 experts on the subject including bureaucrats, scientists, researchers, academicians specializing in the subject, resident welfare association (RWA) heads, local politicians, etc. between January to May 2022. Based upon the analysis of the results of the literature review and the interview data, some recommendations have been suggested to make the ban more effective and inclusive. It is expected that the paper would help the various stakeholders in developing not only new techniques for tackling this problem but also in evolving innovative policies as a way ahead.

Keywords : climate change; interview questionnaire; single use plastics; solid waste management; sustainable development

1. Introduction

When the first man made plastic was discovered in 1862 as Parkesine, it was marketed as an alternative to ivory and horns [Rasmussen, 2021]. Later, Leo Baekeland pioneered the first fully synthetic plastic in 1907 and patented it [Lhamon Jr, 1996]. At first these were perceived and accepted as great inventions that could change the way we packaged, stored and transported goods. Plastic pollution was first noticed in the ocean by scientists carrying out plankton studies in the late 1960s and early 1970s [Vegter et al., 2014]. By the arrival of 2010s plastics pollution had become one of the most crucial environmental issues [Bhagat et al., 2016].

Single-use plastics account for a third of all plastic produced globally, with 98% manufactured from fossil fuels. 300 million tons of plastic is produced each year globally, half of which is for single-use items; which is nearly equivalent to the weight of the entire human population [NRDC, 2022] When 85% of such single use plastics ends up in landfills, marine bodies or unregulated waste; also increasing chances of micro plastic pollution [UNEP, 2022]. Researchers estimate 5-13 million tons of plastic enters the oceans each year; India, with a fairly low per capita plastic use of 11kg and high population of 1.36 billion, produces about 5.5×10^5 tons of mismanaged plastic, 50% of which is single use that has a high possibility to enter the ocean every year and on the current trajectory of production, it has been projected that single-use plastic could account for 5-10% of greenhouse gas emissions by 2050 [Narra et al., 2022].

The effect of single use plastics on the environment, especially on the marine environment has been well articulated in the literature [Baroth, 2022; Chakraborty et al., 2022]. The challenges and opportunities in plastics waste management in India are immense [Bhattacharya et al., 2018; Hossain et al., 2022; Kataki et al., 2022]. Some researchers have studied the transition for plastics recycling and plastics ban related policies [Nagarajan, 2021; Nagarajan, 2022;

Owens et al., 2022, Pathak, 2021; Pathak, 2022]. The behavioral aspects of citizens, manufacturers and other stakeholders towards such policies is also of paramount importance, especially in a developing economy as India [Geetha, 2022; Vimal et al., 2020; Vimal et al., 2022].

The adverse impacts of littered single use plastic items plastic on both terrestrial and aquatic ecosystems, including in marine environment are globally recognized. Addressing pollution due to single use plastic items has become an important environmental challenge confronting all countries. Taking cognizance of the enormity of the problem, the Government of India put a partial ban on select single use plastics which have low utility and high littering potential in India from 1st July 2022 [PIB, 2022]. The list of banned items includes: ear buds with plastic sticks, plastic sticks for balloons, plastic flags, candy sticks, ice-cream sticks, polystyrene (Thermocol) for decoration, plastic plates, cups, glasses, cutlery such as forks, spoons, knives, straw, trays, wrapping or packing films around sweet boxes, invitation cards, cigarette packets, plastic or PVC banners less than 100μ, stirrers, etc. The Plastic Waste Management Amendment Rules, 2021, also prohibit manufacture, import, stocking, distribution, sale and use of plastic carry bags having thickness less than 75μ with effect from 30th September, 2021, and having thickness <120μ with effect from the 31st December, 2022. The Ministry of Environment, Forest and Climate Change also notified the guidelines on extended producers' responsibility on plastic packaging as Plastic Waste Management Amendment Rules (PWMAS), 2022 on 16th February, 2022, clearly mentioning that the Extended Producer Responsibility (EPR) is responsibility of a producer for the environmentally sound management of the product until the end of its life. The guidelines will provide framework to strengthen circular economy of plastic packaging waste, promote development of new alternatives to plastic packaging and provide next steps for moving towards sustainable plastic packaging by businesses.

But a lot of exerts have expressed their concerns on the effectiveness of such a partial ban policy. This research paper is intended to critically study the ban on select single use plastics in India and its related challenges and opportunities towards achieving sustainable development goals. The authors have tried to fill in research gaps pertaining to partial ban policy on single use plastics in India and hope that this research aids all stakeholders in devising future policies on plastics in general and single use plastics in particular.

2. Methodology

The methodology for this paper as shown in Fig. 1 included extensive literature review and conduct of virtual telephonic and questionnaire-based survey interviews related to ban on single plastics in India with 136 experts on the subject including bureaucrats, scientists, researchers, academicians specializing in the subject, resident welfare association (RWA) heads, local politicians, etc. between January to May 2022. The identity of the respondents was kept anonymous by agreeing on a Non-Disclosure Agreement (NDA). The data so collected was analyzed and results are presented here. Based upon the analysis of the results of the literature review and the interview data, some recommendations have been suggested to make the ban more effective and inclusive. It is expected that the paper would help the various stakeholders in developing not only new techniques for tackling this problem but also in evolving innovative policies as a way ahead.

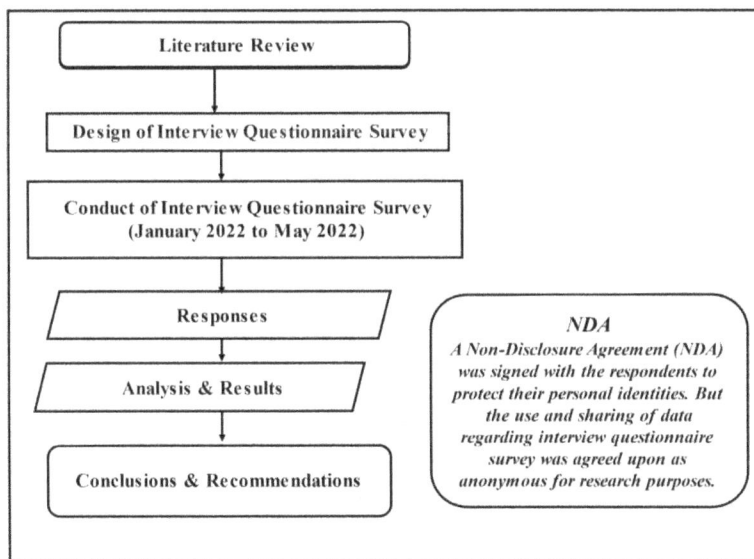

Fig. 1 Methodology diagram of the research

3. Results
3.1. Demographic Profile of Respondents :
A total of 136 responses were received from all over India which were complete in all respects. The demographic profile of respondents has been given in Table 1.

Table 1: Demographic profile of the respondents.

Factor	Respondents (in %)	Respondents (in figures)
Total Respondents	100	136
Age groups (in years)		
(a) <25	8	11
(b) 26-40	35	47
(c) 41-55	42	57
(d) >56	15	21
Sex		
(a) Male	64	87
(b) Female	36	49
(c) Others	0	0
Profession		
(a) Bureaucrats	4.4	6
(b) Scientist/researcher	16.1	22
(c) Academician	30	38
(d) Resident welfare	31	42
association (RWA) heads	18.5	28
(e) Others		

3.2 Interview Questionnaire Survey Results:
3.2.1 Will the partial ban on single use plastics be effective: 88% of the respondents were of the opinion that partial bans are never the solution and no exceptions should have been made. All single use plastics regardless of their size or use should have been banned (fig. 2).

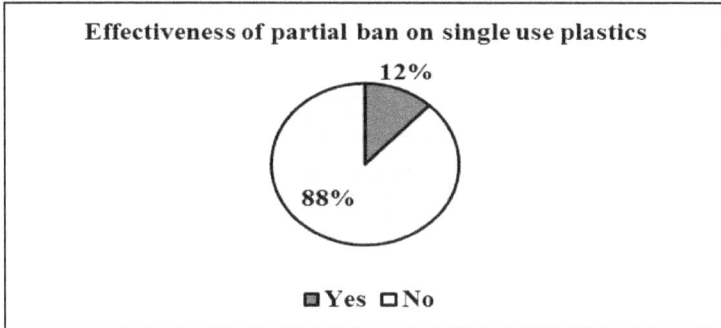

Fig. 2 Effectiveness of partial ban on single use plastics

3.2.2 Method of Disposal of SUPs : A whopping 74% people admitted to discard the SUPs with the regular wastes due to non-availability of separate collection systems, which is an alarming fact as it would on the one hand overburden the landfills and on the other hand pose a serious risk to the humans and their environments along with the surrounding flora and fauna. Only 10% of the respondents disposed off their SUPs safely in a closed dust bin or followed up where their waste went for safe disposal. 4% of the respondents littered around or did unsafe disposal at least once whereas and 12% of them were not certain. (Fig. 3).

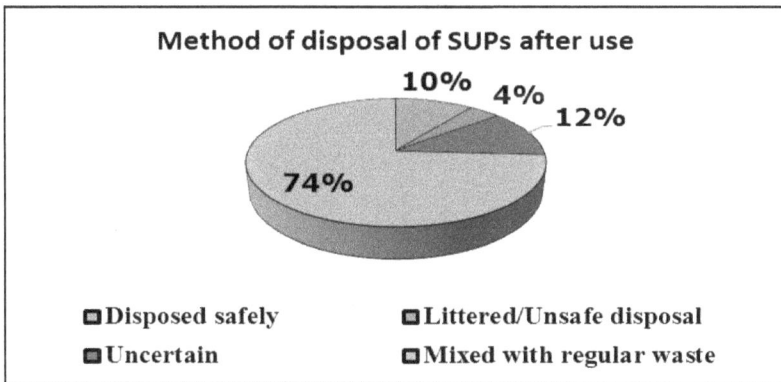

Fig. 3 Method of disposal of SUPs

3.2.3 Knowledge Regarding Problems Associated *with SUPs* : A big section of respondents (88%) knew regarding the harmful effects of unsafe disposal of SUPs, which they were still disposing away with the regular wastes. The rest 12% respondents did not know

149

about the technicalities and harmful effects of their unsafe disposal. These were mainly the RWA people. Most of them had no access to safe disposal systems (Fig. 4).

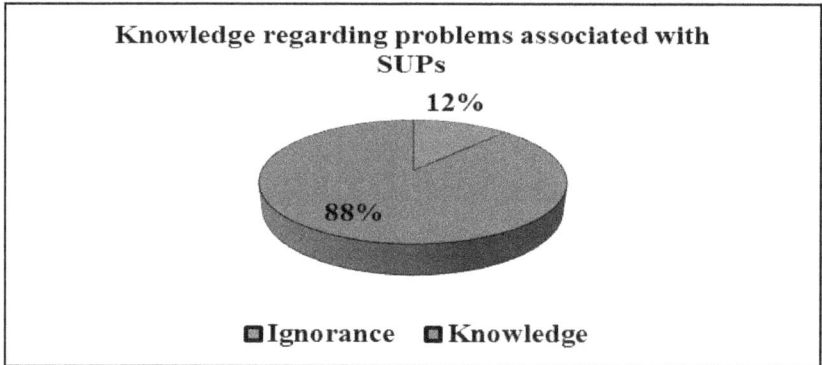

Fig. 4 Knowledge regarding problems associated with unsafe disposal of SUPs

***3.2.4* Access to safe Disposal Systems :** Only a minority (8%) had access to safely dispose SUPs. Rest (92%) were either relying on the traditional waste management systems of resorting to unsafe practices (Fig. 5).

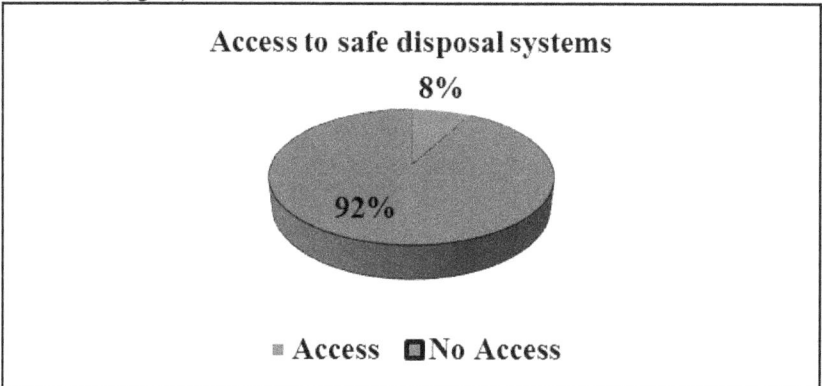

Fig. 5 Access to safe disposal systems

***3.2.5* Problems/Reasons for Unsafe Disposal :** The most common reason (66%) reported for unsafe disposal of SUPs was the unavailability of separate dustbins for them or the lack of them altogether in the vicinity. Second common excuse was mixing of wastes or non-segregation at home/offices (24%). The other reasons included incompetence, laziness, not knowing the associated dangers, lack of awareness on the issue, etc. (10%) as shown in figure 6.

Fig. 6 Reasons for unsafe disposal

3.2.6 Pledge for Safe Disposal : The last part of the interview questionnaire was to make the respondents pledge to safe disposal of SUPs that are in their possession. 100% of the respondents pledged to the same henceforth in future.

4 Discussions

Based upon the literature review and interviews with experts the following discussion has evolved:

4.1 India's Contribution of Single use Plastics (SUP)

As per the Minderoo Report 2021 [Minderoo, 2021]:

- India is ranked 94th in the top 100 countries of single-use plastic waste generation.
- India's domestic production of SUP is 8 million metric tonnes (MMT) annually, and its import of 2.9 MMT.
- India's per capita generation of SUP is 4 kg.
- The largest share of SUP is that of packaging-with as much as 95% of single-use belonging to this category.

4.2 Enforcement of the Ban

- **Choice of Ban Material :** The choice for the first set of single-use plastic items for the ban was based on "difficulty of collection, and therefore recycling".
- **Monitoring :** The ban will be monitored by the Central Pollution Control Board (CPCB) from the Centre and by the State Pollution Control Boards (SPCBs) that will report to the Centre regularly.

- **Stopping Raw Materials Supply :** Directions have been issued at national, state and local levels to all petrochemical industries to not supply raw materials to industries engaged in the banned items.
- **Directions to Industries :** SPCBs and Pollution Control Committees will modify or revoke consent to operate issued under the Air/Water Act to industries engaged in single-use plastic items.
- **Fresh Licensing Required :** Local authorities have been directed to issue fresh commercial licenses with the condition that SUP items will not be sold on their premises, and existing commercial licenses will be cancelled if they are found to be selling these items.
- **Encouraging Compostable Plastics :** CPCB has issued one-time certificates to 200 manufacturers of compostable plastic and the BIS passed standards for biodegradable plastic.
- **Penalty :** Those found violating the ban can be penalized under the Environment Protection Act 1986 – which allows for imprisonment up to 5 years, or a penalty up to Rs 1 lakh, or both.

4.3 Pros of Single Use Plastics (SUP) Ban
- **Business Opportunity for Reusable Bag Manufacturers :** Bans on plastic bags will cause an uptick in business for reusable bag manufacturers (cotton, jute, paper, etc.) and lead to increased employment opportunities.
- **Eliminating Plastic Bags Reduces Cost of Goods :** Stores have to factor in the cost of disposable bags into their prices. By eliminating plastic bags, stores can lower selling prices of their products.
- **Less Littering :** Plastics bags being non-biodegradable, litter and pollute oceans, rivers, farmlands, cities, and neighborhoods. Such bans eliminate SUP bags, which means less litter and less pollution.
- **Diverted Good use of Tax Money :** Banning plastic bags will reduce litter and allow for tax money to be redirected to more important areas.

- **Protection of Birds, Animals and Marine Life :** Birds, animals and marine life forms often mistake plastic bags as food, leading them to consume the litter and become ill or die. Hence, such ban will protect other life forms.
- **Less Drainage Blockages :** Plastic litter often clogs drainage systems, causing unnecessary flooding. Due to such a ban, drainage infrastructures will run more efficiently.
- **Reduction in Petroleum Demand :** Banning plastic bags will minimize the dependency on the limited non-renewable resource such as petroleum that are the backbone of SUP industries.
- **Control the Mosquito Population :** Discarded plastic bags collect rainwater and creates a breeding ground for disease causing mosquitos. Such a ban will lessen the mosquito population.
- **Less Waste in landfills :** SUP's can take 1000s of years to decompose and are hard to recycle. Hence their ban will result in less of them in landfills and open dumping sites.
- **Less Microplastics :** This policy will directly result in less generation of microplastics that have become a cause of concern to scientists worldwide.

4.4 Cons of Single Use Plastics (SUP) Ban

- **Employment Loss :** Bans often lead plastic bag manufacturers to scale back business and may lead to layoffs and unemployment, especially in the unskilled workforce. As per the Ministry of Environment, Forest and Climate Change (MOEF&CC), the single-use plastic manufacturing industry employs close to 2,00,000 people directly and another 4,50,000 indirectly. After the ban, the livelihoods of these people are in peril.
- **Upfront Cost to Shoppers :** Plastic bag bans will require shoppers having to purchase reusable bags, which are costlier than SUP bags.
- **More Resource use in Alternatives :** SUPs use less water, require fewer chemicals, and produce less greenhouse gas than the other two popular options namely cotton and paper bags. Plastic has half the carbon footprint of the cotton and paper bags. It's

counterintuitive to think that plastic could be less harmful than something natural, like cotton, but it is.

- **Alternatives are not all Weather Friendly :** Unlike SUPs, their alternatives are not all-weather type friendly. For example, cotton or paper bags can't be used in rain for carrying items.
- **No Viable Alternatives :** There are several products that need to be packed in polyethylenes and SUPs, otherwise they lose their properties. If clothes are not wrapped in polyethene, they will become dirty soon. If artificial jewellery is kept in open then it would lose its shine. Similar issue are there for medical products.
- **Traders not Criminals :** The traders dealing in SUPs are business owners like others. Whereas, harmful and unhealthy products like tobacco and alcohols are not banned, their SUPs are banned; giving them a feel of criminals, which is not justified.
- **Bane for MSMEs:** The major brunt of the current ban will may be borne by Ministry of Micro, Small & Medium Enterprises (MSMEs) and they will need hand-holding by the government to come up with possible solutions for sustainable alternatives.

4.5 India vs other Countries

- Consensus on SUP in UN: 124 countries, parties to the United Nations Environment Assembly, including India, have signed a resolution to draw up an agreement which will in the future make it legally binding for the signatories to address the full life of plastics from production to disposal, to end plastic pollution.
- 68 countries have plastic bag bans with varying degrees of enforcement
- Bangladesh became the first country to ban thin plastic bags in 2002.
- China issued a ban on plastic bags in 2020 with a phased implementation.
- EU has banned certain single-use plastics for which alternatives are available.

5. Conclusions :

Single use plastics (SUPs) have a negative effect on environment and the ban on them is justified. But a partial ban defeats the very objective of the ban. The unsafe disposal of SUPs is an issue that needs the immediate attention of all stakeholders like governments, bureaucrats, policymakers, municipalities, health care workers, administrators and the general public at large. This paper concludes that the single use plastics should be completed banned as soon as possible in India and worldwide. It would need collaboration concept among the public and the government systems along with NGOs and more research and development put into it to achieve the goals of sustainable development as outlined by the UN.

6. Recommendations :

6.1 There should be complete ban on all SUPs regardless of thickness or use.

6.2 Proper collection and disposal of already manufactured SUPs must be encouraged by mass awareness programmes and social media campaigns by all stakeholders via proper training and sensitization programmes.

6.3 Penalties should be strictly implemented against defaulters and fines imposed to discourage unsafe disposal practices.

6.4 Proper multiple bin systems should be introduced by the governments through their welfare programmes and integrated with the solid waste management practices so that such wastes do not end up with regular wastes in landfills or dumped in the open.

6.5 The use of automation and mechatronic devices must be done in collecting, transporting and safely disposing off the SUPs.

6.6 The practice of disposing billions of SUPs unsafely or with municipal wastes daily need to be stopped altogether and such waste generated till now need to be used as pyrolysis fuel or oil extraction done from them.

6.7 Industry players should not be allowed to bulldoze the government and delay the intricacies of the ban.

6.8 Need awareness and enforcement; affordable and eco-friendly alternatives to make SUPs ban effective.

6.9 More research and Development needs to be done on the technical and policy related aspects of plastics and SUPs for sustainable alternatives.

Acknowledgements
The authors wish to acknowledge the time and contribution of all the interview questionnaire survey respondents without whom this paper would not have been possible.

References
Baroth, A., Mamgain, S., Sivakumar, K., Hatkar, P. S., & Pathan, S. (2022). Role of protected area in reducing marine and plastic litter: A case study from India's first Marine Protected Area and comparison with Non- Protected Areas. *Journal of Industrial Ecology.*

Bhagat, S., Bhardawaj, A., Mittal, P., Chandak, P., Akhtar, M., & Sharma, P. (2016). Evaluating plastic waste disposal options in Delhi using multi criteria decision analysis. *Institute of Integrative Omics and Applied Biotechnology, 7*(11), 25-35.

Bhattacharya, R. R. N., Chandrasekhar, K., Roy, P., & Khan, A. (2018). Challenges and opportunities: plastic waste management in India.

Chakraborty, P., Chandra, S., Dimmen, M. V., Hurley, R., Mohanty, S., Bharat, G. K., ... & Nizzetto, L. (2022). Interlinkage Between Persistent Organic Pollutants and Plastic in the Waste Management System of India: An Overview. *Bulletin of Environmental Contamination and Toxicology,* 1-10.

Geetha, R. (2022). Factors Influencing Plastic Bag Avoidance Behaviour Among the Indian Consumers. *Vision,* 09722629221099601.

Hossain, R., Islam, M. T., Shanker, R., Khan, D., Locock, K. E. S., Ghose, A., ... & Sahajwalla, V. (2022). Plastic waste management in India: Challenges, opportunities, and roadmap for circular economy. *Sustainability, 14*(8), 4425.

Kataki, S., Nityanand, K., Chatterjee, S., Dwivedi, S. K., & Kamboj, D. V. (2022). Plastic waste management practices pertaining to India with particular focus on emerging technologies. *Environmental Science and Pollution Research,* 1-26.

Lhamon Jr, W. T. (1996). American Plastic: A Cultural History. *The

Journal of American History, 83(3), 1028. https://cdn.minderoo.org/content/uploads/2021/12/13191345/Minder oo-Foundation-Annual-Report-2021.pdf

Nagarajan, A. (2021). Dealing with India's Plastic Waste: Why Single-use Plastic Bans may not Work. In *The Crisis of Climate Change* (pp. 164-173). Routledge India.

Nagarajan, A. (2022). The governance of plastic in India: towards a just transition for recycling in the unorganised sector. *Local Environment*, 1-20.

Narra, S., Shettigondahalli Ekanthalu, V., Antwi, E., & Nelles, M. (2022). Effects of Marine Littering and Sustainable Measures to Reduce Marine Pollution in India. In *Handbook of Solid Waste Management* (pp. 1375-1406). Springer, Singapore.

NRDC (2022). https://www.nrdc.org/stories/single-use-plastics-101

Owens, K. A., Divakaran Sarasamma, J., Conlon, K., Kiruba, S., Biju, A., Vijay, N., ... & Khanolkar, C. (2022). Empowering Local Practitioners to Collect and Report on Anthropogenic Riverine and Marine Debris Using Inexpensive Methods in India. *Sustainability, 14*(3), 1928.

Pathak, G. (2021). Nation branding, soft Hindutva, and ecotraditionalism in anti-plastics discourses in India. *Identities*, 1-19.

Pathak, G. (2022). Plastic politics: industry stakeholders and the navigation of plastic control policy in India. *Environmental Politics*, 1-22.PIB (2022). https://pib.gov.in/ PressRelease Iframe Page .aspx? PRID=1837518

Rasmussen, S. C. (2021). From parkesine to celluloid: The birth of organic plastics. *Angewandte Chemie, 133*(15), 8090-8094.

UNEP (2022). https://unep.org/interactive/beat-plastic-pollution/

Vegter, A. C., Barletta, M., Beck, C., Borrero, J., Burton, H., Campbell, M. L., ... & Hamann, M. (2014). Global research priorities to mitigate plastic pollution impacts on marine wildlife. *Endangered Species Research, 25*(3), 225-247.

Vimal, K. E. K., Agarwal, V., & Mathiyazhagan, K. (2022). Barriers in the adoption of buyback schemes for used plastic packaging material–a contextual relationship analysis. *Resources, Conservation and Recycling, 178*, 106084.

Vimal, K. E. K., Mathiyazhagan, K., Agarwal, V., Luthra, S., & Sivakumar, K. (2020). Analysis of barriers that impede the elimination of single-use plastic in developing economy context. *Journal of Cleaner Production, 272,* 122629.

[1]Head (Research & Development),
Juno Terra Technology Private Limited, Delhi (India)
[2]Department of Mechanical Engineering,
Swami Keshvanand Institute of Technology,
Management & Gramothan, Jaipur (India)
[3]TGT, Department of Science,
Air Force School Hindan, Ghaziabad (India)
[4]PGT, Department of Economics,
Air Force School Hindan, Ghaziabad (India)
[5]Data Scientist,
Juno Terra Technology Private Limited, Delhi (India)
[6]Department of Civil and Environmental Engineering,
The NorthCap University, Gurugram, (India)
*Corresponding author: raghavdata26@gmail.com

17. Adsorption and Photocatalytic Degradation of Indigo Carmine Dye Solution using Cuprous Iodide

S SRashmi,
G C Sanjesh,
B G Meghana,
D Archanaand
T N Ramesh[a)]

Abstract

In this study, we have investigated the adsorptive photocatalytic degradation of indigo carmine dye in aqueous solution onto cuprous iodide. X-ray powder diffraction, Infrared spectrum, UV-visible spectrum and scanning electron micrographic techniques were used to characterize CuI. The adsorptive photocatalytic degradation studies were carried out by varying concentration of indigo carmine dye and adsorbent dose of cuprous iodide at different wavelength of radiations. We have optimized the adsorbent dose and the indigo carmine dye concentration for cuprous iodide. Kinetic parameters during the photocatalytic degradation process have been analyzed. Pseudo-second order rate kinetics fits well during the photocatalytic degradation of indigo carmine onto cuprous iodide at ambient conditions (pH 6-7). During the photocatalytic degradation process, the mechanism of adsorption of indigo carmine onto the photocatalyst was evaluated using different adsorption isotherm models.

Introduction

Different types of synthetic dyes like azo dyes, pthalocyanine dyes, VAT dyes, cationic dyes, insoluble dispersive dyes, indigoid dyes are widely used in paper and pulp manufacturing, printing and textile industries [1]. Of which, 15% of overall production of dyes are lost or released as effluents after its utilization around the world [2]. These effluents from the above industries cause irreversible damage to the living organisms by stopping reoxygenation capacity of water and also blocking sunlight thus inhibiting the natural process of aquatic life [3]. Of which, indigo carmine contains carbonyl as chromophore belongs to azo dye, is one of the oldest naturally occurring and important dye used till date. There are several reports on hazardous effect of indigo carmine on living organisms. Reduced hemoglobin level and red blood cell count was found after 45 and 90 days in blood stream on uptake of indigo carmine by pigs [4]. Moderate anemia was observed in mice containing 0.8 or 1.6% indigo carmine [5]. Indigo carmine also causes depressed sperm motility from 70.3% to 1.1% in humans [6]. The effect of indigo carmine on cardiovascular and respiratory effect had been reported indicating that there is 12% decrease in the cardiac rate in human bodies [7]. To overcome these problems, several methods have been developed to remove or degrade indigo carmine dye. The chemical methods involve precipitation, oxidation, chemisorption, photocatalysis. Biological methods involve utilization of microorganisms such as fungi and enzymes for the decolourisation of dyes [8]. There are several reports on the photocatalytic degradation of dye using solar radiation [9]. Photocatalytic degradation were also carried out using calcium oxide as catalyst in UV, visible region and the effectiveness was found to be higher at pH=9, when 0.12g of calcium oxide was used [10]. Indigo carmine had been removed by using adsorption process using calcium hydroxide as an adsorbate and was effective at pH=12 [11]. Adsorption studies have been reported for indigo carmine using mesoporous Mg/Fe layered double hydroxide nanoparticles [12]. Indigo carmine was degraded biologically in aqueous solutions catalyzed by horse radish peroxide and degradation was effective at higher concentration of enzyme at pH=4-6. Electrochemical method has been adopted for the degradation of indigo carmine dye was using boron-doped diamond as an anode in acidic/alkaline aqueous media. [13]. Electrocoagulation method from aqueous solutions of indigo carmine (75mg/L), was effective at $10.91 Am^{-2}$ current density [14]. The electro oxidation process with Ti/Pt and graphite electrodes in the presence of NaCl decolorizes indigo carmine [14].

Photocatalytic degradation of dyes using semiconductors has attracted materials scientists to minimize water pollution. Variety of semiconductors has been used due to its stability and reactivity. Photocatalyst uses solar spectrum to degrade dyes in solution. Research is focused on the use of visible region of electromagnetic spectrum to degrade dyes.

Apart from all the above methods, several degradation techniques use copper/copper reagents. Of which, copper hydroxyphosphate was used as catalyst for the oxidation of azo dyes at optimum pH=4-7, and optimum dose of catalyst at 100mg/100ml solution [16]. Also ZnO/CuO catalysts have been used for the degradation of textile dyes such as methylene blue and methyl orange in visible light radiation [17]. Mesoporous carbon aerogel supported copper oxide catalyst was used in the catalytic ozonization of simulated textile dye.

Photocatalytic degradation of indigo carmine has been carried out using niobium pentoxide having band gap of 3.2eV using mercury vapour lamp at pH=3 and was found to be effective when niobium pentoxide concentration was 0.7g/L.

However, till date there are no reports on the use of copper iodide for the adsorption and photocatalytic degradation of indigo carmine. The rate of change of concentration of dye with time on exposing it to visible/UV region (254 nm/356nm) in presence of photocatalyst such as CuI have been monitored. In this report we have also investigated the rate kinetics during the adsorption and photodegradation of indigo carmine dye usingCuI as a catalyst.

Experimental Section

Reagents used

The chemicals used are of analytical grade. Indigo carmine dye and cuprous iodide were purchased from SD-Fine Chemicals, India.

Preparation of Indigo Carmine Dye Solution

Stock solution of indigo carmine dye was prepared by dissolving 50 mg of indigo carmine dye in 1000 mL of distilled water. Series of dye concentrations ranging 1.072×10^{-4}M, 0.8576×10^{-4} M, 0.6432×10^{-4} M, 0.428×10^{-4} M and 0.2144×10^{-4} M or 0.5mg, 0.4mg, 0.3mg, 0.2mg and 0.1mg/10ml were prepared by transferring 10 mL, 8 mL, 6 mL, 4 mL and 2 mL of the dye solution followed by dilution to 10 mL using distilled water. And the pH of solutions was in the range of 6-7.

Degradations Measurements

The detailed procedure for the adsorption and photodegradation studies of indigo carmine dye solution using CuIphotocatalyst is as follows :

To optimize the adsorbent dosage for the photodegradation studies, 10mg, 20mg, 30mg, 40mg and 50mg of CuI was added to each 10ml of the 1.072×10^{-4} M indigo carmine solution taken in 5 different cleaned and labeled sample vials. Then the above indigo carmine solutions were kept under visible, short-UV (254nm) and long UV radiation (365 nm) and absorbance of all the change in the concentration of the indigo carmine dye solutions were recorded at 570 nm using colorimeter at regular time intervals (every 5/10 minutes). To evaluate the nature of adsorption of indigo carmine onto CuI, indigo carmine solutions of different concentrations ranging 1.072×10^{-4} M, 0.8576×10^{-4} M, 0.6432×10^{-4} M, 0.4288×10^{-4} M and 0.2144×10^{-4} M was examined by the addition of optimized quantity of photocatalysti.e20mg of CuI. The concentration change of indigo carmine dye solutions after adsorption and photocatalytic degradation was monitored using colorimeter (CL-63 model). The maximum absorbance for indigo carmine dye solution was observed at 570 nm and the measurements were performed at a fixed wavelength of 570 nm.

Adsorption Isotherms

Adsorption isotherm studies were conducted to determine the type using various models. The appropriateness of different models were examined to determine the adsorption and photodegradation process of indigo carmine dye using CuIphotocatalyst.

Characterization

Elico CL-63 colorimeter was used to measure the concentration of the dye solutions maintained at pH 6-7 (λ_{max} = 570 nm). The structure of CuIsample was characterized by powder X-ray diffraction (pXRD) using Bruker Advanced X-ray diffractometer with CuKα source (λ= 1.5418 Å). Data was collected at the scan rate of 4° min^{-1} with 2θ steps of 0.05° and scan range of 5-55°. The phases of the sample was indexed and compared with the international center for diffraction database.Fourier transform infrared spectra were recorded using Bruker Alpha Infrared spectrometer in ATR mode. The scan range was 4000 to 400 cm^{-1}, resolution 4 cm^{-1} with 24 scans. UV-Visible spectral data was collected forCuI on the detector using a sphere with a barium sulfate-coated inside. CuI sample was gold coated and morphological features was recorded using JEOL Model JSM-6390LV scanning electron microscope using secondary detector.

Results and Discussion

Cuprous iodide is a wide band gap semiconductor which crystallizes in α, β and γ forms. The low temperature γ-CuI is a p-type semiconductor with a band gap of 3.1 eV crystallizes in cubic structure below 350°C. While β-CuI occurs in wurtzite structure between 390 to 440°C and above 440°C it transforms to α-form having rocksalt structure. Due to its structural diversity, CuI exhibit unique features with diverse band gap, negative spin orbit splitting [19], electro-sensitivity [20] and photosensitivity [21]. γ-CuI is used as light emitting diode with high intensity emission observed in violet region [22]. CuI has been used in field emission display, as catalyst in organic reactions and solid state dye sensitized solar cells [23-25]. p-typeCuI has a high charge carried mobility of 26 $cm^2V^{-1}s^{-1}$ [26]. Also, CuI is poorly soluble in water ($0.0042gL^{-1}$), hence.in this work, γ-CuIwas used as a photocatalyst for adsorptive photo degradation of indigo carmine dye solution.

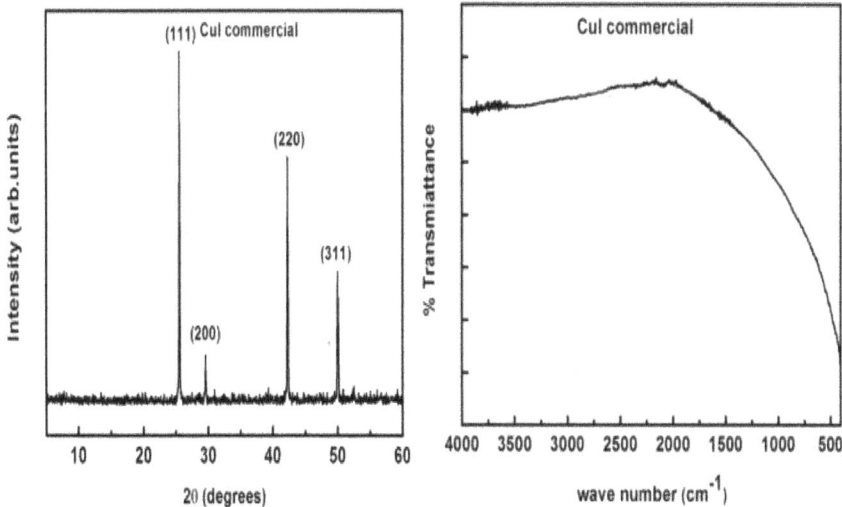

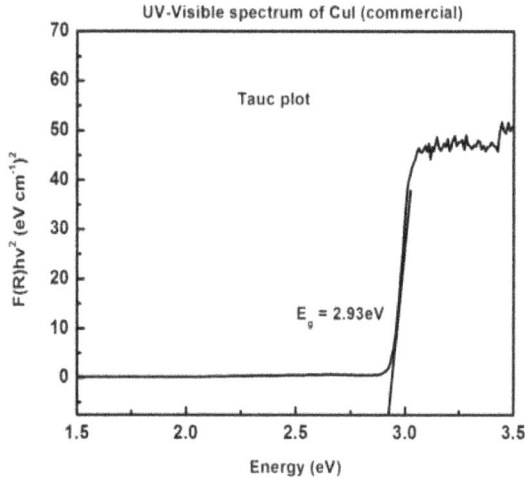

UV-Visible spectrum of CuI (commercial)

Tauc plot

$E_g = 2.93eV$

Energy (eV)

Figure 1.a) powder X-ray diffraction pattern, b) infrared spectrum and c) Diffused reflectance spectrum of CuI commercial sample.

Figure 1a shows the powder X-ray diffraction pattern of cuprous iodide. The sample crystallizes in cubic system having space group F-43m (No. 216) with cell parameters: a=b=c=6.0427 Å; $\alpha=\beta=\gamma=90°$ and cell volume 220 × 106 pm3. The XRD pattern of the CuI exhibit peaks which could be indexed to (111), (200), (220) and (311) planes and matches with γ-CuI. The reflections in the diffraction pattern matches with the data reported in the crystallography open database information card- No. 060711. The full width at half maximum (FWHM) of all the peaks are in the range of 0.14 to 0.24° indicated that the sample is highly crystalline in nature. The average crystallite size of cuprous iodide was calculated using Scherrer formulaand the crystallite size is in the range of 50-86nm.Figure 1b shows the infrared spectrum of copper iodide which does not show any vibrational bands indicating no impurities are present in the sample. γ-CuI is a p-type direct band gap semiconductor of 3.1 eV. Due to the lower electronegativity of iodine compared to oxygen, and the valence band edge made up of copper 3d and iodine 5p states, the electron hole density is much higher on CuI. Figure 1c shows the diffused reflectance spectrum of γ-CuI sample recorded in reflectance mode and the experimentally observed band gap is 2.93 eV (423 nm) which is of slightly lower value compared to 3.1 eV reported in the literature and helps in better utilization of the violet to indigo region of the of visible spectra of electromagnetic radiation. In p-type semiconductor, the population of holes in valence band are high, so, current conduction is mainly because of holes in valence band and holes are major charge carriers.Figure 2 shows the scanning electron micrographs of cuprous iodide sample. We observe irregular platelet morphology.

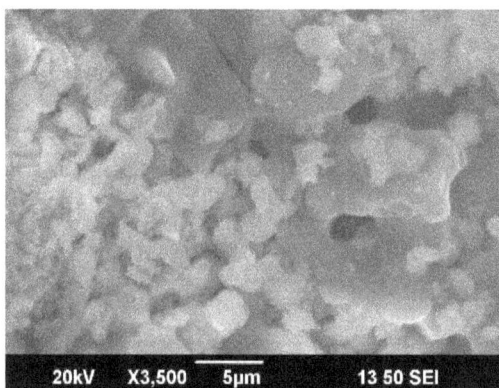

Figure 2.Scanning electron microscopic images of cuprous iodide sample.

Variation of Adsorbent Dose

The effect of dose of cuprous iodide on the adsorption and photodegradation of indigo carmine dye solution was carried out using 10mg, 20mg and 40mg of CuI/10mL of 1.072×10^{-4} M (0.5mg/10mL) separately under UV- visible region. It was found that the effectiveness of percentage of degradation of indigo carmine dye was better in visible region. Since the band gap of CuI matches in the visible region of electromagnetic spectrum, therefore we have carried out all the experiments in the visible light.

Figure 3 shows the effect of degradation of indigo carmine dye as a function of an increase in the dosage of cuprous iodide. The data clearly indicates that the degradation is maximum, when 20mg of cuprous iodide is added to 10ml of 1.072×10^{-4}M indigo carmine solution in visible region.

The percentage of dye degradation is calculated using the following equation:

$$\% \text{ of degradation} = \frac{(A_0 - A_t)}{(A_0)} \times 100 \quad \text{where}$$

A_0 is the absorbance at time t = 0 min and A_t is the absorbance after time 't' min on addition of photocatalyst. A_0 and A_t were recorded at λ_{max} -570 nm for indigo carmine dye solution.

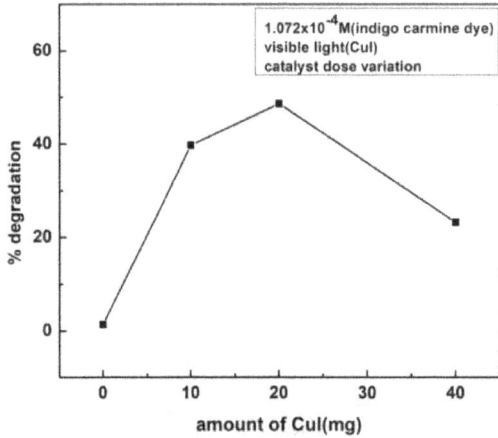

Figure 3.variation of catalyst dosage on degradation.

Variation of dye Concentration

Photocatalytic degradation of indigo carmine dye was carried out at different concentrations of dye solutions (1.072 × 10^{-4}M, 0.8576 ×10^{-4}M, 0.6432 ×10^{-4}M, 0.4288 ×10^{-4}M and 0.2144 ×10^{-4}M or 0.5 mg, 0.4mg, 0.3mg, 0.2mg, 0.1mg dye/10ml solution, where amount of photocatalyst taken is fixed constant i.e., 20mg CuI for each sample solution.

The equilibrium adsorption qe was estimated using

$$q_e = \frac{(C_o - C_e)}{\text{weight of adsorbent (mg)}} V$$

where C_o – initial concentration of dye

C_e – concentration at equilibrium

V – volume of the dye solution

Figure 4. shows the effect of concentration on degradation of indigo carmine dye solution with cuprous iodide catalyst.

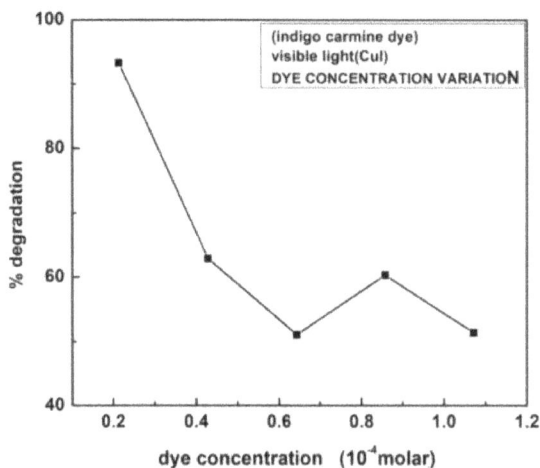

Figure 4.Variation of dye concentration on % degradation.

From the data it was concluded that the degradation was maximum at dye concentration 0.2144×10^{-4}M or 0.1mg dye/10ml solution when 20.0mg of cuprous iodide was used.

The Proposed Mechanism of Dye Degradation is as follows :

Under visible light irradiation, e^-/h^+ pairs are created and the electrons from the valence band get excited to conduction band which results in the formation of e^-/h^+ pairs. The holes present in the valence band of CuI react with surface hydroxyl group of water molecule to produce highly reactive hydroxyl radical (•OH) and the electrons present in the conduction band reacts with the oxygen molecule adsorbed on the surface of CuI to form superoxide anion (•O^{2-}) radical. The highly reactive (•OH) hydroxyl radicals and superoxide anion radicals (•O^{2-}) react with indigo carmine dye adsorbed on the surface of CuI. The more number of •O^{2-} and •OH radicals enhances the photocatalytic activity. The highly reactive hydroxyl radicals generated by γ-CuI that oxidize indigo carmine into smaller fragments i.e carbon dioxide, water, sulphategroup etc. This result demonstrates that CuI can act as good photocatalyst towards degradation of indigo carmine dye.

Different Types of Adsorption Isotherm- Data Analysis

Different types of models proposed were evaluated to understand the nature of adsorption of dye onto the adsorbent during the process of photodegradation [29]. Langmuir isotherm, Freudlich isotherm, Temkin isotherm, Harkin-Jura isotherm, Halsey isotherm and Redlich-Peterson isotherms models were most commonly used to analyze the adsorption of indigo carmine dye on cuprous iodide. The details of the different isotherm models evaluated are summarized in Table 1.

Table 1. Summary of the data analyzed for different types of isotherms

Isotherm	Parameters	Indigo carmine Dye (1.072 × 10^{-4} M)	indigo carmine dye (0.2144 × 10^{-4}M)
Langmuir isotherm	b (mg g^{-1})	0.02	8.695
	Q^o	144	2.875
	R^2	0.926	0.951
Freundlich isotherm	1/n	2.0	0.4411
	K_f	-70.00398	0.0188
	R^2	0.8139	0.879
Temkin isotherm	K_T	0.2	129.411
	B_T	0.138	0.772
	R^2	**1.000**	**1.029**
Harkin-Jura isotherm	A	0.017	0.1285
	B	1.28	-7.2
	R^2	0.890	0.815
Halsey isotherm	N	0.133	2.5
	K	0.0501	0.0082
	R^2	**1.031**	**0.999**
Redlich-Peterson isotherm	βbR	8.5	3.7844
	R^2	0.81	0.976

Adsorption isotherm better fits in the following increasing order based on the correlation coefficient (R^2) value Halsey isotherm, < (1.074) <Temkin isotherm (1.00) While R^2 value of Tempkin and Halsey isotherm are close to 1.00 for both the concentration ($0.2144×10^{-4}$M /$1.072×10^{-4}$M) indicates that adsorption follows multilayer adsorption.

Kinetics of Adsorption Process

Kinetic model was investigated for the adsorption of indigo carmine dye onto cuprous iodide. The pseudo-first order and pseudo-second order rate equations were used to verify the experimental data.Figure 5 shows the graph which fits well with a straight line to predict the adsorption process to be pseudo-second order process.The calculated r or R^2 value is 1.00 indicates that adsorption follows pseudo-second order.If the adsorption involves chemical interaction/bonding due to charge transfer process between the indigo carmine and cuprous iodide, then the reaction is of pseudo-second order.

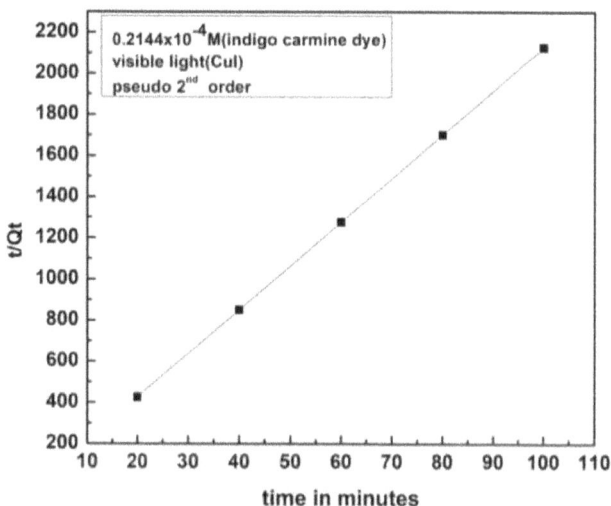

Figure 5.pseudo-second order kinetics indigo carmine dye (in visible radiation, concentration of dye solution=0.2422×10^{-4} M).

Conclusions

From the above results, we demonstrate that that the γ-phase of CuI which crystallizes in cubic structure with band gap of 2.93 eV acts as an efficient photocatalyst(20 mg) for indigo carmine dye (10 mL; 1.072×10^{-4}M) degradation in visible region of electromagnetic spectrum at pH 6-7 (298-300K).CuI degrades 51% in 100 minutes when the dye concentration is 1.072×10^{-4}M, while at lower concentration of indigo carmine dye solution (1.072×10^{-4}M), 96% was degraded.

Acknowledgments
Authors gratefully thanks Tumkur University for the facilities. T N Ramesh thank Chemistry Department, Bangalore University for providing XRD and IR facilitates.

References
1. Heinrich Zollinger *"Color Chemistry. Synthesis, Properties and Applications of Organic Dyes and Pigments*, (Wiley VCH; 2nd Edition, 1991) pp 1-4 1987
2. S.H.Lin andC. F.Peng., "Treatment of textile waste water by electrochemical method, Water Research, **27**,1743-1748 (1993).
3. C.I.Pearce, J.R.Lloyd andJ.T. Guthrie, "The removal of colour from textile waste water using whole bacterial cells'': a review. Dyes Pigments **58**, 179-296(2003).
4. G.L.Borell, "Automatic detergent feeding control''– US Patent, 2,859,760,1958
5. A. K. Subramani, K. Byrappa, S. Ananda, K.M.L. Rai, C. Ranganathaiah, "Photocatalytic degradation of indigo carmine dye using TiO_2 impregnated activated carbon'', Bulletin of Materials Sci.**30**, 37-41(2007).
6. A. Mittal, J. Mittal andL. Kurup, "Batch and bulk removal of dye,indigo carmine from wastewater through adsorption''.Journal of Hazard.Mater.137, (591-602),2006.
7. Y. R.Sheykin, Christopher Starr, P. L.Li, M. Goldstein "Effect of methylene blue,indigo carmine and Renographin on human sperm motility'' Urology **53**, 214-217(1999).
8. L. El.Gaini, L.E.Sebbar, A.Meghea, andM.Bakasse., "Removal of indigo carmine dye from water to $Mg-Al-CO_3$calcinated layered double hydroxides'' Journal of Hazardous Materials, **161**, 627-632(2009).
9. B.Neppolian, H.C.Chooi, S.Sakthivel, B.Arabindoo andV.Murugesan, "Solar |UV- induced photocatalytic degradation of three commercial textile dyes'' **89**, 303-317(2002).
10. S. H.Lin andC.M.Lin, "Treatment of textile waste effluents by ozonation and chemical coagulation", Water Research **27**, 11743-1748(1993).

11. A.Carlos, Martinez-Hutle andE.Brillas, "Decontamination of waste water containing organic dyes by electrochemical methods' Applied Catalysis B: Environmental **87**, 105-145(2009).
12. E.Brillas, B.Boye, B.M.Angekl, J.Carlos Calpe, J.Antonio, "Electrochemical degradation of chlorobenzoic herbicides in acidic aqueous medium by the peroxi-coagulation method'' Chromophere**51**, 227-235(2003).
13. N.Daneshvar, H.Ashassi-Sorkhabi, A.Tizpar, Decolorization of orange II by electrocoagulation method,Separation and Purification Technology,**31**, 153-162(2003).
14. M.Cardona, "Optical properties of the silver and cuprous halides," Physics Review, **129**, 69-78 (1963).
15. S.F.Lin, W.E.Spicer and R. S.Bauer, "Temperature-dependent photoemission studies of the electronic states of CuBr," Physics Review B, **14**, 4551(1976).
16. D.Chen, Y.Wang, Z.Lin, J.Huang, X.Chen, D.Pan and F.Huang, "Growth strategy and physical properties of the high mobility p-type CuI crystal," Crystal Growth and Design, **10**, 2057-2060(2010).
17. A.Gruzintsev andW.Zagorodnev,"Effect of annealing on the luminescence of p-CuI crystals," Semiconductors, **46**, 149-154(2011).
18. J.-H.Lee, D.-S.Leem andJ.-J.Kim, "High performance top-emitting organic light-emitting diodes with copper iodide-doped hole injection layer," Organic Electronics, **9**, 805-808(2008).
19. P. M.Sirimanne, T.Soga andT.Jimbo, "Identification of various luminescence centers in CuI films by cathodoluminescence technique," Journal of Luminescence, **105**,105-109(2003).
20. V. P. S.Perera andK.Tennakone, "Recombination processes in dye-sensitized solid-state solar cells with CuI as the hole collector," Solar Energy Materials and Solar Cells **79**, 249-255(2003).
21. J.Vidal, X.Zhang, V.Stevanovic,J-W. Luo andA.Zunger, Large insulating gap in topological insulators induced by negative spin-orbit splitting, Physical Review B **86**, 075316 (2012)

22 .T.Jow, Bruce and J.Wagner Jr, "On the Electrical Properties of Cuprous Iodide", Journal of the Electrochemical Society **125**, 613-620(1978).

23. M.Ferhat, A.Zaoui, M.Certier, J.P.Dufour, B.Khelifa, Electronic structure of the copper halides CuCl, CuBr and CuI, Materials Science and Engineering: B **39**, 95-100(1996)

24. S.A.Mohamed,J.Gasiorowski, K.Hinger, H.D.R.Zahn, M.C.ScharberS.S.Obayya, M..K..El-Mansy, N.S.Sariciftci, D.A.Egbe andP.Stadler, "CuI as versatile hole-selective contact for organic solar cell based on anthracene-containing PPE–PPV", Solar Energy Mater. Solar Cells **143**, 369–374(2015).

25. Y.Liu, J.Zhan, J.Zeng, Y.Qian, K.Tang andW.Yu, "Ethanolthermal synthesis to γ-CuI nanocrystals at low temperature", J. Mater. Sci. Lett. **20**, 1865–1867(2001).

26. K.Zhao, O.Guy,N.Ndjawa, L.K.Jagadamma, A.El-Labban, H.Hu, Q.Wang, R.Li, M.Abdelsamie, P.M.Beaujuge andA.Amassian, "Highly efficient organic solar cells based on a robust room-temperature solution-processed copper iodide hole transporter", Nano Energy **16**, 458–469(2015).

27. P.Stakhira, V.Cherpak, D.Volynyuk,F.Ivastchyshyn, Z.Hotra, V.Tataryn andG.Luka, "Characteristics of organic light emitting diodes with copper iodide as injection layer", Thin Solid Films, **518**, 7016-7018(2010).

28. M.Grundmann, F-L.Schein,M.Lorenz, T.Böntgen, J. L. Holger andV.Wenckstern, Cuprous iodide – a p-type transparent semiconductor: history and novel applications, Phys.Stat. Solidi A, **210**, 1671-1703(2013).

29. N.Ayawei, E. A.Newton andD.Wankasi, Modelling and Interpretation of Adsorption Isotherms, Journal of Chemistry, Article **ID 3039817**, 11 pages (2017).

[a]**Department of Chemistry,**
University College of Science,
Tumkur University, Tumkur
[a]*Corresponding authorb: adityaramesh77@yahoo.com*

18. Role of Sustainable Food in Environment Conservation and Chronic Disease Prevention

Dr. Samina Yasmin

Abstract

More than 3 billion people are malnourished and large sections of the population of 7 billion on the Earth eat the diets low in quality today. Even as the world's population is rapidly expanding, it is estimated there will be close to 10 billion people on our planet by 2050. The goal of policy formulation while considering sustainable food development should be to ensure a future when the entire population on Earth has both enough food available to eat as well as access to high quality and nutritious foods.

Thinking about a successful food future must focus on the earth system as a whole, rather than local levels. The "anthropocene" is a term used to describe the current geological epoch, a time period defined by humanity being the dominating driver of change in atmospheric, geologic, hydrologic, biospheric and other earth systems. In other words, humanity's influence is at its greatest point in the history of our planet. The term "anthropogenic" is an adjective that denotes "originating in human activity." In terms of anthropogenic activities, agriculture is the largest cause of global environmental change which include climate change, deforestation, desertification, and damage to coastal reefs and marine ecosystems. It is high time the initiatives are taken in the right direction to ensure a safe, disease free and resources-intact future to the coming generations.

We know that the food (monocrops) are obtained by industrial agriculture, the methods of cultivation of obtaining this food is the major cause of air and water pollution, is responsible for rapid depletion of healthy top soil, and uses harmful chemical pesticides and fertilizers.

Sustainable farming should be promoted which will eventually lead to use of lesser fossil fuels, will produce less green house effects, will be human labour dependent and will reduce use of energy based- intensive technology and chemicals. Sustainable diets can reinforce our role for better environment. Sustainable food system has tremendous benefits of protecting our forests, will act against climate change, help contribute to food security, improve health, increase survival of threatened species, preserve water resources. This will help attain a healthy and sustainable food fut6which is the urgent need to prevent chronic diseases.

Keywords : Sustainable, disease prevention, diet, anthropocene, sustainable farming.

Need for Sustainable Food System

It is quite obvious that Food systems encompass the entire range of actors and their interlinked value-adding activities involved in the production, aggregation, processing, distribution, consumption and disposal of food products that originate from agriculture, forestry or fisheries, and parts of the broader economic, societal and natural environments in which they are embedded.

The food system comprises sub-systems and interacts with other key systems, making it clear that a structural change in the food system might originate from a change in another system. A policy promoting more biofuel in the energy system will have a significant impact on the food system.

Therefore, a sustainable food system is a food system that delivers food security and nutrition for all in such a way that the economic, social and environmental bases to generate food security and nutrition for future generations are not compromised. Thus, it has to be economically sustainable, provide broad-based benefits for society and have a positive impact on the natural environment.

A sustainable food system forms an important element of the United Nations Sustainable Development Goals (SDGs). The SDGs call for major transformations in agriculture and food systems in order to end hunger, achieve food security and improve nutrition by 2030. To realize the SDGs, the global food system needs to be reshaped to be more productive, more inclusive of poor and marginalized populations, environmentally sustainable and resilient, and able to deliver healthy and nutritious diets to all.

Utility of Food Systems Approach

A food system has to be considered in the context of rapid population growth, urbanization, growing wealth, changing consumption patterns, and globalization as well as climate change and the depletion of natural resources. The developments in food systems have yielded many positive results, especially over the past three decades in developing countries. These results include the expansion of off-farm employment opportunities as food industries have developed, and the widening of food choices beyond local staples, thus satisfying consumers' preferences in terms of taste, form and quality.

The associated rapid structural transformations have also resulted in increasing and significant challenges, with potentially wide-reaching consequences for the state of food security and nutrition. These include the many highly processed, high-calorie and low nutritional value food items that are now widely available and consumed; limited access of small-scale producers and agri-enterprises to viable markets; high levels of food loss and waste; increased incidences of food safety, and animal and human health issues; and an increased energy-intensity and ecological footprint associated with the lengthening and industrialization of food supply chains.

Therefore, a better understanding of how a diverse range of food systems functions is critical to ensuring that these systems develop in such a way that minimizes their negative impacts and maximizes their positive contributions.

Scope of the Present Approach

Since there is complexity in the food systems, the approach requires a more holistic and coordinated method. Many food security and nutrition challenges are complex problems whose solutions are contested and which transcend disciplinary, divisional, and institutional boundaries. In increasingly globalized food systems, these challenges result from interactions across different scales and levels. They require integrated actions taken by all stakeholders at local, national, regional, and global levels, by both public and private actors, and across multiple fronts. These fronts include not only agriculture, but also the trade, policy, health, environment, gender norms, education, transport and infrastructure, and so on. It requires a synergetic merging rather than a destructive clashing of the ideas emerging from these various angles.

The food security programmes which were adopted till now tend to adopt a production-focused approach, which seeks to directly influence food security through increasing the supply of food. In a few regions of the world, particularly Sub-Saharan Africa, inadequate food production is still the major cause of food and nutrition insecurity. However, the dramatic pace of food system changes over the past decades has brought about complex interactions and feedback loops that impact food security and nutrition in many different ways.

The focus on food production leads to the neglect of other areas in which the root causes of the food system underperformance, as well as the leverage points to bring about the biggest impacts can often be found. Furthermore, the interwoven interactions and feedbacks in the food system mean that direct interventions in one area risk creating or exacerbating problems in another.

Other approaches adopted recently have given a new momentum to the systems thinking. The value chain development approach, for instance, uses systems thinking to examine the way value is created and captured not only by producers, but also by other stakeholders, including workers, governments and consumers. Essentially, this development emphasizes systemic analyses and integrated interventions to improve the chain's performance. Achieving broad-based developmental impacts, thus, requires taking a broader look at the interactions of all food value chains at the food system level.

Another increasingly popular approach, which is the market systems approach, recognizes markets as complex adaptive systems to address systemic constraints to market linkages that can affect multiple value chains. The market systems approach tends to be constrained to one market and as such subject to a similar narrow perspective challenge as the value chain approach.

Structure of Food System

The food system wheel framework is centred around the main goals of Food and Agriculture Organization (FAO), which include poverty reduction, food security and nutrition. These are embedded in the broader performance of the system, referring to the three dimensions of sustainability: economic, social, and environmental. Such performance is determined by the behaviour of diverse actors, or the conduct of stakeholders in the food system (people-centric).

This conduct in turn take place in the structure of the system, which consists of a core system, societal elements and natural elements. The core system includes a layer of activities through which food products flow (production, aggregation, processing, distribution and consumption, including waste disposal) and a layer of services supporting the flow. These activities are embedded in a societal context and a natural environment. The former includes all related policies, laws and regulations, socio-cultural norms, infrastructures and organizations. The latter includes water, soils, air, climate, and ecosystems and genetics.

Development of Sustainable Food System

Sustainability is examined on a holistic basis in the sustainable food system development. In order to be sustainable, the development of the food system needs to generate positive value along three dimensions simultaneously: economic, social and environmental. On the economic dimension, a food system is considered sustainable if the activities conducted by each food system actor or support service provider are commercially or fiscally viable. The activities should generate benefits, or economic value-added, for all categories of stakeholders: wages for workers, taxes for governments, profits for enterprises, and food supply improvements for consumers.

On the social dimension, a food system is considered sustainable when there is equity in the distribution of the economic value-added, taking into account vulnerable groups categorized by gender, age, race and so on. Of fundamental importance, food system activities need to contribute to the advancement of important socio-cultural outcomes, such as nutrition and health, traditions, labour conditions, and animal welfare. On the environmental dimension, sustainability is determined by ensuring that the impacts of food system activities on the surrounding natural environment are neutral or positive, taking into consideration biodiversity, water, soil, animal and plant health, the carbon footprint, the water footprint, food loss and waste, and toxicity.

Any proposed measures to address a problem or to take advantage of a new opportunity will have to be assessed against all other dimensions of sustainability to ensure there are no undesirable impacts. This holistic vision allows us to use potential synergies and to reveal often hidden trade-offs, to ensure that while our targeted impact is positive, the net overall impact on the value added of the food system activities will also be positive. An immediate result of this is the need for new or improved impact metrics.

Change and Development Paradigm

Since the structure of the food system is dynamic and driven by complex and varied trends such as urbanization, population growth, climate change, and forces such as technological change and innovation, the policy change has to keep track with it. The structure generates incentives for actors and influences their capacities, which ultimately determine their conduct. Actors in the food system are also interdependent on each other and can impact each other's incentives and capacities to act.

The overall performance of the food system, measured in terms of sustainability, is the result of the intertwined conduct of all actors in the system. Firms, farms, consumers, for instance, all can have the power to influence food system performance and initiate change. Such performance, in turn, will generate positive and/or negative feedback that influences the conduct of actors and the structure of the system in an evolutionary process.

For a development organization such as FAO, the goal here is two-fold. First, to understand how the structure generates incentives for and influences capacities of actors, and orient them toward behaviour that leads to an observed system performance. Second, to facilitate the emergence of positive feedback loops that generate a self-sustained process of sustainability performance improvement.

This value added sets in motion four feedback loops that relate to economic, social and environmental sustainability, and directly impact poverty, hunger and nutrition. The four feedback loops are: an investment loop, driven by reinvested profits and savings; a multiplier loop, driven by the spending of increased worker income; a progress loop, driven by public expenditure on the socio-cultural and natural environments; and an externalities loop, driven by economic, social and environmental impacts within the broader food system and on other systems.

Each of these feedback loops can be positive or negative, but the more positive they are, the more sustainable the food system will be. By facilitating, through catalytic support, positive feedback loops for both behaviour change and value creation, a transformative change of food systems is promoted that will help countries to achieve the Sustainable Development Goals. It will generate wealth that contributes to poverty reduction, while using natural resources responsibly and protecting the environment. Together with an improved food supply, it will ensure food security. Finally, with the right socio-cultural and natural environments, it will make more nutritious food products available, accessible and desired, thus contributing to nutrition security.

Improvement in Performance

A systems approach to improving performance is based on the holistic analysis and aims to change behaviour by targeting the structural elements that affect both the capacities and incentives of stakeholders, including by addressing stark differences in their level of organization, technology and economic power to foster more balanced relationships.

A joint vision should be developed for improving performance, and an integrated set of solutions that are supported by multi-stakeholder partnerships and can achieve improved results at scale should be evolved. Besides, facilitation, rather than getting directly involved in the system, can generate a self-sustained process of performance improvement.

Conclusion

The present food consumption patterns in industrialized countries are having a detrimental impact on both human health and the environment. In this context, it is essential to raise public awareness concerning the environmental and nutritional impacts of our food choices. The most interesting result emerging from the Double Pyramid Model is the strong correlation between the environmental impact of food and their nutritional characteristics. Specifically, it has been demonstrated that the foods whose consumption should be moderated for health reasons are also those that have a greater impact in terms of soil use, water consumption, and carbon dioxide emission.

The healthy diet is essential to achieve a sustainable level. More plant-based foods should be eaten and the our consumption of meat, animal products, and other foods, like salted snacks and sweets, should be rdeduced, as they offer little in terms of nutritional value. In order to estimate the extent to which an individual's food choices can influence their environmental impact, three dietary regimes were analyzed as part of this study. All the menus were balanced from the nutritional perspective, but they differed in relation to the amount of animal products included.

The solely plant-based diet shows the best results in terms of environmental impact, outperforming both the vegetarian and the omnivorous diets. Even adopting a semi-vegetarian diet offers individuals with the possibility of reducing their environmental impact compared to that generated from a dietary regime rich in animal products. By limiting the intake of animal flesh to just twice a week, it would be possible for an individual to reduce his environmental impact, generated by food consumption, by up to one-third.

References
1. Stehfest E, Bouwman L, van Vuuren D, den Elzen M, Eickhout B, Kabat P. Climate benefits of changing diet. Clim Change (2009) 95:83–102 10.1007/s10584-008-9534-6
2. Garnett T. What is a Sustainable Healthy Diet? A Discussion Paper. Oxford: Food Climate Research Network; (2014).
3. FAO, IFAD, WFP. The State of Food Insecurity in the World 2014. Strengthening the Enabling Environment for Food Security and Nutrition. Rome: FAO; (2014).
4. Popkin BM. Global nutrition dynamics: the world is shifting rapidly toward a diet linked with noncommunicable diseases. Am J Clin Nutr (2006) 84:289–98.
5. Popkin BM, Adair LS, Ng SW. Global nutrition transition and the

pandemic of obesity in developing countries. Nutr Rev (2012) 70:3–21. 10.1111/j.1753-4887.2011.00456.x

6. World Health Organization. Global Status Report on Non-Communicable Diseases 2014. Geneva: World Health Organization; (2014).

7. Chopra M, Galbraith S, Darnton-Hill I. A global response to a global problem: the epidemic of overnutrition. Bull World Health Organ (2002) 80:952–8.

8. Nishida C, Uauy R, Kumanyika S, Shetty P. Diet, nutrition and the prevention of chronic diseases: report of a joint WHO/FAO expert consultation. Public Health Nutr (2004) 7:245–50. 10.1079/PHN2003592

9. FAO. Sustainable Diets and Biodiversity. Rome: FAO; (2010).

10. Macdiarmid J, Kyle J, Horgan G, Loe J, Fyfe C, Johnstone A, et al. Livewell: A Balance of Healthy and Sustainable Food Choices. WWF Report. Aberdeen: Rowett Institute of Nutrition and Health, University of Aberdeen; (2011).

11. Baroni L, Cenci L, Tettamanti M, Berati M. Evaluating the environmental impact of various dietary patterns combined with different food production systems. Eur J Clin Nutr (2006) 61(2):279–86.

12. Norden.Nordic Nutrition Recommendations 2012. Copenhagen: Nordic Council of Ministers; (2014).

13. Health Council of the Netherlands. Guidelines for a Healthy Diet: The Ecological Perspective. The Hague: Health Council of the Netherlands; (2011).

14. Barilla Center for Food & Nutrition. Double Pyramid 2014. Fifth Edition: Diet and Environmental Impact. Parma: BCFN; (2014).

15. Environmental Product Declaration Database. Available from: www.environdec.com

16. LCA Food Database. Available from: www.LCAfood.dk

Assistant Professor,
Department of Zoology,
Agrawal P.G. College, Agra Road,
Jaipur

19. Chemical Pollution : A Potentially Catastrophic Risk to Humanity and its Solutions

Narendra Nirwan[1],
Gayatri[1],
Neelam Nagora[2,]
Kamal K. Verma[3]

Abstract

Chemical technologies are essential for modern societies and provide many desired benefits.The chemicals may be released during the lifecycle of these chemical technologies and cause adverse effects on human health and the environment.The chemical industry is recognized as one of the most powerful sources of environmental pollution. Indeed, chemical pollution has now been recognized as one of the planetary boundaries and it adversely impacts other planetary boundaries such as climate change and biosphere integrity. Chemical pollution can be caused by a variety of chemicals from a variety of sources and can involve a variety of health effects from simple digestive problems to chemical intoxication and sudden death by poisoning.This pollution can be reduced by less consumption or usage of polluting products and treatment of wastes, discharges and disposals of a pollutant. In this article we have presents a comprehensive perspective of the hazard of chemical pollution to humanity, cognitive health and food security.

Keywords : Asthma, Green products, Immunity system, Pesticides

Introduction

The increasing amount of chemical pollutants in our environment by the various natural and human activities are chemical Pollution.Some natural disasters (such as volcanoes) can release chemical pollutants, most chemical pollution occurs through manmade manufacturing or other human activities. Chemical pollutants mostly result from various human activities like the manufacturing, handling, storing, and disposing of chemicals. These occur in industrial places and activities such as oil refineries, coal power plants, construction, mining & smelting, transportation, agricultural use of pesticides and insecticides, as well as household activities. The chemical industry is recognized as one of the most powerful sources of environmental pollution. Since all of the chemical manufacturing processes use raw materials and consumables from each component of the environment, it is clear that damages resulting from the activities in the chemical industry are not due to the very industrial processes only, but because of the exhaustion of natural resources too.

The chemical industry indirectly charges the environment with emissions of sulfur dioxide, nitrogen oxides and particulate due to energy production in heat power stations. Production of oil and coal used as fuels and raw materials in the chemical industry also charge the environment by destroying fertile land due to mining activities and oil extraction. Emissions of carbon dioxide (CO_2), with their long-term effects on the climate, atmosphere and oceans, are a striking example, but many othersubstances have been released in the form of industrial and agriculturalemissions. Trillions of tonnes of chemically active material are dischargedinto the environment by mining, mineral processing, farming,construction and energy production [1,2]. In addition to the anthropogenic dispersal ofgeogenic chemicals, humans have synthesized more than 140,000chemicals and mixtures of chemicals [3], most of which didnot exist previously. Indeed, a recent analysis of global inventories ofchemicals estimates this figure could be over 350,000, which is manytimes larger than previously reported [4]. New syntheticchemicals are constantly being developed: recently, the USA aloneproduced an average of 1500 new substances a year [5]. Manyof these substances are known to be toxic in small doses, sometimes incombination with other pollutants, or as breakdown products afterrelease into the biosphere and geosphere.

We have considered some of the bulk chemical products, which are the main cause of pollution [6].

1. Sulfuric Acid : Sulfuric acid is one of the basic chemicals with anextremely large scale of annual production throughout the world. Its applications cover different areas of human activity, starting with fertilizers and ending with explosives. It is applied mainly in the chemical industry as acid, dehydrating and sulfonating reagent.

2. Nitrates-Containing Fertilizers : Nitrates-containing fertilizers were the most frequently used ones in the past. Mainly they are potassium, sodium and ammonium salts of nitric acid. The natural resources of these salts are large, but not sufficient to meet the demands of agriculture, and therefore, their industrial manufacturing has become inevitable.

3. Inorganic Toxics : Toxic metals should have a restriction on maximum environmental release based on relative toxicity levels and accumulation rates in ecosystems. If it is inevitable that heavy metals will be released in waste, treatment is necessary before the waste is released into the environment. In a series of steps, electrolysis should be used to reduce precious metals (Cu, Ag), which can then be refined and sold. Then, biological processing with the appropriate microbes should be used to reduce the toxicity of very reactive ions (Hg, Cd, Mn). Last, the waste solution should be made slightly alkaline to precipitate as many metal hydroxides as possible before being released into the environment.

4. Organic Toxic : Toxic organic compound emissions that are not pesticide applications should be reduced by setting a fixed standard of emissions and Eco-toxicity in a cap-and-trade system which can gradually be lowered. Ideally, this would eventually lead to zero emissions, as most organic compounds can be degraded by microbes and thus treated effectively. If compounds are found to be excessively toxic, a blanket ban should be introduced.

5. Agrochemicals : Agrochemicals should be subject to a taxation system in which the Eco-toxicity of the compound determines the levy. However, some dangerous pesticides such as atrazine should be incorporated in a cap-and-trade system of dangerous agrochemicals that would gradually be lowered to allow time for transition to less dangerous chemicals. Again, excessively toxic compounds will need to be removed from the market by a blanket ban.

Eight Ways Chemical Pollutants Harm the Body
1. Oxidative Stress and Inflammation : When antioxidant defences are depleted, inflammation, cell death, and organ damage occur.

2. Genomic Alterations and Mutations : An accumulation of DNA errors can trigger cancer and other chronic diseases.

3. Epigenetic Alterations: Epigenetic changes alter the synthesis of proteins responsible for childhood development and regular function of the body.

4. Mitochondrial Dysfunction: A breakdown in the cellular powerplant may interfere with human development and contribute to chronic disease.

5. Endocrine Disruption: Chemicals found in our environment, food, and consumer products disrupt the regulation of hormones and contribute to disease.

6. Altered Intercellular Communication: Signaling receptors and other means by which cells communicate, including neurotransmission, are affected.

7. Altered Microbiome Communities: An imbalance in the population of microorganisms in our body can make us susceptible to allergies and infections.

8. Impaired Nervous System Function: Microscopic particles in air pollution reach the brain through the olfactory nerve and can interfere with cognition.

Chemical pollution involved a variety of health effects from simple digestive problems to chemical intoxication and sudden death by poisoning.Some chemical pollutants can impair the immune, endocrine and reproductive systems. Common environmental chemical pollutants include pesticides and herbicides, volatile organics (VOCs) such as benzene, toluene; and chloroform, heavy metals such as lead, mercury, and arsenic; air contaminants such as carbon monoxide, ozone, particulate matter (PM), and second-hand smoke; and persistent organic pollutants, such as the dioxins, PCBs, and DDT [7]. Environmental chemicals can cause a broad spectrum of effects, which depend not only on the route of exposure and dose but on the susceptibility of the recipient of the pollution. Age, gender, and genotype can have major effects on whether or not exposure causes a problem. We know that children are not little adults, both as to behaviors, metabolism, and responses. Pollutants may also cause lesions, alter the liver function or darken the skin, trigger asthma symptoms in those diagnosed with the disease, and cause headaches, upper respiratory infections, dizziness and nose, throat or eye irritations. We can control the side effect of chemical pollution by reducing levels of Volatile Organic Compounds (VOCs), filtering your drinking water, using chemical-free cleaning products, reducing toxins in your garden, using green cleaning products, and always recycling batteries and stabilizing the environmentally friendly industry.

Conclusion

Human beings, as well as animals, need clean food, water and air which means a healthy environment. It is necessary to protect the ecosystem that makes survival possible. If we do not stop pollution, it is sure that the world will come to end. The government has always been showing sensitivity to the conservation and cleanness of the environment. It is also our duty to protect and improve the environment for the benefit of living in the present and future. In general, being aware of the impacts that the chemicals you are using can have is very important. Chemical pollution involved a variety of health effects from simple digestive problems to chemical intoxication and sudden death by poisoning.It is very essential to control chemical pollution. This pollution can be reduced by less consumption or usage of polluting products and treatment of wastes, discharges and disposals of a pollutant.

Reference
1. Cribb J., 2021. Earth Detox: How and why we must clean up our planet. Cambridge University Press, Cambridge
2. Pure Earth; Green Cross Switzerland, 2016. World's worst pollution problems- The toxics beneath our feet. Pure Earth and Green Cross Switzerland NY, USA and Zurich, Switzerland. http://www.worstpolluted.org/2016-report.html.
3. UNEP, 2019. Global chemicals outlook II- From legacies to innovative solutions: Implementing the 2030 agenda for sustainable development. United NationsnEnvironment Programme, United Nations https://www.unenvironment.org/

exploretopics/chemicals-waste/what-we-do/policy-and-governance/global-chemicalsoutlook.

4. Wang Z., Walker G.W., Muir D.C.G., Nagatani-Yoshida, K., 2020. Toward a global understanding of chemical pollution: a first comprehensive analysis of national and regional chemical inventories. Environ. Sci. Technol. 54, 2575–2584.

5. GAO, 2019. Substantial Efforts Needed to Achieve Greater Progress on High-Risk Areas. https://www.gao.gov/ products/ GAO-19-157sp.

6. Beschkov V.,POLLUTION CONTROL TECHNOLOGIES – Vol. III - Control of Pollution in the Chemical Industry. http://www.eolss.net/Eolss-sampleAllChapter.aspx

7. https://cfpub.epa.gov/si/si_public_record_report.cfm?Lab=NHEERL&dirEntryId=188070

[1]SPC Government College, Ajmer, India
[2]Government Girls College, Ajmer, India
[3]Seth RL Saharia Government PG College, Kaladera, Jaipur, India

20. Long Term study of Surface Gases Variability Trends using Satellite based Data at Southern Region of Rajasthan

Dhanraj Meena[1],
Himani jasora[2]

Abstract

In this study, we present long-term total column measurements of carbon monoxide (CO), Nitrogen dioxide (NO_2), Sulfur dioxide (SO_2), ozone (O_3) at an urban location, Udaipur (24.59N, 73.73E, 423 m above mean sea level), in Rajasthan from January 2010 to December 2020. The long-term mean total column concentrations of CO, NO_2, SO_2, and O_3 were 2.09 (x 10^{18} mol/cm^2), 1.9 (x 10^{15} mol/cm^2), 0.12 DU, and 270.4 DU, respectively. CO, NO_2, and SO_2 were the lowest during the monsoon season, whereas O_3 concentration peaked during summer. The former could be attributed mainly to the near-surface anthropogenic sources (e.g. automobiles, residential cooking, agricultural land-clearing, and biomass burning) and increased humidity. In contrast, the latter was clearly due to enhanced chemical production of O_3 during the pre-monsoon (i.e. summer) season. The mean lowest concentration of all gases was observed during the post-monsoon season due to efficient wet scavenging by precipitation. The averaged decadally and multi-annual patterns showed mixed trends, declining in 2020 due to movement restriction. Total column concentrations of CO, NO_2, SO_2, and O_3 register 1.8%, 6.9%, 7.7%, and 1.3% enhancement since 2010 in the Udaipur region. From the interannual comparison, the column CO and O_3 concentrations have increased by 1.5% and 3.5%, respectively, from 2019, despite the imposed movement restrictions. Upon the investigation of atmospheric parameters, average Temperatures are linked to the boundary layer height variability. The correlation between CO, NO_2, SO_2 and O_3 was average. Contrarily, O_3 depicted a reverse pattern with the highest concentrations during summer and monsoon and lowest in the winters. The mean wind speeds, PBL height and RH at Udaipur during 2010-2020 were five m/s, 820 m, and 38%, respectively. O_3 followed a positive correlation with Temperature, the negative with CO, NO_2 and SO_2.

Keywords : Surface Gases, long-term variability, Southern Region of Rajasthan

1. Introduction

Carbon monoxide (CO) is considered one of the most critical atmospheric trace gases that play a vital role in the oxidative chemistry of the troposphere [1][2]. Nitrogen Dioxide (NO2) is a choking, brown-coloured, extremely reactive gas with a robust oxidising nature that enables it to form corrosive nitric acid and toxic organic nitrates [3]. Amongst, nitrogen dioxide (NO_2) and sulfur dioxide (SO_2) has the second and third highest exceedance rate in India, respectively, after particulate matter less than 10 μm (PM10), Air Quality Monitoring Program, initiated by CPCB, 2012 [4]. Combustion is one of the principal processes which emit trace gases and aerosols into the atmosphere including several hazardous pollutants such as CO, NO_2, SO_2, O_3, volatile organic compounds (VOCs), metal oxides, and particulate matter (ex: BC, PM2.5, PM10) [5][6]. Meteorological parameters may also influence urban air pollution [7]. Water vapour increases the free radical scavenging rate, especially in low nitrogen environments whereas the linear relationship between temperature and O_3 results in higher O_3 concentrations with thermally accelerated chemical reactions in the atmosphere [8][9]. Ozone gas being convective, is a significant greenhouse gas because it absorbs 9.6 μm radiation emitted from the Earth's surface and is known to have adversative effects on human health and ecosystem productivity [10][11].

The primary industries in Rajasthan are cement, tourism, ceramics, chemicals, textiles, steel, handicrafts, marble, and recently IT and ITeS. Reports suggest that industrial, mining, and locomotive activities are the major causes of air pollution in Rajasthan [12]. Industrial zones were created to encourage industries at Kota, Jaipur, Udaipur, Bhilwara, Bhiwadi and Jhunjhunu in Rajasthan. Rajasthan is among the largest producers of raw minerals, with over 70 minerals from a commercial point of view. The state is also the largest manufacturer of cement-grade limestone. Approximately 26% of the country's proven limestone reserves are possessed directly by the government. A significant portion of air pollution comes from factories, a source of workplace hazards and health consequences. The RSPCB is responsible to monitors the air quality of the state [13][14]. According to a recent study, the most known North-West Indian Region, Rajasthan, is facing a surge in all kinds of pollution [15]. The 2020 Lancet Report revealed that out of total deaths, more than a million deaths in Rajasthan are due to pollution. This number will rise as the air worsens due to ambient particulate matter and other pollutants. RSPCB is responsible for controlling and implementing Rajasthan Air Pollution rules and policies amended from time to time. Rajasthan pollution levels have become a growing concern led by commercial progress fuelled by industrialisation, infrastructure development, and taking air pollution levels to high-risk levels [16]. Thus, for the present study, we selected Udaipur, Rajasthan.

The Goals of the Present Work are as Follows :

1. A long-term study of satellite observation of Surface Gases (CO, NO_2 , SO_2 , and O_3) at Southern Region, Rajasthan
2. Investigate the impact of meteorological parameters on air pollutants using statistical methods.

2. Importance of Site

Udaipur (24.5854° N, 73.7125° E) is located in the foothills of Aravalis. Maharana Udai Singh established Udaipur in 1557 AD. Udaipur district is particularly mineral-rich, showcasing a large variety of essential minerals. Udaipur is a commercial hub of the world, with marble mining and processing as an essential occupation of people. In the Udaipur district, RIICO has already developed the industrial areas in ten places and acquired the land at four/five places for developing industrial areas. There are 49 large and medium-scale industries in the Udaipur district. These industrial ventures are mainly in synthetic yarn, tyre tubes, cement, tiles, marble slabs, gases, synthetic threads, oil refineries etc. The city is a hotspot of significant tourist attractions and is renowned worldwide. Hence, transport like buses, automobiles, and two-wheeled and three-wheeled vehicles contribute significantly to particulate and gaseous pollutants. With an annual minimum of 10% vehicle increases, industrial plants and marble factories located on Udaipur's outskirts also join in the deteriorating air quality. In recent years, PM2.5 and PM10 have increased due to combined fossil fuel combustion, industrial process and biomass combustion. According to the Indian Population census, Udaipur city registers at least 20% in annual population growth due to its weather, relaxing environment and beautiful places to visit nearby [17]. This region also experiences four seasons each year. Hence it is quite a lively site to investigate the air pollutants over a long period [9].

3. Data Collection and Analysis

Since 2000, globally measured CO columns have been provided continuously by the MOPITT at 1-degree (lat-long) resolution and are available daily. The data in this work is collected from 2010-2020 to study the Udaipur region. OMI retrieved Daily gridded data for NO_2, SO_2, and O_3 (viz. OMNO2 v003, OMSO2 v003, OMTO3 v003), at a resolution of $0.25° \times 0.25°$. From daily CO, NO_2, SO_2, and O_3 datasets, monthly and yearly means are calculated for 2010-2020. The MOPITT and OMI datasets are available at NASA's Goddard Earth Sciences Data and Information Services Center (GES DISC) or available at http://mirador.gsfc.nasa.gov/[18][19][20]. Temperature and Relative Humidity (RH) data is acquired from The Atmospheric Infrared Sounder (AIRS), which is an advanced sounder with 2378 infrared channels and four visible/near-infrared channels designed to provide highly accurate atmospheric temperature profiles and a variety of additional Earth/atmospheric products [20][21]. Other meteorological parameters, Wind speed and PBL height are taken from the Modern-Era Retrospective Analysis for Research and Applications, version 2 (MERRA2) data from 2010 to 2020. It is a weather assimilation database, also the first long-term global reanalysis to assimilate spatial observations of aerosols and represent their interactions with other physical processes in the climate system [22]. The average daily data used in this study are directly accessible from the above sources. Open source tools like python and its libraries are used for data cleaning, statistical analysis, and visualisation. Only data points with simultaneously available meteorological parameters and atmospheric pollutants are selected for this study.

4. Results and Discussion

This paper presents ten years of continuous measurement of CO, NO_2, SO_2, and O_3 from 2010-2020. The missing data intervals are due to instrument calibration and interval checking. Daily data coverage for the entire study period was very high, with more than 80% of data available. The Monsson and Summer are the best covered, with up to 90% data availability. Such data coverage helps perform time-series statistical analysis. We present these air pollutants' monthly, seasonal and decadal characteristics over Udaipur using the monthly mean and annual mean data computed from daily observations [20].

Figure 1 shows the monthly variation of CO, NO_2, SO_2, and O_3 at the Udaipur site from monthly mean data. The mean and percentiles were plotted as a box plot as a measure of variability for an individual month. The daily averaged mean CO, NO_2, SO_2, and O_3 column over the entire study period ranged from 1.6 - 2.8 $x10^{18}$ mol/cm^2, 1.0 - 3.1 $x10^{15}$ mol/cm^2, 0.02 – 0.8 DU, and 230- 300 DU, respectively, with a mean and standard deviation of 2.09± 0.14 x 10^{18} mol/cm^2, 1.93 ± 0.39 x 10^{15} mol/cm^2, 0.13± 0.08 DU, and 270.49± 12.9 DU. The highest values in CO and NO_2 are observed in the winter season, along with a large variability range of 10-20%. Figure 1 shows that the CO, NO_2 and SO_2 follow an annual periodicity, with an opposite trend with O_3. CO and NO_2 concentrations showed a perfect correlation with maxima during winter and minima in the monsoon season (Fig. 1a and b), possibly due to a mutual outcome of large near-surface anthropogenic emissions, boundary layer progressions, slow photochemical loss owing to lower solar insolation, as well as local surface wind pattern [14]. Beig et al. [23] reported that similar seasonal behaviour was detected at other urban sites, for example, Pune (Maharastra) and Ahmedabad (Gujarat). However, a rural site Gandanki did not exhibit a similar seasonal pattern, where the impact of local emission sources is less [24].

In Figure 2, the mean differences are shown. A yearly average is computed for each year from daily and monthly averages at

Udaipur. A long-term average is calculated from the annual averages of concentrations during 2010-2020. The difference between the average concentration of CO, NO_2, SO_2, and O_3 every year is subtracted from its long-term average value. The most significant negative difference in CO for 2015 is also in SO_2 and O_3, but not NO_2. In 2020, all the pollutants will be very close to the mean values [7]. Except for NO_2, an alternate year trend is seen. Since 2010, the CO, SO_2 and O_3 column values have started to diverge, but at the end of 2020, they are very close to the mean value suggesting a symmetrical distribution and not random. In the year 2020, the movement restriction halted air pollution. This is reflected in 2019 and 2020 data, where all the pollutants reduce. This lays the foundation of our hypothesis, are these pollutants correlated? Do air pollutants bear the climate change? How well do the meteorological parameters and air pollutants correlate?

Figure 3(a-h) shows the multi-annual comparison of air pollutants from yearly mean data. In figure 3(a), CO concentration has risen by 1.2% since 2010, 1.4% higher than its previous year, 20 19 (Figure 3b). Hence we conclude that the CO inventory has risen a little despite the movement restrictions. From Figure 3(c-d), it is clear that the NO_2 inventory has risen by 6.9% since 2010, which is 3.6% less compared to 2019. Hence NO_2 concentrations show a long-term increase, with a slight decrease in 2020. SO_2 shows similar trends to NO_2 but has risen by 7.7% in the long term and declined by 8.7% in 2020, which matches with concurrent studies(Figure 3e-f). The ozone trends, as seen in figure 3 (g-h), correlate with CO, 1.3% since 2010 and 3.5% compared to 2019 [10][11]. From figure 3, the air pollutants are rising in the Udaipur region at a steady pace. Preventing emissions must be implemented strictly to avoid health hazards and related ailments.

Figure 4 shows decadal trends of meteorological parameters at the Udaipur site from the monthly mean values. Temperature, PBL height and wind speed are important factors influencing the dispersion of air pollutants. The seasonal temperature variation was the most pronounced in summer, with maxima during April-May [5]. This could also be the effect of relatively high solar insolation correlated with PBL height. In the monsoon season, the relative humidity shows strong effects depleting most of the observed air pollutants. During the pre-monsoon season, RH showed its lowest values. At the same time, the post-monsoon and winters are pleasant in this region. This region shows a relatively high period of humidity relative humidity from July to September [25] (Yadav et al. 2016). All meteorological parameters exhibit a seasonal cycle from 2010 to 2020. The top panel shows temperature variability indicating the year 2018 recorded a 1.3% increase in temperature since 2010, which is 0.3% higher than the previous year. The temperature is significant for the rest of the years, but there is no clear trend. The wind speed has shown a constant decline since 2012; it has dropped to 6.8% since 2010, which is 0.5% less than in 2019. The PBL height shows an alternate trend with no clear increasing a decreasing value, but it has declined to 6% since 2010, which is 0.27% higher than in 2019. In conclusion, we can say that the Temperature, winds, PBL height, and RH have decreased by 3%, 6%, 6.2% and 16%, respectively, since 2010.

Figure 5 shows the variability of air pollutants with meteorological parameters, T vs RH (left) and Wind speed v PBL height (right). There is a contrast between the left and right panels among all air pollutants using monthly mean data. This region's CO, NO_2, and SO_2 decrease in a monsoon while peaking during summer. The CO shows cross-correlation between winds and PBL. However, O_3 relates positively, but NO_2 and SO_2 negatively correlate with temperature. Except for O_3, all pollutants decline with winds and PBL. From the distribution, a strong season dependence is observed. Various weather conditions such as high temperature, low relative humidity and high solar radiation are favourable for terrestrial ozone production [3][13][26].

Pearson's coefficient, Spearman's correlation coefficient, and Kendal's coefficient usually determine the strength of the relationship. Scores ($< \pm 0.10$) are considered very mild, ($< \pm 0.20$) are mild, (($< \pm 0.30$) are moderate, and ($> \pm 0.30$) and above are considered strong correlations. Using monthly mean data, figure 6 shows the correlation coefficient between pollutants and meteorological data observed in the Udaipur region between 2010 and 2020. The Pearson, Spearman, and Kendall coefficients are calculated to generate the correlation seen from the previous analysis. The colour scale shows the correlation based on the value of the coefficient. CO has a weak negative correlation with RH, wind, PBL, and O3 but a clear average positive correlation with SO_2 and NO_2. SO_2 and NO_2 show a weak negative correlation with all meteorological parameters. O3 has a strong positive correlation with PBL and a moderate correlation between temperature and wind speed [13][27]. There is a positive correlation between PBL and Temperature, followed by wind speed. Similar results are obtained with the remaining correlation methods, and the results are validated. In India, about 60% of SO_2 emissions can be attributed primarily to coal and petroleum product consumption from industry (36%) and transportation (7.8%), as well as biomass and non-energy consumption. Positive correlations between CO, NO_2 and SO_2 may indicate similar anthropogenic sources. In addition, the negative correlation between CO and NO_2 and CO and O_3 underscores the production of O_3 by photochemical oxidation of carbon-bonded compounds (CO, CH_4) in the presence of NO and NO_2 [13].

Conclusions

Here, we presented continuous measurements of CO, NO_2, SO_2, and O_3 from an urban site, Udaipur, in India, from January 2010 to December 2020. The data coverage over the entire study period was excellent, with more than 80% of the data available. We have performed statistical analysis between air pollutants and meteorological parameters to characterise their monthly and annual variability and studied their influence. The Long term means of air pollutants (CO, NO_2, SO_2, and O_3) at Udaipur, Rajasthan, were 2.09 (x 10^{18} mol/cm^2), 1.9 (x 10^{15} mol/cm^2), 0.12 DU, and 270.4 DU, respectively. The seasonal and annual characteristics of air pollutants show an increase in the inventory affected by meteorological parameters. Total column concentrations of CO, NO_2, SO_2, and O_3 register 1.8%, 6.9%, 7.7%, and 1.3% enhancement since 2010 in the Udaipur region. From the interannual comparison, the column CO and O_3 concentrations have increased by 1.5% and 3.5%, respectively, from 2019, despite the imposed movement restrictions. CO, NO_2, and SO_2,concentrations are highest in winter due to the combined effects of significant anthropogenic emissions near the surface and surface winds [28]. The lowest concentrations of all trace gases were observed during the monsoon season, mainly due to relatively low near-surface emissions (excluding transport and industry) and wet cleaning of pollutants. Percentage change over many years indicates that Udaipur has a high potential for pollution.

Furthermore, it is suggested that air pollution is a regional problem and is not limited to climate change and dynamics. However, long-term continuous measurements of meteorological parameters and pollutants are essential to better understand the characteristics of air pollutants in Rajasthan, including urban areas at high health and economic risk. Increasing the sample size, using 20 years and 40 years of data, will help to get a statistically significant correlation. Another way is to add particulate matter (PM 2.5 and PM 10) to the study. From different statistical tests, the correlation does not change significantly; the grouping method can also help us in future work.

Author Contributions

Dhanraj Meena : Investigation, Writing an original draft Himani jasora: Conceptualization, Methodology, Proof-reading

Declaration of Competing Interest

The authors declare that they have no known competing financial interests or personal relationships that could have appeared to influence the work reported in this paper.

Acknowledgements

MOPITT and OMI processed datasets used in this study were produced with the Giovanni online data system, developed and maintained by the NASA GES DISC. The authors are thankful to Beaudoing, H. and M. Rodell (NASA/GSFC/HSL) for providing access to MERRA model online for scientific research.

References

[1] Girach, I. A. and Nair, P. R., "Carbon monoxide over Indian region as observed by MOPITT", <i>Atmospheric Environment</i>, vol. 99, pp. 599–609, 2014.

doi:10.1016/j.atmosenv.2014.10.019.

[2] Nandi, I., Srivastava, S., Yarragunta, Y., Kumar, R., and Mitra, D., "Distribution of surface carbon monoxide over the Indian subcontinent: Investigation of source contributions using WRF-Chem", <i>Atmospheric Environment</i>, vol. 243, 2020. doi:10.1016/j.atmosenv.2020.117838.

[3] United States Environmental Protection Agency. Review of the Primary National Ambient Air Quality Standards for Oxides of Nitrogen. Doc # 2018-07741, Document Citation: 83 FR

[4] CPCB: National ambient air quality status and trends in India-2010. In: Central pollution control board, ministry of environment and forests, NAAQMS/ 35 /2011-2012. 2012.

[5] Khare, M.: Air pollution – monitoring, modelling, health and control. In Tech Janeza Trdine 9, 51000 Rijeka, Croatia, 2012.

[6] Andreae, M. O. and Merlet, P., "Emission of trace gases and aerosols from biomass burning", <i>Global Biogeochemical Cycles</i>, vol. 15, no. 4, pp. 955–966, 2001. doi:10.1029/2000GB001382.

[7] Akpinar, S., Oztop, H., Kavak Akpinar, E., "Evaluation of relationship between meteorological parameters and air pollutant concentrations during winter season in Elazığ, Turkey. Environ. Monit. Assess . vol. 146(1–3), pp. 211–224, 2008.

[8] Walcek, C. J. and Yuan, H.-H., "Calculated Influence of Temperature-Related Factors on Ozone Formation Rates in the Lower Troposphere.", <i>Journal of Applied Meteorology</i>, vol. 34, no. 5, pp. 1056–1069, 1995. doi:10.1175/1520-0450(1995)034<1056:CIOTRF>2.0.CO;2.

[9] Jacob, D. J., "Factors regulating ozone over the United States and its export to the global atmosphere", <i>Journal of Geophysical Research</i>, vol. 98, no. D8, pp. 14, 817–14, 826, 1993. doi:10.1029/98JD01224.

[10] Akimoto, H., "Global Air Quality and Pollution", <i>Science</i>, vol. 302, no. 5651, pp. 1716–1719, 2003. doi:10.1126/science.1092666.

[11] Cooper, O. R., "Increasing springtime ozone mixing ratios in the free troposphere over western North America",

Nature, vol. 463, no. 7279, pp. 344–348, 2010. doi:10.1038/nature08708.

[12] Kuldeep, K., Kumar, P., Kamboj, P., and Mathur, A. K., "Air Quality Decrement After Lockdown in Major Cities of Rajasthan, India", *ECS Transactions*, vol. 107, no. 1,pp. 18479–18496, 2022. doi:10.1149/10701.18479ecst.

[13] Saxena, A, and Shani R., "Impact of lockdown during COVID-19 pandemic on the air quality of North Indian cities." Urban Climate, vol. 35, no. 100754. 2021

[14] Porush K, Kuldeepa, Nilima G., "An assessment of ambient air quality using AQI and exceedance factor for Udaipur City, Rajasthan (India)." International conference on Innovative Development and Engineering Applications. vol. 8. 2021.

[15] Balakrishnan, K., Dey, S., Gupta, T., Dhaliwal, R. S., Brauer, M., Cohen, A. J., et al., "The impact of air pollution on deaths, disease burden, and life expectancy across the states of India: The Global Burden of Disease Study 2017". The Lancet Planetary Health, vol. 3(1), pp. e26-e39. 2019.

[16] Sharma, S., Zhang, M., Gao, J., Zhang, H., & Kota, S. H. "Effect of restricted emissions during COVID-19 on air quality in India." Science of the total environment, vol. 728, no. 138878. 2020.

[17] 2011 Census of India. Registrar General and Census Commissioner of India. Retrieved 2022-06-18. https://censusindia.gov.in/census.website/

[18] Porush K, Kuldeepa, Nilima G., "An assessment of ambient air quality using AQI and exceedance factor for Udaipur City, Rajasthan (India)." International conference on Innovative Development and Engineering Applications. vol. 8. 2021.

[19] orush K, Kuldeepa, Nilima G., "An assessment of ambient air quality using AQI and exceedance factor for Udaipur City, Rajasthan (India)." International conference on Innovative Development and Engineering Applications. vol. 8. 2021.

[20] Balakrishnan, K., Dey, S., Gupta, T., Dhaliwal, R. S., Brauer, M., Cohen, A. J., et al., "The impact of air pollution on deaths, disease burden, and life expectancy across the states of India: The Global Burden of Disease Study 2017". The Lancet

Planetary Health, vol. 3(1), pp. e26-e39. 2019.

[21] Sharma, S., Zhang, M., Gao, J., Zhang, H., & Kota, S. H. "Effect of restricted emissions during COVID-19 on air quality in India." Science of the total environment, vol. 728, no. 138878. 2020.

[22] 2011 Census of India. Registrar General and Census Commissioner of India. Retrieved 2022-06-18. https://censusindia.gov.in/census.website/

[23] Martin, R., Interpretation of TOMS observations of tropical tropospheric ozone with a global model and in situ observations. Journal of Geophysical Research, 107(D18). 2002.

[24] Deeter, M. N., Edwards, D. P., Gille, J. C., and Drummond, J. R., "Sensitivity of MOPITT observations to carbon monoxide in the lower troposphere", <i>Journal of Geophysical Research (Atmospheres)</i>, vol. 112, no. D24, 2007. doi:10.1029/2007JD008929.

[25] Beaudoing, H. and M. Rodell, NASA/GSFC/HSL (2020), GLDAS Noah Land Surface Model L4 monthly 0.25 x 0.25 degree V2.1, Greenbelt, Maryland, USA, Goddard Earth Sciences Data and Information Services Center (GES DISC), Accessed: [Data Access Date], doi:10.5067/SXAVCZFAQLNO

[26] Acker, J. G. and Leptoukh, G., "Online Analysis Enhances Use of NASA Earth Science Data", <i>EOS Transactions</i>, vol. 88, no. 2, pp. 14–17, 2007. doi:10.1029/2007EO020003.

[27] Global Modeling and Assimilation Office (GMAO) (2015), inst3_3d_asm_Cp: MERRA-2 3D IAU State, Meteorology Instantaneous 3-hourly (p-coord, 0.625x0.5L42), version 5.12.4.

[28] Beig, G., Gunthe, S., and Jadhav, D. B., "Simultaneous measurements of ozone and its precursors on a diurnal scale at a semi urban site in India", <i>Journal of Atmospheric Chemistry</i>, vol. 57, no. 3, pp. 239–253, 2007. doi:10.1007/s10874-007-9068-8.

[29] Lal, S., Naja, M., and Subbaraya, B. H., "Seasonal variations in surface ozone and its precursors over an urban site in India",

Atmospheric Environment, vol. 34, no. 17, pp. 2713–2724, 2000. doi:10.1016/S1352-2310(99)00510-5.

[30] R. Yadav, L. K. Sahu, G. Beig, and S. N. A. Jaaffrey, "Role of long-range transport and local meteorology in seasonal variation of surface ozone and its precursors at an urban site in India," Atmospheric Research, vol. 176–177. Elsevier BV, pp. 96–107, Jul. 2016. doi: 10.1016/j.atmosres.2016.02.018.

[31] Barupal, T., Bhodiwa, S., Lal, C., & Sompura, Y., "Evaluation of air quality change of udaipur city during banned crackers deepawali (2020) and unbanned crackers Deepawali", Biomaterials Journal, vol. 1 no. 3, pp. 3-8, 2022.

[32] Yarragunta, Yesobu, Shuchita Srivastava, D. Mitra, and H. C. Chandola. "Seasonal and Spatial Variability of Ozone Inferred from Global Chemistry Transport Model Simulations over India." ISPRS Annals of Photogrammetry, Remote Sensing & Spatial Information Sciences 4, no. 5, 2018.

[33] N. Ojha et al., "Variabilities in ozone at a semi-urban site in the Indo-Gangetic Plain region: Association with the meteorology and regional processes," Journal of Geophysical Research: Atmospheres, vol. 117, no. D20. American Geophysical Union (AGU), Oct. 19, 2012. doi: 10.1029/2012jd017716.

**[1]Department of Physics,
Govt. College Sawai Madhopur, Rajasthan, India
[2]Department of Physics,
Pacific University Udaipur, Rajasthan, India**

www.ingramcontent.com/pod-product-compliance
Lightning Source LLC
Chambersburg PA
CBHW050222270326
41914CB00003BA/535

.